THE SEYMOUR DESK

The Seymour Desk

Andrew S. Harrison

Onion River Press
89 Church Street
Burlington, VT 05401

info@onionriverpress.com
www.onionriverpress.com

ISBN: 978-1-966607-09-0
Library of Congress Control Number: 2025906064

To Dirck, for starting me on this crazy adventure.

Acknowledgements

This project would not have been possible without the support of friends and family who tolerated my questions and updates. Special thanks go out to my aunt Barbara Mulhern and my dad's cousin Dr. Jamie Hall for filling in lots of gaps and to former colleagues and close friends Dr. Heather Gigliello and Jerry Kuhn for serving as my first editor and cover designer, respectively. Finally, my heart goes out to my wife Cathy Hawkins-Harrison who never once questioned my sanity over the last three years. At least not verbally.

Contents

1

I'm an Idiot

I'm an idiot. No, I take that back. Let me clarify. I simply say and do idiotic things. A lot of idiotic things. It has become an art form for me. Trust me. I've been perfecting it for over 60 years. Fine tuning. Molding.

Usually, it's a daily little thing—some ill-timed verbal retort. I'm not trying to gloat, but I'm pretty good with a one-liner that's usually considered funny by all parties—with the emphasis on "usually."

Unfortunately, my gift is also my curse because a well-timed quip doesn't normally allow me enough time to ponder the big question in our PC world: *How is my target audience going to take this?* Therein lies my paradox: to be whimsical and spontaneous at the cost of perhaps pissing off those I love. It is my cross to bear. For example, a few years ago when my wife, Cathy, and I were having a brief romantic moment and exchanging a kiss, she made *that face* that indicated she was not really excited about the three-day growth on my face. Rather than apologize and say something like *I'll get right on it, boss,* I retorted, "Hey, do I complain about your mustache?" For the record, she doesn't have a mustache. I thought it was hilarious and was quite proud of my whimsical and spontaneous self. She was not.

Of course, my cross to bear gets heavier as I often *do* idiotic things rather than simply *say* them. For example, in one of my most idiotic moments, I decided to ask Cathy to marry me after a volunteer gig in the mountains of Mexico where I couldn't adequately shave or shower for two months. *Think Tom Hanks in* Cast Away. Another whimsical and spontaneous (and quite romantic) moment, I assumed. She did not, though she did say yes. *If you are getting the sense that she is a saint, you are not wrong.*

Again, I do and say lots and lots of idiotic things on a continuous basis, but I still do not consider myself an idiot. Except when it comes to the Seymour desk. Sometimes my idiotic tendencies are about what I *don't* do or say.

The Beginning

The story of the Seymour desk really begins with the passing of my dad, Dirck, at the ripe old age of ninety-three and a half in early November 2020. My mom's passing preceded his by about three years. While her death caught us slightly off guard, his death did not. After a two-year battle with a whole host of ailments, he passed and left us with a whole host of decisions that all sons and daughters face with the death of their last parent. One such decision was the distribution of their earthly possessions among the four children and six grandchildren.

If you are looking for juicy drama and infighting at this point, you should look to the Kardashians. In fact, my mom and dad were fairly meticulous about making the transition as painless as possible. As they say, the apple doesn't fall too far from the tree, and my three siblings and I moved through their modest, but in most cases, quite symbolic, possessions with the same efficiency. The only real jostling occurred over a brass figurine of a weird-looking dude with a huge erection that was part of my mom's brass collection. You get the gist of the family's unique sense of humor. *Once again, tree and apple.* But in addition to these small special trinkets that meant something to someone, there were a lot of pieces of furniture and works of art that had some story behind them—and the Seymour desk was no different.

The Seymour desk is defined as a tambour secretary desk. "Tambour" refers to sliding accordion panels that cover small vertical compartments, and "secretary" refers to a hedged leaf that when opened is covered with green felt. It is a gorgeous mahogany piece popular back in the late 1700s to early 1800s, and was used as a working desk. *Think quill and inkwell.* Though I have vague memories of the piece in my paternal grandparents' manse in Cooperstown, New York, and better recollections of the desk in my parents' home, I cannot remember when my parents inherited it, though it was presumably after my grandmother Carlotta's death in 1991. I never made a big deal about it other than perhaps saying at some point, "Huh, cool desk!"

For the record, when Carlotta died in 1991, Cathy and I were in the depths of raising a three-year-old son, Noah, while considering another (my daughter, Sam, was born in 1992, so I guess we were more than considering), looking at buying our first home, and teaching full time at our respective schools. I'm not making excuses, but the fact that I didn't really notice a new piece of furniture in my parents' home doesn't really shock me.

You may at this point judge me about my laissez-faire attitude to this whole thing, but as Clint Eastwood once said, "A man has got to know his limitations." Mine is noticing the finer details of the many things happening around me. The subtleties of such details in life have never really rocked my Richter scale, which drives Cathy crazy. For example,

Andy: How long has that house been painted green?

Cathy: (with a sigh and eye roll) About two years. How can you not notice these things? You make this same drive twice a day going to and from school.

Andy: I'm usually thinking about how much I love you during those trips? (the whimsical and spontaneous thing)

Cathy: Sigh (with an eye roll and a headshake)

Wash. Rinse. Repeat.

Again, while I am not surprised at this meh attitude more than thirty years ago in terms of the Seymour desk, it did begin to create the foundation of my Idiot moniker. Even when my parents moved into their last home in 2003—one of those older clientele communities of houses where the occupants still want their own home but not the endless outdoor care that goes with it—and the desk sat prominently in their new dining room, I never gave it much thought. While I may have now and then acknowledged its fine ornate post-colonial craftsmanship, it was never a piece I imagined in my own house. Why bother? Cathy and I simply prefer a more rustic type of wooden furniture, and I figured I would let my other siblings fight over it when the time came.

This all changed when my aging parents started hinting that they would prefer the Seymour desk go to me because of its historical value. *At what point do you start to look around your house and say, "I really want the brass figurine with a huge penis to go to so and so?"* Anyway, they were adamant about the desk's future destination.

And, in hindsight, it made sense. I like history. I majored in history. I initially taught history. Additionally, the desk contained written materials from some of the desk owners dating back to the late 1700s, and my parents probably assumed that I would enjoy looking through them for their historical value. But as I came to realize over time, my passion—at least from an occupational sense—was not history. Don't get me wrong. Cathy and I love to travel to different places and take in the historical and cultural aspects a region or city has to offer. When others are heading to the beach or an amusement park, we are heading to a local museum.

But as my educational career progressed from years to decades, I began to teach fewer of the normal history classes and more of the social sciences like sociology, criminal justice, and even a forensic science and a law class. As my class-load became more centered around the present than the past, the less interested I was in getting a desk that was more than 200 years old. So much so, that Cathy and I were fairly certain that we'd donate it to a museum so others could appreciate it. Well, that was the initial thought.

My Burden

I guess, as I look back, what angers me most about my idiocy relevant to the desk was my stubbornness in the whole ordeal. The more my parents suggested that I dig into the desk a little bit, the more I wanted nothing to do with it. I felt put upon: *Why are they hefting this burden onto me?* To make matters worse, when I began to go through the materials in the Seymour desk well after the fact, I discovered that my dad had started his own research. He'd taken pages of notes in his cryptic handwriting—asking the same questions and coming to the same conclusions that I did much later in the process. This, more than anything that I learned during my desk adventure, hit me the hardest. I now think that his desire for me to jump on the Seymour desk train was less about passing it along to his history-buff son after he died than joining him on a project while he was still alive. While my mom had more or less succumbed to the evils of Alzheimer's before she passed, my dad's mind was as sharp as a tack until almost the very end. Of course, at the time, the thought of working with my dad on a very intimate level about a desk I cared little about seemed like torture. Before you again judge, think about working with your own eighty-to-ninety-year-old father who is way more stubborn than you are—and for the record, I am really stubborn. What could a stupid desk from the past offer me that I didn't already have in the present?

How wrong I was! Wrong for not taking the time while Cathy and I visited every month to at least start the lengthy process that has now consumed me for the last three years. Wrong for not bonding with my dad on something that he was passionate about and that I would become equally passionate about when it was too late. Wrong for letting my stubbornness get the best of me. Again.

I kick myself now for not taking the desk and its contents seriously. I would have loved to have co-authored a book with my dad rather than simply writing it in his honor. *I'm such an idiot.*

Again, when Dirck (we all called my father Dirck) passed away on November 2, 2020, our country was in the depths of Covid. He may not have died from the virus, but it surely affected all of us as we trudged down the long road to his passing. It affected home care, visits to the hospital, his ability to get out of the house, and his final weeks under hospice care. At that point, my school had a very stringent policy about traveling out of state. But I did sneak over to see him a few times, and, thankfully, I saw him the day before he died (*shhhh*).

Even in the aftermath of his death, Covid changed the norm. Rather than focusing our efforts on calling hours and a funeral for my dad, we had no choice but to put those matters on the back burner and redirected our efforts elsewhere. Following his death in November 2020, we slowly began the process of putting the house on the market and distributing the articles within it—including the Seymour desk. Again, though the distribution on paper of my parents' worldly possessions was relatively painless, the actual execution of such things is normally never easy, in both a physical and philosophical sense. But, in our case, things couldn't have gone much more smoothly.

We moved through our parents' physical possessions with relative ease, while at the same time taking into consideration the wishes of the grandchildren. It was our version of an NFL draft board, but rather than grabbing quarterbacks and defensive linemen, we were selecting furniture, paintings, and other knick-knacks. *The third pick in the first round of the Harrison draft goes to Andrew Harrison, and he chooses the Seymour desk!*

By January 2021, we had all carried off our wares so the painters could get to work. Our efforts in a relatively short period of time paid off (literally) when a prospective buyer fell into our laps before the paint was even dry and the house was officially on the market. The sale of the house closed in May 2021.

While the frantic pace of the sale caught all of us off guard, I made a point to reflect on the house's meaning beyond the bedrooms, kitchen, and such. I am generally not one to wax poetic—blunt perhaps, but not poetic—but standing in an empty house now totally devoid of its furniture, paintings, and little bronze thingies, I realized that a family home held an aura well beyond its owners and their possessions. Holidays would never be the same. It was at that point that I decided to take my piece of inherited possessions from my parents seriously—it was all I had, other than a lifetime of memories. If my parents felt so adamantly about a silly desk, then I would respect their wishes.

Now What?

This was my mindset when I unloaded the Seymour desk from the rented U-Haul into the basement of my house in January 2021. Only then, I finally had a chance to take in my new desk: to marvel at the marbling design of the mahogany, to play with the accordion doors and go through its drawers. In the drawers, as Dirck had mentioned on countless occasions, were stacks and stacks of materials decades old, and in a few cases, centuries old. The amount of paperwork blew my mind. I was dumbstruck. *Emphasis on dumb.* I assumed that there were a few pieces of artifacts and nothing more—*and we all know what happens when we assume.*

At that point, I knew that the first order of business was to meticulously go through each of these written materials with the proverbial fine-toothed comb. Analyzing and organizing was the mantra. While I may not acknowledge a house that had been repainted years before, I have become a zealot in terms of academic organization. *Thank you, Mom.* I ordered a box of latex gloves, three ring binders, plastic notebook sheaths, and one of the electric magnifying lamps that any good stamp and insect collector has. I was in total geek mode. Then I set up shop in our living room using my daughter's old card table.

For the next several months, I methodically went through each item, briefly analyzing it, categorizing it, and safely putting it into a plastic sheath and placing it in a three-ring binder. Although teaching high school classes online during Covid was perhaps the lowest point in my career, it was a blessing in one regard. I wasn't going anywhere, and working on the desk's contents became a nice break from the heady work of planning lessons for students who stared at you from the confines of their own bedroom. *Strange times.* In due time, the written materials—mostly personal letters, some dated as far back as 1798—were all organized in their respective folders.

I then moved on to the Seymour desk itself. *Seymour desk?* But before you say to yourself, "This guy doesn't seem to be the idiot he claims to be," the emcee from offstage says, "But wait, there's more!" While I was well aware of its name, I honestly had no idea why it was called the Seymour desk. Really. Absolutely no idea. I was that stubborn, in hindsight. I simply never bothered to ask.

Never giving the Seymour aspect of the desk much thought, I assumed that it had passed from my grandmother Carlotta Creevey Harrison to my dad and then eventually to me. Before that, I figured that it was owned by one of my founding fifth great-grandfathers, Noah Webster (author of the Webster's dictionary) or Oliver Ellsworth (one of the framers of the U.S. Constitution and the chief justice of the Supreme Court). *Why all the hoopla unless it had some connection to those two?* So, my initial thought was that the Seymour desk was so-called because of the style of the desk. Think of the Franklin stove as another example.

A quick search on Google—my BFF as I dove into this project before Ancestry.com rolled into town—turned up nothing. Then, I remembered two articles that were cut out from the *Journal of the Museum of Fine Arts* based in Boston among the other materials in the desk.

The first article showed a black and white replica of the same style of desk that I now owned. It was donated to the Museum of Fine Arts in 1930 by a person named Dudley Leavitt Pickman. According to the writer, this Federal period desk was probably built around 1790 and in the style of "American Secretary" type desks at that time. It then goes on to detail the components of the desk—that could have easily been about my own desk. From the "mahogany" wood to the "three drawers with beaded edges and lines of satinwood inlay" to "a hinged writing leaf, with green baize, rests on sliding supports when in use" to the "upper part or cabinet of the secretary has an unusual curved front containing tambour doors" to finally "The interior of the cabinet contains fitted drawers and filing compartments." *Yup, my desk to a T...but nothing referencing the "Seymour style."* A quick search confirmed what I now began to realize. "American Secretary" was a common style in the late 1700s to early 1800s (the Federal period) that usually had tambour or accordion doors. But who or what was Seymour in all this? The second article gave me answers. *Or so I thought.*

This article, also about a desk, is far more recent based on the texture of the paper and its brilliant color. Again, the style of the desk described is quite like the 1930 acquisition and my own. It is a beautiful piece. While I am partial to my own tambour desk, this desk pictured is gorgeous. The heading underneath the desk reads, "Recent Acquisition—Tambour Desk, About 1796-98—John Seymour and Son (1794-1816)." *Whaaaat? Now things began to click.* My desk had nothing to do with style per se but rather a cabinet maker back in the day.

I glanced at the page from the magazine a few more times and realized that I needed to dig deeper. I googled "Museum of Fine Arts Boston," and bingo, an extensive website appeared. A few new searches here, a few clicks there, and a page showing five tambour secretary desks appeared that were all in the collection at the museum. Four of them were made by the Seymour team. *Who are these guys?* The desk described in the magazine article was the last item listed on the website's page. When I clicked on the link, an extensive description was given, including the year 2000, which was when it was donated to the museum. *Whaaaat? Did my dad actually find the* Journal of the Museum of Fine Arts *in question and rip out this page? Ugh. I'm such an idiot.*

Clearly, the Seymour furniture makers were not your average furniture hacks down the road. Another deep search on the museum website found that there were close to twenty pieces of furniture by either the father, John Seymour, or his son, Thomas, between the last decade of the 18th century and the first decade of the 19th. Could it be like how we refer to Revere Ware? If you missed this lesson in history, when not charging through the streets of Boston on horseback yelling something about the Redcoats, Paul Revere produced copper ware that eventually became the namesake for a style of pots and pans still popular today. *Could this be the same scenario with my desk? Back to the drawing board.*

John Seymour was born in Dorset, England, in 1738, and he built a modest trade as a furniture maker there. In 1783, he moved to the former colonies with his family to hopefully build a more lucrative business as a so-called cabinet maker. His son, Thomas, who would become his partner in the trade, was thirteen at the time. Initially settling in Portland, Maine, John moved his family to Boston in 1793. The growing prosperity in the Boston area meant a desire for finer things like exquisite furniture, and though Seymour's business initially struggled, it grew dramatically after the turn of the century because of the quality of his and son's craftsmanship. If you were someone of moderate wealth and prestige, you commissioned the Seymours to build you a piece of furniture such as a desk or a cabinet or a table. *Think Tiffany & Company.* Thomas eventually took over the business and started his own company: Boston Furniture Warehouse. Like many artists, their artwork gained more prestige and value well after their deaths, as illustrated by the number of pieces in the Museum of Fine Arts. Neither man died wealthy.

In my mind, this was all making sense. Someone on my dad's side purchased a Seymour mahogany tambour desk from the famous Seymours sometime after 1794.

As I mentioned earlier, my paternal grandmother, Carlotta Creevey Harrison, is a direct descendant of Noah Webster and Oliver Ellsworth, both prominent founding fathers during the late 1700s and the early 1800s. Their daughter and son, respectively, married in 1813, and the lineage joining the two major Connecticut families began. *Could Noah Webster or Oliver Ellsworth have been the original owners of the desk?* The timing definitely fit, and both men had the means to afford it.

As my heart quickened and my research on the Seymours progressed (picture me scrolling frantically down the Google page), I noticed a link that caught me off guard and pulled me from the normal historical minutiae.

A Kindred Spirit

The title on the link read, "Card Table, a $25 Garage-Sale Bargain, Is Sold for $541,500" from the *New York Times* on January 19, 1998. *Whaaaat? I was definitely intrigued.* The story details a retired school teacher by the name of Claire Wiegand-Beckmann from Secaucus, New Jersey. She, in her retirement, liked to do the yard and garage sale thing. One person's antiquing is another person's homebrewing—my current semi-retirement gig. She purchased an old and battered desk (nothing like my desk in terms of its size and ornateness) at a yard sale around the mid-1960s to fit in a designated spot in a recently purchased house. The desk was for $25, bargained down from $30.

In 1997, Mrs. Wiegand-Beckmann appeared on PBS's *Chubb's Antiques Roadshow* and was told by the appraisers, brothers Leigh and Leslie Keno, that the desk was worth at least $200,000. She was dumbfounded. What made the piece worth that much was the authenticity of the Seymour stamp on the underside of the desk. Additionally, the fact that no one had done anything significant to improve it made it even more valuable, giving credence to the adage that "less is more."

Under the guidance of the two Keno brothers, Mrs. Wiegand-Beckmann put the piece up for auction at Sotheby's in January 1998. The *New York Times* article states, "Israel Sack Inc., a New York dealer of fine American antiques, bought the table, which was one of six made by the Boston furniture maker John Seymour & Son. The meticulously constructed table has its original finish and is considered to be in good condition." So here is a diminutive retired teacher sitting among some of the biggest antique buyers in the world, watching the price skyrocket to $490,000—which at that point is the highest amount ever paid for a piece of Federal furniture. I was ecstatic for this woman. She, like most teachers, probably scraped and saved her way through her school years to eventually retire relatively comfortably with a state pension. But with one antiquing moment, she was a half million richer. Then my reality as the new owner of the Seymour desk came crashing down on me. *What have my parents dropped in my lap?*

Money is a relatively foreign element to me, simply because my wife and I, like Mrs. Wiegand-Beckmann, lived our whole lives as educators with reasonable salaries. We have lived, by necessity, relatively frugal lives. Whether it was job selection or simple genetics, I've never really understood the desire to have the most or the newest toys in town. *I wouldn't get a second look from Melania Trump.* I really was perplexed about the potential of having a piece of furniture worth six figures in my home of general modesty. How did I explain that to my brothers and sisters? *Oh hey, that brass figurine with the erect penis is pretty cool, but is it worth a half million dollars?* Did I auction it? Did I donate it to a museum in Connecticut—which up until that point was my general plan due to the fact that the desk may have belonged to either Noah Webster or Oliver Ellsworth? Did I keep it for the kids and grandkids? *Ugh!*

During this moment of head scratching, I did what I've always done: called my brother Matt. He and I are a year and a half apart and have always been close. And while we definitely have different tastes, we have always been able to hash things out, knowing that ultimately we'd come to the same conclusion. So, I laid it all out to him over the phone, explaining how uncomfortable I was inheriting a desk that might be far more valuable than anything else left by our parents. He, in typical Matt style, laughed his endearing laugh and said something like "Geez, I thought you were going to ask advice about Cathy or your kids. Run with it, bro. Mom and Dad really wanted you to have the desk, so fuck the rest. Good luck. Buy me a new car if it pans out." So, I ran with it.

Run With It, Bro!

The first part of my new marching orders was simple: Was there the Seymour label somewhere on the desk? Up until that point, I hadn't really scoured the desk from top to bottom. Sure, I had opened the drawers, played with the tambour doors, and opened the hedged desktop, but I hadn't done a full Nicolas Cage on the piece. Now, I was on a mission.

The key to the Claire Wiegand-Beckmann desk was the seal or label of the makers, John Seymour and Son, on the backside of the table top. According to the Keno brothers, it is quite rare to find these still intact due primarily to the element of time. Then I remembered that the article about the piece donated in 2000 had a picture of the label in addition to the photo of the desk itself. In this particular case, it was on the backside of the desk—the side that would butt up against a wall. So, into the basement I went, and I scoured the desk, paying close attention to the backside. Nothing. I pulled out the drawers, even the small ones, and turned them over. Nothing. I looked at the underside. Nothing. While I was slightly disappointed, I wasn't devastated. Obviously, having a Seymour label would have facilitated matters greatly, but I quickly moved on to Plan B: Find an expert to look at the desk and tell me the good or bad news.

How would I find someone who knew a thing or two about antique furniture dating back to the Federal period? Well, in all honesty, I hadn't a clue. But I did have an inkling who would. One of the perks of teaching high school social studies in general, and criminal justice, sociology, and forensic science and the law specifically, is that you get to meet a lot of interesting and dedicated people in those fields. And if I was lucky enough, they were willing to come in and discuss their area of expertise. One of those people was Kim Rumrill, who was a criminalist at the New Hampshire Forensic Lab in Concord. I could go on and on about the various ways she helped me do my job over the years, but this time it was her husband I was interested in.

Alan Rumrill was the executive director at the Historical Society of Cheshire County in Keene, New Hampshire, the biggest town/city in the southwest corner of the state—and one town over from the school where I taught. Alan is *that guy* in terms of historical information for the area, and he even has a weekly byline in the local paper about some person, event, or place in the region's past. I found his contact information easily enough; then I contacted Kim so she could tell him that some nut job she knew would be contacting him about a silly desk. In late January 2021, I sent him an email explaining my dilemma. I had to assume that he knew some auctioneers who worked with antique furniture, given the nature of his own expertise. He did not disappoint. He quickly responded with a name from a town due east of Keene called Peterborough, New Hampshire. I contacted Charlie Cobb via email, and he encouraged me to complete an online appraisal form as a first step.

Charlie Cobb runs a business called the Cobbs Auctioneers in Peterborough. His antique and auctioneer website is excellent, and I found the appraisal link easily enough. A big stumbling block was describing the desk's history or provenance, which in many ways is what gives an antique its value. But that's why I needed help from an expert in the first place. I didn't know the desk's history. Thankfully, that issue was solved with a simple email from Charlie Cobb after I submitted the information, including photos, in late February 2021. He wrote back on March 1, 2021:

> First of all your desk is not made by the Seymours but is probably made by a rural cabinet maker, the desk is not a significant one but it is nice, seems to be NH even though the history ties it into Conn which is why there is a tie in up here as well, should you want a formal appraisal I could do that for a fee which of course would be refundable should you use us to sell it.
>
> My best, cm cobb

And there it was: "not made by the Seymours." Honestly, I was a bit relieved. One avenue in this process was now eliminated. I was further enlightened when Charlie discussed the premise of selling the desk when he wrote:

> This antique market is very different from the old days, there is not a lot of support for the middle of the road furniture so with that in mind I feel your secretary is worth $2500. However should you decide to place it in auction I don't think it would bring more than $1200-1400. This may be a disappointment but it is the reality of today's antique market place.

Though it still didn't answer my question of why the desk was so named, at least I didn't have to explain to my brothers and sister how I could afford a Lexus on a teacher's salary.

So, back to square one. I put the name game aside for the time being and concentrated on my side of the family—Noah Webster and Oliver Ellsworth. If I was going to eventually donate the desk to their estates (both of their respective homes are now museums in West Hartford and Windsor, Connecticut), I needed to dig into their pasts. And the more I dug, the more the idiot moniker kept ringing in my ears.

2

Ships in the Night

It didn't take long for that idiocy to rear its ugly head again when I asked myself what I really knew about Noah Webster and Oliver Ellsworth. Honestly, not much, and what I thought I knew for sure was, for the most part, wrong. My official knowledge of my somewhat famous ancestors was this: Noah Webster's oldest daughter, Emily Schotten Webster, married Oliver Ellsworth's youngest son, William Wolcott Ellsworth, in 1813, and this carried a lineage through my grandmother Carlotta to my dad, Dirck, and eventually to my three siblings and myself. Noah was a lifelong teacher before deciding to write a dictionary, and Oliver served on the U.S. Supreme Court at some point. And one of them must have purchased a desk that I now owned. But which one?

Unfortunately, though not surprisingly, the more I dug into their lives, the more that L on my forehead began to burn. *Wait a minute. When did the idiot become a loser?* At this point, my working mantra became: Assume you know nothing about whatever you're researching because it's probably true. I decided to jump feet first into the lives of these two men and their ancestors, hoping I would discover something about the mystery desk.

Right off the bat, I learned that other than the connection between the two men through marriage, their lives never really connected. Pick up any biography of either man and you'll only find a few references to the other. However, they were contemporaries, and both had significant dealings with the same historic events. Additionally, both had significant influence on American culture, though from different perspectives. They were ships in the night.

In the end, while I had hoped that I would find an answer to the desk question, I found that I was more intrigued by the two men's lives, not only for their influence on our country but also in seeing some of the same traits in myself. As I trudged through their lives, the desk question became almost an afterthought.

Noah: America's Educator?

Here is what I thought I knew about my famous ancestor from Hartford. Noah Webster lived in Hartford, Connecticut. He taught for a living. At some point, he wrote a dictionary and became rich. While indeed all three of these facts have some truth to them, I soon realized there was so much more to the man. Additionally, I felt that he and I were kindred spirits, since I started my teaching career in Hartford and lived in West Hartford for a time. In fact, my first-born child, Noah Benjamin Harrison, was named in part due to my familial connection to a famous teacher.

Noah Webster c. 1867

Noah Webster was born in 1758 in the western division of Hartford (now known as West Hartford). His father, Noah, Sr., was a descendant of one of Connecticut's founding fathers: Governor John Webster. Additionally, his mother, Mercy Steele Webster, was the great-great-granddaughter of William Bradford II, a Mayflower traveler and the first governor of the Plymouth Bay Colony. Noah indeed had some prominent New England relatives. He was the fourth of five children, and he spent his childhood working the family farm during the growing and harvest seasons and going to school. While most of the Webster family had a long history of good standing throughout New England, at least one did not—and it was perhaps no fault of her own.

Noah's great-aunt, Mary Reeve Webster, lived in Hadley, Massachusetts (about twenty miles directly south from my home in Northfield, Massachusetts) with her husband and son. They were simple, poor farmers by all accounts, but it is documented that she, as we say in school, had a mouth on her. So much so that she was soon despised by her fellow citizens of Hadley. In something out of a colonial version of *Mean Girls*, she was accused of being a witch. Other than her mouthiness, the evidence ranged from putting spells on horses and cattle so they wouldn't pass by her house to causing a chicken to fall through a neighbor's chimney to causing the painful death of a prominent Hadley citizen. In the spring of 1683, she was officially accused of witchcraft and went on trial in Boston. Luckily, she was acquitted by the sitting judge.

Unfortunately for Mary, things did not improve upon her return to Hadley. It was not the first time nor the last time that an acquittal in a court would not placate the masses. For the next year and a half, she continued to be persecuted and "disturbed" (basically, people would go into her home and beat her up) until things went a little too far when a few lads broke into her house, dragged her outside, and strung her up under a tree until they believed she was dead. Remarkably, she survived the ordeal and lived for another eleven years. As legends go, she was given the nickname Half-Hanged Mary.

Oliver: Yale's Loss, Princeton's Gain

Truth be told, whatever knowledge I thought I knew about Noah Webster—and after doing some research, I realized that I had barely scratched the surface—I knew even less about my other founding grandfather, Oliver Ellsworth.

In the simplest sense, Oliver lived his entire life in Windsor, Connecticut (a few towns north of Hartford) and was a half generation older than Noah Webster. While I was growing up, I heard little to nothing about Oliver and a bit more about his contemporary, Noah.

Oliver's great-grandfather, Josiah, moved from England, as many did, and settled in Windsor in 1654. Josiah's sixth child, Jonathan, a storekeeper and tavern keeper, married Sarah Grant in 1669, and they had a slew of children. As many did. Their seventh child, David, born in 1709, married Jemima Leavitt in 1740 and had four children—though only three survived infancy. Oliver, the middle child and the only one to survive to adulthood, was born on April 24, 1745.

Oliver Ellsworth, c. 1891

Oliver's official education began in 1757 when he was twelve under the tutelage of Reverend Joseph Bellamy, a teaching pastor within the Congregational Church in Connecticut, and it continued until he was seventeen. The Congregational Church, while still the prominent church throughout New England at the time, was going through an evolution, which occurs within many religions and their sects. This particular shift is known as the Great Awakening. Like many awakenings throughout any religion's history, this was no different. The newer generation of Christian thinkers felt that their viewpoint on the relationship with God was more appropriate. *Wash. Rinse. Repeat.*

While Noah Webster's religious awakening didn't occur until well into the 19th century, Oliver Ellsworth's faith was front and center from day one. In a nutshell, he felt that his purpose on earth was to be God's servant to mankind and that was more important than worrying about an afterlife. His efforts as a lawyer, politician, and judge always came back to this premise. *Amen, brother. Or fifth great-grandfather.* Additionally, the old fire and brimstone sermons were (at the time) a thing of the past.

Given his religious education under Joseph Bellamy, attending Yale University, a center for religious training, was the next obvious choice. This was especially logical since Oliver was from Connecticut and Yale had a long history of producing men of the pulpit. He entered the college in 1762. Unfortunately, Yale was also in its own religious turmoil—like the rest of New England—over the Old and New Light or Divinity (New Awakening), which immediately rubbed Oliver the wrong way, especially given his last five years of indoctrination under Joseph Bellamy. In general terms, the whole student body was at serious odds with the Old Light-leaning administration under President Thomas Clap. Oliver, in due course, was disciplined for "cleaning the yard" in the fall of his freshman year, which on the surface sounds absurd. The term "cleaning the yard" was a guise for meeting in the courtyard to organize the student body's next demonstration against Old Divinity teachings and was thus banned by President Clap.

Of course, I really began to admire his style following a more serious event his sophomore year. For no apparent reason, he was either caught drinking wine or spiking the cafeteria food with said wine—or perhaps both. The details are sketchy. Whatever the case, Oliver's parents had enough of his antics and he was sent home from

Yale. So, my fifth great-grandfather was expelled from Yale for drinking. *Hell ya!*

Oliver, with the help of his parents, was admitted to the College of New Jersey (Princeton) the following fall, and it was clearly a much better fit. Princeton was founded in 1746 and used the New Divinity as its foundation. In addition to having a similar religious basis to Oliver's upbringing, it also had a much more diverse population than Yale did. Whereas Yale was much more locally represented, Princeton had students from all over the colonies, which gave Oliver his first glimpse of a national population and a broader perspective that would serve him well as a politician. He graduated in 1766 with a theological degree and began his career as a pastor. That career did not last long.

As I've seen with many prospective teachers over the years, simply having a boatload of knowledge about a particular topic doesn't mean that someone can stand up in front of a roomful of students and connect with them. The same applies to Oliver and his first attempt at a sermon under someone else's tutelage. His mentor read the sermon and immediately said it sounded more like an argument before the court. He suggested that Oliver change directions. So, taking the hint, Oliver headed toward a law career and passed the bar in 1771. He spent the next five years trying to make a practice out of a law degree. Ironically, while he used the law degree to propel him into a political career, he never fell back into a standard law practice again during his lifetime of public service.

In the meantime, he married Abigail Wolcott in 1772, and they had nine children, with seven living to adulthood. Abigail Wolcott Ellsworth's lineage was no slouch in its own right; her uncle, Roger Wolcott, was colonial governor of Connecticut in the 1750s. The couple lived their entire lives in their homestead in Windsor, Connecticut.

Noah: Not Your Normal College Career

While Oliver Ellsworth was finishing at Princeton and becoming a lawyer, Noah Webster was growing up in West Hartford. At the age of sixteen, like many who could afford it, he enrolled at Yale University in 1774. While you can't swing a dead cat without hitting a twenty-year-old college student with a backpack and a cup of Dunkin' coffee today in New England, there were only a limited number of colleges back in the day. If a college education today seems somewhat elitist, it was tenfold in the 1770s. Thankfully, Noah's parents saw that he wasn't farmer material, and they found the money to send him to Yale.

Noah's college career at Yale, spanning from 1774 to 1778, was nothing less than chaotic. First and foremost, Yale in New Haven, Connecticut, in the late 1700s, was not the well-oiled and prestigious machine that it is today. Founded in 1701 as a religious school, it focused on training Protestant Congregationalists, as previously mentioned. But, by the time Noah arrived, it was additionally touted for training would-be lawyers. Beyond that, it did not have the reputation of other colleges across the thirteen colonies—and especially not of its neighbor, Harvard, to the northeast. In Noah's time, Yale had a reputation for poor living conditions, mediocre teachers, and horrible food. Additionally, he did not come from the same wealth as his forty other classmates, and paying the tuition bills throughout his four-year college career was a constant struggle.

If that wasn't enough to make a college freshman drink like, well, a college freshman, then the turbulent circumstances swirling around the colonies in general and New England specifically, were. In the spring of their freshman year in 1775, Noah and his classmates had to deal with the American Revolution brewing right down the road at Lexington and Concord, Massachusetts. Think "one if by land, two if by sea." Anywhere along the New England coast between New York and Boston was fair game to the English, and that included New Haven. Like many towns, the local militia trained and prepared for the inevitable, and in this case, that militia included the students of Yale. Not only did the 100 or so Yale students train for potential combat, but forty of them wound up later serving in the war. Disruption became the norm.

In August 1776, the student body was sent home due to a typhoid outbreak. Six months later, in January 1777, Yale was shut down again due to the threat of the Redcoats and relocated to Glastonbury, Connecticut, where it remained until the fall of 1777. In November 1777, Yale reopened again in New Haven, but then it closed again due to the war in the spring of 1778. Not your typical four years of college bliss.

As I delved into Noah Webster's tumultuous four years at Yale in the middle 1770s, I couldn't help but think of the similarities to my dad's four years at Yale in the mid-1940s. As Noah had to deal with the revolutionary years, life in the 1940s for Dirck was preoccupied by World War II. After graduating from the Berkshire School in the hills of western Massachusetts in the spring of 1943, Dirck entered Yale the following autumn at the height of the war. A year and a half later, he turned eighteen, dropped out of Yale (by the grace of a few teachers, he passed his sophomore year), and enlisted in the Navy. He was finally deployed in August 1945, but he missed active duty by only a few days when the Japanese finally surrendered around the same time. Dirck served for another year and returned to Yale in the fall of 1946, graduating in the spring of 1948. He would comment on numerous occasions that his college career was not much to speak of other than graduating in the same class as George Bush, Sr. Again, I find it remarkable that two distant but direct relatives had a crappy college career for the same reasons 170 years apart.

After graduating from Yale in the spring of 1778, Noah took up his first teaching gig in February 1779 in Glastonbury, Connecticut. He only lasted the winter term. Here I had assumed (yeah, yeah, I know the saying) that he'd spent his whole life as an educator. *Wrong. Wrong. And more wrong.* He, on a multitude of occasions, joined a teaching staff, or in some cases even started his own school or academy, only to walk away some time later. Disenchanted with the whole education thing, he decided to focus on what many Yale undergraduates did—becoming a lawyer.

Quite different from today, a would-be lawyer needed only a bachelor's degree and two years of tutelage under a practicing lawyer. As fate would have it, Noah joined Oliver Ellsworth for the task. *What about ships in the night, Harrison?* His stint with Oliver as an underling did not last long. *Aaaahhh!* Working as a teacher in Hartford during the day to pay the bills and working for Oliver and studying at night drove Noah to a near breakdown within months. By the summer of 1779, he'd quit both endeavors. His battle with mental illness in the form of acute anxiety due to overwork and an insatiable need to be successful and wealthy was a demon he would wrestle with his whole life. Well before the availability of Xanax and Valium, psychological help, and techniques to unclutter one's brain, I can only imagine the struggles that Noah went through without the least bit of support. Eventually, after a long two years and a second legal sponsor, he passed the bar exam in the spring of 1781.

Oliver: From Lawyer to Politician

While Noah Webster was starting and stopping an educational career and attempting a legal one, Oliver Ellsworth was pausing his own legal career and starting a political one. He was elected to the colonial General Assembly in 1773, the office of Justice of the Peace in 1774, and he took on many apprentices—including Noah Webster—until federal and state politics officially became his passion. His first call of duty occurred following the Battle of Lexington in Concord, Massachusetts, in April 1775. The Connecticut General Assembly almost immediately thumbed their noses at Big Brother and authorized support to the Boston rebels. As a congressman for Connecticut, Oliver was given a position on the Committee of the Pay Table and Council of Safety. Serendipity stepped in at this point when Oliver, a relative unknown outside the borders of Connecticut, visited General Washington to request money to pay the Connecticut troops. While Oliver's role in the process was minimal and Washington did the political thing, "Go talk to the Continental Congress," they began a close relationship that would continue for another 25 years.

Oliver's war efforts at home earned him a spot in the Continental Congress in 1777, but his appointment was delayed when his first son and his namesake died in May 1778 at six years old. My research turned up these infant and young child deaths continuously in the 1700s, 1800s, and even the early 1900s, and I can't even imagine the pain, having raised two children of my own. While families were much bigger back in the day for a multitude of reasons, I always wondered whether parents had the same deep remorse given the knowledge that most lost a few along the way. So, when I read Oliver's reaction and delayed appointment to put his familial affairs in order, I realized that of course they did.

Thus, he did not enter Philadelphia officially until the fall of 1778, and at that point, the war with Great Britain was in full swing. Oliver soon realized the state of running a country and a war at the time was not a pretty picture, and much of the disharmony was not solely due to fighting the British. In addition to financing a war, the Continental Congress had to deal with sectionalism that would continue well after the Civil War and perhaps still exists today.

One of Oliver's first appointments was joining a five-member group to create a federal court to deal with admiralty or maritime issues occurring between colonies and states. Before I trudge on, it is important to mention that maritime and admiralty matters were not small items. Keep in mind that commerce was all about the open seas. There were no trains, cars, trucks, or planes. Other than the arduous movement of goods over land, the high seas and rivers were the main way to transport goods from state to state and country to country. Thus, stopping and robbing a ship of its contents was a lucrative business. But it does beg the question, was it still illegal if the ship's owner was involved with our enemy of war?

George Washington was concerned with the contraband (confiscated goods from British ships) that might fall into the hands of non-combatants (i.e. pirates), and he wanted Congress to tackle the potential problem. While the adage of "all's fair in love and war" comes to my mind, General Washington did not want to open that can of worms so early in the fighting. The initial plan was for the individual states to deal with their own contraband prizes within their own borders and offshore of those borders as well. A federal court would only step in if there was a controversy.

Oliver Ellsworth was then placed on the Committee of Appeals to serve as an arbiter, and by October 1778, the committee had decided thirty-eight cases on appeal. But the states were not necessarily happy about a federal government intervening into state court affairs. For many, the war was being fought to cut ties with an overreaching authority by the British. Nevertheless, Oliver's time creating a maritime court and overseeing it during the war would serve him well, as he did the same as a senator ten years later.

Noah: From Lawyer to Author

As Oliver Ellsworth was wrestling with other bigwigs in Philadelphia who were trying to run a country while also financing a war, Noah Webster, with a new lawyer shingle hanging from his doorway, thought that his financial woes were a thing of the past. Unfortunately, Noah neither was a very good lawyer nor did he really enjoy doing it. *Noah, my man, you got some real problems here!* On the other hand, he seemed to really enjoy academia and especially writing. Many of Noah's issues with teaching were not only internal but also with the resources available to him—specifically American-based resources. At that time, on both sides of the Atlantic, children used what was called the *Dilworth Speller* or *The Guide to the English Tongue.* Well before the classic *Run, Tip, Run* (yes, I am really dating myself), the *Dilworth Speller* served the same purpose: helping students read and pronounce words and syllables correctly. Just as Noah eventually had an obsession with dictionaries that did not reflect the American language, so he felt similarly about the *Dilworth Speller*. It needed work, and it needed to be from an American perspective.

So, he wrote his own textbook named *A Grammatical Institute of the English Language* in 1783. It was eventually nicknamed *Blue-Backed Speller,* and it became one of the most popular books of its time—selling over 100 million copies. This very popular and lucrative book paved the way for a long history of writing, social activism, and limited financial security. By the time of Noah's death in 1843, *The Elementary Spelling Book*—its official title after 1829—averaged about a million copies sold per year. *If you never heard of it, you are not alone. But then again, I'm an idiot!*

While eventually quite profitable, the book took a while to gain traction, and Noah's promotion of the product may have been the problem. After its initial publication, Noah barnstormed the country (keeping in mind that the country was only thirteen states) to promote his new publication. Though he proved to be a brilliant writer, he wasn't much of an orator in a business sense. He always assumed that he was the smartest in the room, and he may well have been, but he had problems relating to those he needed most. I'm no businessman, but he didn't do himself any favors as a marketer.

In addition to promoting his speller to anyone who would listen, he was also on a campaign to push for copyright laws in every state where he planned to sell his speller. In his mind, it did him no good to promote a textbook to be used across the country if someone else was going to turn around and copy his efforts. He was quite successful in this regard.

In the end, the popularity of the speller overshadowed his failings as a promoter. As I did my research and read between the lines of some of the narratives, I couldn't help but think that Noah was somewhat of an aloof prick who could not relate to those around him, including his own kids. And perhaps, as he aged, he realized that sitting in his office and plodding through the alphabet as he wrote his dictionary was really his niche and leaving the promotion to someone else was in his best interest.

Oliver: From Politician to Lawyer to Delegate

By 1783, while Noah Webster was barnstorming the country with his new speller, Oliver Ellsworth was back in Windsor, Connecticut, after his stint with the Continental Congress. He had rejoined Connecticut's General Assembly and restarted his law practice. In 1785, he was selected to the Connecticut Superior Court as a judge, but his time in Connecticut's political systems did not last long. He probably would have been comfortable maintaining his home and family in Windsor and working in any of these roles for the remainder of his life, but he was called into federal service again to serve as a representative for the state of Connecticut at the Constitutional Convention in the summer of 1787.

Up until the Broadway musical hit, *Hamilton* most were unfamiliar with the Constitutional Convention beyond its eventual outcome. If you were taking a pee break during this part of your early U.S. history class, here is the brief skinny. In November 1777, while the war was raging with the British, the Continental Congress pieced together the Articles of Confederation, our first national government constitution, and it was ratified by the thirteen states in March 1781. As I would often tell my students, the Articles were an overreaction to the colonial government experience of the time. In theory, the colonies were rebelling against a repressive British government, so it would behoove the Continental Congress to create a central government that did not do the very same thing. But they overcompensated. They created a central government that had little to no power, which became quite evident once the war ended.

It did not take long for many of the big names of the time to propose revamping the Articles of Confederation to beef up central government powers to run a country on a more efficient basis. *I know, I know, it doesn't seem really efficient now.* In the summer and early fall of 1787, the best and the brightest from twelve states met in Philadelphia to initially revamp the Articles.

Oliver Ellsworth joined Roger Sherman and William Samuel Johnson to represent Connecticut in the summer of 1787. The number of delegates per state varied in number—as little as two from New Hampshire and as many as eight from Pennsylvania. The total number of delegates was fifty-five, representing all thirteen states except Rhode Island, who believed they had everything to lose by shifting power to the national government. While there may have been as many as fifty-five delegates in the tiny and un-air-conditioned Independence Hall, the reality is that many delegates came and went over the course of the four-month period. While not on the original drawing board, it became clear almost immediately that the idea of revising the Articles would be scratched and replaced with the thought of creating a new document.

Noah: George and Ben's Bro

The summer of 1787 also provided a needed distraction for Noah Webster from the drudgery of selling his written works and pushing for copyright laws in every state. He decided that he would not miss the events of the summer of 1787 in Philadelphia for anything, which was news to me. I had always assumed that he'd lived his life in relative obscurity, chained to his desk researching word after word to create a colossus dictionary. This was not the case. He was a major player in the politics of the day—not like Oliver who was down in the mud and wrestling with the others, but critiquing from afar. But, in this case, not too far.

Like many during this time period, Noah was dismayed by the chaos after the American Revolution. With his debts paid from the sales of his speller and the admission fees earned from a Northeast lecture series, Noah pulled up stakes in New Haven, Connecticut—his home off and on throughout the entirety of his life—and moved to Philadelphia to join the fun. To pay his new bills, he took up a six-month stint at the Episcopal Academy in April 1787. For Noah Webster, known as America's Educator, this would be his last official job as a teacher. Of course, the real reason for the move was to influence the proceedings that began a month later in May 1787. While Noah was not among the three delegates from Connecticut (Roger Sherman, David Johnson, and, of course, Oliver Ellsworth), he spent a lot of time with the powers that be in Philadelphia during the time period. He, like his three Connecticut brethren, was a Federalist and supported a much stronger central government. But his influence on our nation's new government went far beyond the connection to the three delegates from Connecticut.

Between 1784 and 1785, Noah wrote and published his essay "Sketches of American Policy." For a man who spent much of his writing career focusing on language, this came out of left field. Researching the major thinkers of the day in Europe, he wrote a four-part series looking at the history of the relationship between governments and the governed. By all accounts, the series earned high praise from all corners of the new country, but it was the fourth and last installment that got the most attention.

Named "Plan of Policy for Improving the Advantages and Perpetuating the Union of the United States," it literally spelled out the reasons for a new constitution and the necessary components to be included. Even though the Constitutional Convention was two years away but clearly in the works, the essay became the standard for all those who were seeking and justifying a strong central government. One such individual was George Washington, who met Noah for the first time at Mount Vernon in early summer of 1785 while Noah was promoting his speller and a need for copyright laws in Virginia. They got along swimmingly, especially after Noah gave George Washington a copy of his newly published *Sketches*. Their bromance would continue for decades.

To this point, George Washington was fifty-three at the time of their first meeting to Noah's twenty-seven. To Noah, Washington was an icon, a father figure, and a true hero in their midst. Like Kobe Bryant playing against his elder and icon, Michael Jordan, once Noah got beyond his awe, the two got down to brass tacks. *Brass tasks? Hmmmm. Let it go, Harrison.*

According to Harlow Giles Unger in his biography of Noah Webster, *Noah Webster—The Life and Times of an American Patriot,* "Webster and Washington got along famously. Webster gave the general a copy of the *Sketches*, and the two spent the afternoon discussing the most controversial issues of the day—national unity, the need for a strong federal government, abolition of slavery, agriculture, and education."

Things went so smoothly that the two met again in the fall of 1785 while Noah was still in the South. Hoping for Washington's help in the passage of a copyright law in Virginia, they again discussed the virtues of Noah's *Sketches* and finally the education of Washington's grandchildren. Washington felt a need to import a tutor from Europe. Noah, a wise man, especially when considering the state of American education at that point, suggested that a tutor from anywhere other than the United States would not look good in the public eye. So taken by the young educator and writer, Washington wished to hire Noah as said tutor and as his private secretary. Noah declined gracefully. Noah agreed, instead, to send Washington a list of suitable American tutors, which he did in a later correspondence. This correspondence would continue until George Washington's death in 1799.

With the immediate issues in 1787, Washington's praise for Noah's *Sketches* received almost two years previously resurfaced when he was gearing up for the Constitutional Convention. He was so influenced by the contents of the fourth installment of *Sketches* that it was rumored that Washington (who was unsurprisingly chosen as the president of the Constitutional Convention and oversaw all proceedings) met with Noah at his temporary digs in Philadelphia two days into the convention. While there is no official record of their meeting nor any evidence of a direct link to Noah's political document, George Washington began pushing hard for a new constitution rather than revising the Articles of Confederation, as Noah had strongly suggested. Additionally, many of the necessary components advocated for by Noah (for example, a two-house congress—each selected under differing guidelines) were included and, in some cases, Washington used his exact language.

Noah's other BFF was none other than the new nation's second most famous icon—Benjamin Franklin. In Franklin's case, their relationship was far deeper and for different reasons. Franklin had his hands in many projects, and one of those was the creation of his own educational speller well before Noah stepped into the arena. Whereas Noah wanted to focus on the spelling of words, Ben Franklin wanted to create a new alphabet. Thankfully, Noah's ideas of an improved American system to teach children to read and write prevailed. I can only imagine how that initial conversation went:

Noah: Yo Ben! I'm working on a new spelling textbook for children that would be easier for the American student to learn to read and write while at the same time helping teachers instruct.

Ben: Nice. I want to revamp the whole Roman alphabet that has been the norm for centuries.

Noah: Ummmm.

Ben: First off, I want to eliminate the letters C, W, J, Y. Useless garbage. Don't need them.

Noah: Maybe you ought to lay off the mead for a while, especially at your age.

Ben: Whatever. When are the concubines showing up?

They met for the first time in the winter of 1786 and continued to work together until Benjamin Franklin passed away in 1790. The matter at hand was the re-creation of the new government in the summer of 1787, and though Noah had not been officially invited to the ball, he made sure to connect with those who were. However, it was Franklin who sought Noah out once the document was complete in 1787—not only for his support, but for his keen ability to explain matters in the simplest terms so all could understand.

Oliver: We Are Partly National; Partly Federal

While there is plenty of documentation of Noah's backroom influence with the real power brokers of the convention, Oliver Ellsworth does not appear to have been one of his confidants. Perhaps it was simply not Oliver's style.

Well documented in every U.S. history textbook across the country, there were a lot of contentious moments during these months involving multiple battle-lines. The initial and biggest stumbling block was representation in Congress. One of the worst decisions made in creating the Articles of Confederation was a one-house Congress where each state had one vote, with no regards to their population. While at the time it made some sense in terms of how each state viewed itself, it had to be fixed before moving on to the other matters at hand.

The Virginia Plan, as it is referred to today, was proposed early in the convention. It asked for two houses of Congress, both appropriated by the population of each state. States like Virginia, New York, and Pennsylvania felt that they should have more weight in making decisions for the whole country since most of the nation's population lived in those states. Not surprisingly, the smaller population states like New Jersey (*crazy, I know*) and Delaware were furious and proposed that Congress should remain as it was—one state, one vote. Of course, neither group held enough of a majority to make either proposal law, and any passage of either would have ended the convention before it really started.

Connecticut—again, represented by Ellsworth, Sherman, and Johnson—was technically in both camps. While it had a large enough population to technically put it in the Virginia Plan camp, they felt that without a house represented equally, they would always be in the financial shadow of their neighbor to the west, New York. In early June, the Sherman and Ellsworth team proposed a two-house congress—one based on population and the other equally or two senators per state. The Connecticut Compromise, or Great Compromise, eventually passed in mid-July, but not without a lot of turmoil. Again, while Roger Sherman gets a lot of credit for the language of the compromise, it was Oliver's persuasiveness that pushed the contentious proposal forward. In the *Founding Federalist* book, it reads,

Ellsworth displayed his rhetorical skill by fashioning a straight-forward message: accept the equal state vote in the Senate or risk the disintegration of the nation; in other words, union or no union, national harmony or quite possibly confederate sectionalism. Courtroom experience had taught the attorney-delegate to condense a complex debate into a single question and then to repeat the obvious answer to his audience.

His best one-liner to sum it up was "We are partly national; partly federal," which I find inspiring for two reasons. First, this six-word sentence says everything you need to know about the United States politically. We've always put a lot of emphasis on the uniqueness of individual states and their own governance, while at the same time we've always stressed the need for national unity and status. It took the Civil War almost seventy-five years later to truly affirm this.

Second, Oliver had an ability to persuade others through clear, undebatable rhetoric that hit home with as little pedantic hyperbole as possible. It was his gift. With this, I truly found a kindred spirit. I've spent a lot of time in administrative meetings and have been called many things in reference to my general disposition, but I have also been told that I have a way of getting through all the chaff to deal with the respective problem at its root level. He was also *that guy* whom those in charge sought out to get a problem solved. This would be the case throughout his political career. He made it clear that if the larger states did not accept this compromise and agree to a senate represented equally, then the nation would fall apart. With that, the proposal passed and a Congress and its two different houses have remained the same since.

As in a lot of major endeavors (I would put creating a new government into that category), once this significant stumbling block was eliminated, all other issues were dealt with in due process with the end in sight. Subsequently, Oliver was chosen to serve on a five-member committee to write the official document based on all previously agreed material. The committee was called the Committee of Detail. While one would assume the selection was an honor, the work immediately became arduous and presented new speed bumps. Issues like voting standards within each state, citizenship, state residency in terms of representation in Congress, payment and term length for representatives, counting slaves in the states' populations, and election of senators were all dealt with in due course. The new constitution was passed by the twelve states at the convention on September 17, 1787.

Now the real work began. The full states themselves would have to ratify the document.

Noah: The Federalist

The ink wasn't even dry on the U.S. Constitution when Noah Webster began writing a pamphlet supporting it in mid-September 1787—again with the urging of Benjamin Franklin. It was titled, "An Examination into the Leading Principles of the New Federal Constitution Proposed by the Late Convention Held at Philadelphia." Not the catchiest title, but it served its purpose. While never known to be able to argue his points verbally, Noah's ability to explain his viewpoint on paper was beyond reproach.

The article received high praise from Alexander Hamilton, James Madison, and John Jay, the major proponents of the U.S. Constitution. Apparently, Noah had found a new niche. While the three men above, especially Alexander Hamilton, were given credit for writing some of the most influential arguments for ratification of the Constitution with their *Federalist Papers,* Noah's pamphlet was easier to understand for the general public—especially those in the South who feared the Constitution the most. Maybe Lin-Manuel Miranda should start a new musical. *How does a teacher, lexicographer, son of a farmer...*

Oliver: Seal the Deal

Connecticut's ratification convention occurred in January 1788. Compared to other states' conventions, it was a relative cakewalk. Whether it was the nature of Connecticut's position in the Constitution debate or Oliver Ellsworth's efforts to promote the document, it passed easily with a vote of 128 to 40. Oliver opened the convention with a speech, but his brilliance in the whole ordeal was his in-depth knowledge and general rationale. Like a student defending his thesis, he argued every point with an informed counterpoint and answered every question that he was asked. Additionally, he, like many of his peers including Alexander Hamilton and James Madison, began writing extensive anonymous persuasion papers. As did Noah Webster for that matter.

While Connecticut approved the U.S. Constitution relatively quickly (the fifth state to do so), there were plenty of other states that needed all the help they could get. The beauty of Oliver's 1788 version of podcasts was his ability to appease both camps of political thought. While Alexander Hamilton made no bones about pissing off the states' righters by endorsing a president for life and getting rid of state government entirely, Oliver did what he did best by taking the most pragmatic approach possible. Probably the most important bone thrown to the states was the fact that the U.S. Constitution was a document that spelled out the powers given to the federal government and any powers not specifically given to the federal government would fall to the states by default.

Education is an excellent example. Nowhere in the Constitution does it mention the federal government's authority to deal with education within each state's borders. Thus, every state (within reason) has the right to define and create the criteria of education there.

While Alexander Hamilton (and Noah Webster, I later learned) would be appalled at the notion that the federal government would not be the supreme authority in terms of education, Oliver Ellsworth would grin. This idea of reserved powers was solidified with the Tenth Amendment to the Constitution in 1791, which reads, "the powers not delegated to the United States by the Constitution, nor prohibited by it to the States, are reserved to the States respectively, or to the people."

Convincing the general populace that state power would not be totally stripped away was one thing, but convincing the same populace that the new powers given to the federal government were not as bad as they sounded was something totally different. Again, ever the pragmatic lawyer, Oliver Ellsworth simply approached the issue with common sense. He argued that these enumerated powers given to the federal government spelled out in the Constitution were nothing more than powers that the average citizen would assume the federal government would have in the first place.

As an example, having thirteen separate armies made no sense in Oliver's argument; it made logical sense that one government body would oversee that element. He went further in a famous quote, "Wars have now become rather wars of the purse than of the sword," which in his mind justified the need for the federal government to tax in order to fund its army.

He would argue further that the sole purpose of government is to protect its citizens from tyranny and only a well-funded military could do that. It is important to note that the United States was pretty much the laughingstock of the world at that point, primarily because of its general inability to defend itself. And I know what people are saying: *Didn't we just kick some British ass?* Sort of. The reality is, the British just pulled up stakes and left the mainland. We, in 1787, were still having problems with the British and the French on the open seas, and the British had not evacuated forts from the periphery of our territory. *Laughingstock.*

The first order of business of a new national government was to increase our coffers and beef up the military—especially the navy—and put on some big boy pants to hang with the other big boys. Along the same lines, Oliver Ellsworth also argued that to play with the big boys, we needed one voice in terms of international commerce and trade. One trade policy was necessary to compete with the other markets of the world, rather than thirteen separate trade agreements. From a Connecticut perspective, a state without a significant port city, it would be at the mercy of New York City and whatever trade restrictions it would impose on other states who used its vast port.

Oliver's argument was based solely on reason—let the national government handle global and military affairs as anyone would assume they should, allow them to tax to carry out those affairs, and let the states run their own affairs within the confines of their borders without significant oversight of the federal government. Of course, the extent of that oversight has been an issue since the U.S. Constitution's creation and implementation.

Finally, Oliver continued the ideal of two significant entities—state and national government existing harmoniously—through an analogy. In one document, he discusses a two-lane street with both governments running side by side and enough room to maneuver but not run into each other. He would cringe at the viral videos of road-ragers today.

As another example, he envisioned a new court system at the federal level along the same lines where the state courts would interpret state law and the federal court would interpret federal law. But he went further, which became the focus of the development of the federal court system (only the U.S. Supreme Court was spelled out in the U.S. Constitution) and the foundation of the appellate courts today.

While Alexander Hamilton and James Madison worried about rogue state governments ignoring the legal mandates from the federal government, Oliver worried about a rogue federal government imposing its will on the masses with no recourse internally. He felt that a new federal government court system should have the power to negate policy and law if it violated the specifics of the U.S. Constitution. Little did he know that he was way ahead of the curve. *Smart and intuitive, man.*

Whether or not his writings had any profound effect beyond his own ratification convention, it's tough to know. The deciding ninth vote made the U.S. Constitution law in June 1788, when New Hampshire ratified the U.S. Constitution. The other three states attending the convention (Virginia, New York, and North Carolina) ratified in due course in the same year. Rhode Island decided to join the party in May 1790. *Yawn.*

Noah: We Can Occupy Ourselves for Hours

Noah Webster, in the meantime, took his recent success over the popularity of the *Principles* document and his pamphlet supporting the Constitution and moved to New York City to work on his own publication, called the *American Magazine,* in the winter of 1787-88. It became a voice for a Federalist mindset.

While George Washington never declared himself connected to any political party, all presidents since then have. At that time, there were Federalists, who supported a strong central government, and the Anti-Federalists or state-righters or, eventually, the Democratic-Republicans. They supported more power delegated to the states and their governments. Without going off track, these two mindsets are the basis of political arguments today. Should our national government deal with only those areas specifically mentioned in the U.S. Constitution and leave the rest to the states, or should it deal with all types of issues that need to be addressed? *I'll leave you to debate that issue over Thanksgiving dinner with your relatives.*

Whatever the case, Noah Webster was clearly in the Federalist camp, and his new magazine was a platform to support that party's agenda. He, like Alexander Hamilton, continued to make their party's stance known through literary platforms, as did members of the opposing party. It is no different today. While there are definitely websites and blogs that have no bones about letting you know where their allegiance lies, news websites are no different—though perhaps a bit more subtle. Look at a hot topic on Fox News and then on CNN and you'll get a whole different interpretation of the same topic. *Nothing changes.*

Unfortunately, Noah's success as a writer of educational materials and political propaganda did not carry over to sales of the *American Magazine*. In December 1788, he abandoned ship and returned to Hartford, Connecticut. On the upside, he met and married the love of his life, Rebecca Greenleaf, the daughter of a wealthy entrepreneur in the Boston area. As it has been said, he married *up* for the simple fact that even though he was a known name, he still wasn't making a lot of money. Thus, he fell back on his law degree to make ends meet. The couple had their first child, Emily, in August 1790. Emily, their oldest, would eventually marry William Wolcott Ellsworth, Oliver Ellsworth's youngest son, in September 1813. But that is for another chapter. Noah and Rebecca would have seven more children—all girls except for their only son, William. *No wonder he wanted to lock himself in a room for hours.*

For a while, at least, Noah was happy to live the life of a doting husband and father in Hartford. His law practice began to grow, and he eventually got involved in local politics. But, for better or worse, he couldn't stay out of the national political scene, and he wrote op-ed pieces for anybody who cared to read them. For the next ten years or so, he wrote extensively in a multitude of magazines and newspapers, much of it in support of the Federalist agenda and their two presidents—George Washington and John Adams.

Additionally, between 1789 and when he began his dictionary opus in 1806, he wrote about almost everything—from politics to language to infectious diseases. Needless to say, while many respected his thoughts on the American education system of the time and even his Federalist leanings, others felt that he was out of his element. His transition from a part-time teacher and an even more part-time lawyer to a writer of textbooks (e.g. *Blue-Backed Speller*) to an essayist and finally to a lexicographer of an enormous dictionary seems like a descent into lunacy. Think of the countless hours of sitting, day after day, plugging through the alphabet researching and writing definitions, origins, and usages for thousands of words (keep in mind that there was no Google). While the topic is clearly not my cup of tea, I can honestly relate.

Indeed, the more I delved into this distant relative, the more I began to move from a sense of awe (given the magnitude of his dictionary completed in 1825 and published in 1828) to a mere acknowledgement of his happy place. It has been said by many people that "Andy can occupy himself for hours by himself," and I have never denied the fact. I am an introvert surviving in an extroverted world, which also means that I am most comfortable when working hours upon hours on projects and such all by myself.

As I dug deeper into this project, I, too, became more attuned to the realities of my own happy place—researching and writing. When I pictured Noah doing the same thing for hours a day for more than a decade, I thought, *I get it.* While most were awestruck by the depth and scope of his dictionary, he, like myself, probably never once considered the process debilitating.

Oliver: More Courts, Please!

About the same time Noah was returning to Hartford, his Connecticut compadre and eventual relative by marriage was leaving for New York City—the capital city at that point. Our new government didn't get under way until the spring of 1789, with George Washington at the helm and a new legislature slowly making its way to New York. Oliver Ellsworth was chosen by his state's legislature to serve as one of two senators. Per the U.S. Constitution, senators were chosen by the state legislators up until 1913, when it became a direct election as dictated by the 17th Amendment.

Once in office in New York, Oliver and a few others were chosen to head up a committee to design the federal court system and propose the creation of new courts. Article III of the U.S. Constitution was fairly bare in terms of the federal courts in general and the U.S. Supreme Court specifically as compared to Article I (Congress) and Article II (President). Either by design or by desire, the framers decided to deal with it later. So, by April 1789, the subcommittee had submitted what is known as the Judiciary Bill of 1789. Its contents are the foundation of our federal court system, at least in principle.

Ultimately, the questions before this subcommittee were: One, what would the power of the Supreme Court look like given its relative vagueness in the Constitution? Two, what would the lower courts look like at the federal level? And three, what would the relationship between the federal courts be, as well as the other branches of federal government and the states? Oliver was truly walking into virgin territory here.

Article III begins, "The Judicial Power of the United States, shall be vested in one Supreme Court, and in such inferior Courts as the Congress may from time to time ordain and establish." The task for the new committee was to do just that create a new federal court system beyond the Supreme Court. With Oliver on the committee, the Judiciary Act of 1789 was passed in September of that year.

So, what did the Judiciary Act of 1789 do? Basically, two things. One, it created two sets of new federal courts (U.S. District Court and U.S. Circuit Court of Appeals); and two, it clarified the roles of federal courts in general and the roles of the three separate federal courts specifically. While the U.S. Constitution was relatively vague about the powers of the federal courts as opposed to the other two branches, the act was careful to eliminate the vagueness written into the U.S. Constitution. Oliver and other committee members, in an effort to placate the state righters, spelled out what a specific federal court can do and left all other situations to the states. *Federalism 101.*

Noah: John Jay Did What?

While not much is written about Noah Webster's viewpoint on the Judiciary Act of 1789, I can only assume that based on his Federalist leanings, he supported the increased power to the national government—at least from the courtroom standpoint. But that doesn't mean that he was quiet on other political matters of the time. He continually wrote about the deteriorating issues with England and France.

These issues became the focal point for both Noah Webster and Oliver Ellsworth. In the early 1790s, problems with the English continued and intensified in 1792 when war broke out between the French and England again (think of all the *Rocky* sequels) and the English started impounding American ships that were trading with the French. The Democratic-Republicans in Congress called for a severe reaction, starting with a heavy tariff on English goods. But the Federalists, including Oliver Ellsworth, pushed for less drastic measures. They argued that the United States still could not afford another all-out war with the English and that England was still our biggest trading partner. Since Oliver and a few other Federalists had the president's ear, they convinced George Washington to send an envoy to England to negotiate a treaty rather than go for the more drastic route. After several names were batted around, in 1794, Washington sent John Jay, then chief justice to the U.S. Supreme Court, to do the work. John Jay returned six months later and presented the treaty to President Washington in March 1795. As the U.S. Constitution dictates, all treaties must be passed by the Senate by a two-thirds vote. The treaty was quickly ratified by a slim margin in the Senate along party lines. *Nothing changes.*

The treaty achieved several goals, but most importantly it avoided another war with England. While in the president's eyes averting another war was paramount, the general public was not really happy that the United States was backtracking and falling into its old subservient ways with the British. To make matters worse, the negotiations with the English were kept secret from everyone other than the president, his advisors, and a select group of senators, including Oliver Ellsworth. When many of the House of Representatives got wind of the secret negotiations and the eventual treaty, they went ballistic, especially knowing their constituents were not happy with the end results. They demanded to know what instructions the president gave to John Jay prior to his departure to Great Britain. In their minds, the president would have never given him such conciliatory instructions. Rather than allow the House, and especially the Democratic-Republicans, to have their way, President Washington and his Federalist posse told them to "go suck eggs," as my dad would say.

Ever the Federalist supporter, Noah Webster jumped in with both feet and his pen. By 1793, he had decided to leave Hartford and his cushy lawyer job and return to New York City. Given the high tension around the world and the United States in the thick of it, he started up a new newspaper called *American Minerva*. It became the vehicle for all things pro-government, though just as before, it didn't garner a lot of readership beyond the hardcore Federalists. But when the Jay Treaty debate rolled around, it regained its legs.

John Jay, one of Noah's biggest supporters, sent the terms of the treaty to him, and Noah soon printed them in the paper. Like George Washington and Oliver Ellsworth, Noah insisted that the terms of the agreement were the best at that moment in time, even though it was panned publicly throughout the country. One true test of his writing skills in support of the treaty was the backlash from Democratic-Republicans far and wide, including Thomas Jefferson. For a time, Noah was in his haven as a political rabble rouser.

Oliver: He'll Be the Judge of That!

Matters became more complicated for Oliver Ellsworth when John Jay decided to hang up his chief justice robe upon his return from his sojourn to Mother England. At this point, it's important to explain that the process back in the day of replacing a U.S. Supreme Court Justice was not as lengthy and painstaking as it is today. The president would simply select a judge to serve at the federal level, and the Senate would approve it with a quick vote. *Sorry, folks, no questions about what may or may not have happened at a keg party at college.*

President Washington initially proposed that John Rutledge, who served as chief justice to the South Carolina Supreme Court, be chosen in late June 1795, but his appointment was rejected by the Senate. Washington turned to his close ally since the American Revolution—Oliver Ellsworth. Oliver, our nation's third chief justice of the U.S. Supreme Court, was approved by the U.S. Senate in March 1796, and he served in that capacity until December 1800.

His first moment as chief justice came quickly as the House wanted input from the U.S. Supreme Court on whether the House of Representatives had the right to give official input on the Jay Treaty. It was complicated in Oliver's case, because days earlier he'd been a vocal figure in support of the treaty as a senator. As a judge, he now had no official voice on the matter. But times were different, and judges weighed in politically all the time—which would be taboo today. Oliver indeed weighed in, sending a memorandum to both members of the Senate and the president himself. His arguments were simple. As the U. S. Constitution clearly states in Article II, Section 2, the president "shall have Power, by and with the Advice and Consent of the Senate, to make Treaties, provided two-thirds of the Senators present concur." The House of Representatives had no legal right to access Washington's initial instructions to John Jay unless the president wished it so. When the president once again told the House to go suck eggs, he used Chief Justice Ellsworth's legal basis as a guide. What Oliver didn't realize, at least publicly, was that this one decision began a precedent of judicial review that was solidified in a landmark case in 1803 called Marbury vs. Madison. Both decisions defined the U.S. Supreme Court's greatest power—to clarify what the U.S. Constitution really says. Good or bad depending on your political leanings, it still holds extreme weight today.

Noah: Dictionary Avoidance, Part One

Meanwhile, Noah Webster was also enjoying his favor with the president and his Federalist allies in the president's cabinet while at the same time trying to call out the opposition whenever possible. According to the book *The Life and Times of Noah Webster—An American Patriot*, "As he intended, Webster became the government's eyes and ears in New York, reporting every effort to undermine the Washington administration." Strangely enough, though, once the Jay Treaty chaos subsided, Noah turned his attention to the other big story raging in New York City—yellow fever. *Whaaat? When is he going to do the dictionary thing?*

Never seemingly satisfied with living in the moment, Noah focused all of his attention on researching and finding a cure for the disease. Gathering all the information at his disposal, especially from the top doctors at the time, he wrote a book on the disease and how he felt it could be eradicated—by cleaning up filth and unhealthy sanitary practices that plagued New York City. While his efforts didn't solve the yellow fever and malaria problem—that was another 100 years down the road—they did lead to massive sanitary projects in not only New York City but other cities on the East Coast.

Oliver: He Went to Paris...

Oliver Ellsworth's tenure as chief justice was fairly uneventful, other than an indirect interpretation of a Sedition Act of 1798 (one of many attempts to restrict the people's right to publicly denounce the government) and a few smaller cases dealing with the interpretation of the language of the U.S. Constitution. Ironically, Oliver's most notable accomplishment as a chief justice had nothing to do with his role, at least not directly. The John Jay treaty had settled matters with the English, at least for the time being, but matters started to heat up with the French. Keep in mind that George Washington had made the personal decision not to run for a third term and laid the precedent for another century and a half. Federalist John Adams ran for the presidency and won in 1796.

The French, like the English years before, began seizing commercial American ships heading to English ports since the French and English were at odds again. *A friend of my enemy is now my enemy mentality—or middle school relationships 101.* Adams had initially proposed a peaceful solution, much like Washington did, under the argument that any war with France would not be a good idea. The peaceful route seemed doomed when, in April 1798, the president informed Congress that his official representatives to France were asked to pay an entrance fee (i.e., bribe) before any negotiations could begin. When Adams informed Congress, he gave fake names to the three French emissaries who requested money before talking—X, Y, and Z. Thus, the XYZ Affair, mentioned in every American history textbook, was named.

Needless to say, both the president and Congress were irate, and preparations for war began. But before matters totally got out of hand, Adams attempted to negotiate with the French one last time, with no bribery attached. The French agreed. But the matter continued to broil when he proposed a representative—U.S. Minister to France William Vans Murray—whom no one in Congress was comfortable with. *Think Dennis Rodman going to North Korea.*

Matters finally calmed down when Oliver Ellsworth was able to convince Adams that two additional representatives would quell the opposition in Congress. Of course, Oliver was one of the representatives, in addition to another from North Carolina, Governor William R. Davie. Congress and Adams were happy again.

In the fall of 1799, the three envoys made their way to France and a deal was made. The result was a treaty much like the one with the English. War was once again averted. Thankfully, the reestablishment of a friendly relationship with France probably helped along the Louisiana Purchase in 1803, which the U.S. got for a bargain price and almost doubled the size of the country.

Noah: Finally, a Dictionary. Sort of.

The XYZ Affair obviously shifted Noah Webster's attention from cleaning up New York City to dealing with the French. In this case, rather than supporting a negotiation like he did with the Jay treaty, he proposed an alliance with England to gang up on the French. Adams ignored his calls, and Webster realized that he no longer had the president's ear, as he did with Washington. Additionally, he saw the power of the Federalist Party waning at the expense of the Democratic-Republicans. He was right. Thomas Jefferson, a Democratic-Republican, was elected in 1800.

Thus, in the spring of 1798, Noah dropped his efforts at the *Minerva*, and moved back to Connecticut. *Really, dude?* Leaving New York City and life as a political agitator for good, the Websters purchased a beautiful home in New Haven in 1798. It had initially been lived in by the notorious Benedict Arnold, America's first high-profile traitor. In 1781, the Arnold house in New Haven was confiscated by the state of Connecticut and sold to a local war hero. When the wife of said hero decided to sell the estate in 1798 Noah purchased it in cash and lived there for almost ten years. He seemingly had no qualms about the home's history.

While Hartford had been the heart and soul of Connecticut since the state's beginnings, New Haven was the place to be in the early part of our nation's history. Always a college town thanks to the founding of Yale, it also served as a port city into the rest of Connecticut. For much of Noah's life from 1798 until his death, New Haven would be his family's home. Much like their short time in Hartford, both he and his wife, Rebecca, became socially and politically involved in the port city.

Still living off the proceeds from his previous educational works, Noah Webster set to work on his newest pet project—disease. *When is this guy going to write his stupid dictionary?* His 712-page book called *A Brief History of Epidemic and Pestilential Diseases* was completed in 1799. In typical Noah fashion, it was quite thorough in its depth and research, but unfortunately most of its conclusions in terms of cause and prevention were wrong. Of course, people were still bleeding patients to cure almost everything at the time, so he wasn't alone.

For the next ten years, Noah would continue to write. In 1804, he published an updated version of the *American Spelling Book,* which would bankroll his other endeavors for the rest of his life. He also produced a set of encyclopedias over the first decade of the 1800s that were specifically for children. These books were titled *Elements of Useful Knowledge,* contained a total of four volumes, and covered material ranging from history and geography to animal classification.

In 1801, Noah started his first attempt at a dictionary. It was called *A Compendious Dictionary of the American Language* and it, like most of his other works, was geared toward the American student. It contained more than 40,000 words, and though it wasn't the opus that would come later, it, according to biographer Harlow Giles Unger, "was, nevertheless, the most innovative and comprehensive dictionary ever produced at that time—and it was uniquely American." The work was officially published in 1806.

Unfortunately, when the *Compendious* was finished and published in 1806, it had many critics. First, many still supported the works created by other noted lexicographers at the time. Others questioned the inclusion of new words or definitions of those words as a temporary usage. To me, it raised a question. At what point is the new usage of a common word simply temporary or one that will last the test of time?

No matter. His first official dictionary, though limited in scope, would serve as the stepping-off point for his biggest work to date and the one that he would become most known for. It would consume his life off and on for the next twenty years. And, while Noah's life was apparently on the rise again at the age of fifty, Oliver Ellsworth's life and career was winding down.

Oliver: Separation of Church and State Be Damned

After a long and arduous trek to France, negotiating a treaty, and returning to the States in 1801, Oliver Ellsworth decided to call it quits as a justice of the U.S. Supreme Court at the ripe old age of 55. Whether it was his continuing issues with gout, his general fatigue from being away from home, or the fact that the Democratic-Republicans gained the White House in 1800 under Thomas Jefferson, he was done with federal politics and wanted to return to his roots in Windsor, Connecticut. He reconnected with his family, took up his duties working at their general store with his two sons, and began writing for the *Hartford Courant* (the oldest continuous newspaper in the United States, if you ever get on *Jeopardy*). He generally wrote about agriculture, of all things. Of course, he couldn't totally walk away from politics. In 1802, he was reelected as a state senator and quickly became embroiled in a hot topic of the times.

The First Amendment of the U.S. Constitution deals with five things—speech, press, religion, petition, and assembly. Each of these has been defined and redefined over the years, and some of those new definitions have not been pretty. *Look up* Westboro Baptist Church vs. Snyder *and try not to vomit.* For much of my teaching career, I taught a Civics class and really enjoyed instructing about the subtle nuances of each freedom—but especially those relating to the freedom of religion.

This piece of the First Amendment reads, "Congress shall make no law respecting an establishment of religion, or prohibiting the free exercise thereof." In layman's terms, it means: one, you have the right to practice any religion (or not) within reason; and two, the government must be separate from the general support and acknowledgement of one religion over another. This last part gave rise to the much-used expression "separation of church and state" and led to the elimination of prayer in public school and such. While the separation piece started with Thomas Jefferson, I was never quite sure about the official context until I started reading about the 1802 Baptist Petition to the Connecticut General Assembly.

As in most states in the Union in the early 1800s, Christianity in general and Congregational Churches specifically were the foundation of local towns and cities in Connecticut. While tough to picture today in New England, the church was the social hub of every town. Thus, in Connecticut as well as many other states, tax money was dispersed to local churches as if they were fire departments, police departments, or schools today. This was never really questioned, except that as the Baptist, Quaker, and Anglican churches grew, they felt that they should receive the same monetary compensation as the Congregational Church had over the years. The state legislature in Connecticut agreed, as long as those churches could document the number of active persons. All good. But then the Baptists threw a wrench into the matter. *Did they have wrenches in the early 1800s?* In 1802, the Baptist Church in Connecticut petitioned the Connecticut General Assembly, asking whether less than active members and even non-goers or non-believers should be obligated to pay a religious tax if they did not use said churches. *Oh, damn.*

In due course, a select committee took up the charge, and Oliver probably sprinted to the front of the line on it. As a side note, Baptists had taken up similar petitions in other states with similar tax laws, and they'd requested the input of then President Jefferson to support it. He did indeed write a letter in support, which is where the quote "a wall of separation between Church & State," was first written. Whatever the case, Oliver Ellsworth, rumor has it, stood up in front of the Connecticut General Assembly, dropped a copy of the petition on the ground, put his foot down upon it, and stated, "This is where it belongs." *Oh, damn!* While it may not have the same ring to it as "Give me liberty or give me death!" from Patrick Henry, or even "Go ahead; make my day!" from *Dirty Harry*, it does show where Oliver's allegiance to his faith most likely stood.

But Oliver, ever the pragmatist, once again took a more subtle route on paper in protest of the petition. Rather than argue from a religious standpoint, he stressed that the church in America functioned much like schools in terms of their importance to the community, and one could not argue that if one had no children, then they should not have to pay a school tax. The schools and churches served the majority of their citizens in a practical and fundamental capacity, and all citizens should contribute, regardless of their circumstances, for a betterment of the community as a whole. In a sense, Oliver viewed the church as a public service, much like plowing the streets or buying a new police cruiser, and he probably wasn't wrong for that time and place. Not surprisingly, the petition never made it out of committee. Of course, while Oliver may have won the day in 1802, he ultimately lost the war. We no longer have tax money directly supporting churches.

Oliver would continuously serve as a member of the upper house in Connecticut for the rest of his life. He also accepted another stint on the state's supreme court in the spring of 1807, but he had to decline the appointment because of his declining health. Oliver died on November 26, 1807, at the age of sixty-three.

As I write this, I realize that he died at the same age that I am currently, which immediately makes me pause. Did people back in the day look at their mid-sixties as a chance to retire from the normal grind and move on to bigger and brighter things? Probably not. Retirement as we know it was an abstract thought, with death always right around the corner. While many today might look at death at sixty-three as time lost, I know now that Oliver Ellsworth's life was anything but wasted. In addition to being a great husband and father by all accounts, he served his home state of Connecticut and his country in every way possible. All while never really receiving, nor, I would say, desiring, the same limelight as others of his time. His faith propelled him to honor his God by helping others as a public servant despite his personal feelings at times. It would be nice if all public servants brought the same attitude to their jobs.

Noah: Dictionary Avoidance, Part Two

Noah Webster, still in New Haven and still trudging through his dictionary, became equally frustrated with the politics at that time. The Democratic-Republicans would hold the White House for the next decade or so, there were threats of another war with England (that would come to fruition in 1812), and the cost of maintaining a house in expensive New Haven took its toll on him. His solution was to sell the house in New Haven, pack up all his belongings, and move to Amherst, Massachusetts, to become a farmer in 1812. *Whaaat? I thought he was writing a dictionary?*

His move to Amherst was indeed perplexing. While there was some familial connection to the hinterland of western Massachusetts (i.e., Half-Hung Mary), Amherst was nothing compared to the urban-like mecca of New Haven. While Noah's financial reasons for selling seemed plausible, the new location felt a bit drastic. While his youngest children were quite excited about the change of venue, his two oldest, Emily and Julia, were not. They had become quite accustomed to the hustle and bustle of urban life in New Haven. Around the time of the drastic move, Emily, twenty-two and already engaged to William Walcott Ellsworth, Oliver's youngest son, married in 1813, and Julia, nineteen, soon followed in 1816. Both marriages took place in Amherst, Massachusetts. I can only imagine the conversation at the dinner table when their father, Noah, dropped the impending move on the family. *Did teenage girls back in the day yell, "Whatever!", storm upstairs, and slam their doors for effect?*

While Amherst may be the center of New England college life today, in the early 1800s it was nothing more than a sleepy farming town with slim pickings for the two teenage girls. Equally perplexing was Noah's relatively easy transition into a gentleman farmer and a vibrant community member. While most Americans at this point were farmers, Noah, up until 1812, was not. He was a writer and an educator. But he dug right in (pun intended) to the new way of life. From fruit trees to livestock, he found a new sense of achievement outside the day-to-day grind of writing his opus.

Once settled in the pastoral life of rural western Massachusetts, you would assume his daily schedule would be set. Get up, do your chores, and jump into the dictionary that he had been putting off for years. Of course, it seems that he did everything but write the dictionary. First and almost immediately, he took on the civic responsibility of serving as justice of the peace and state representative in the Boston legislature. Additionally, rather than continue his dictionary, he decided instead to write a complete etymology of the English language, which he called *Synopsis of Words in Twenty Languages*.

Having put aside his dictionary for the time, he began looking at the origin of words through the multitude of different languages.

Though Latin and Greek were very influential to modern languages at that time, as well as the Germanic languages, Noah's claim was that all European languages could be traced to the Arameans and Semites, who lived in what we now consider Syria 1,000 years before the birth of Christ. In the end, Noah was wrong. The two language groups were not connected or at least not enough to positively prove the case. While his work to connect all European languages was foolhardy, the depth of Noah's research into the history of the English language is breathtaking. The book was completed in 1817 but never published.

Additionally, Noah was continually distracted by global events, even though that was one of his reasons for moving. He, like many New Englanders, was unimpressed by the leadership in Washington, D.C., beginning with the election of Thomas Jefferson in 1800. As a staunch Federalist, he had never seen eye to eye with the favored farmer son.

Finally, Noah threw himself into the creation of a new institution of higher learning—Amherst College. It began as a prep school in 1814 that was called Amherst Academy. Some four years later, Noah and a group of organizers and benefactors concluded that the prep school should become a new college in New England. The first cornerstone was laid on August 9, 1820. Keep in mind that colleges were rare—which is ironic because the area around Amherst is now known as The Five College Consortium (Amherst, Mount Holyoke, UMass-Amherst, Smith, and Hampshire).

My initial aha moment in terms of a connection between Amherst College and Noah Webster came several years ago when my son and I decided to play golf at the Amherst Golf Course about 30 miles from my house in Northfield. As I always do with new golf venues, I did a little research on the course and quickly learned that it was owned by Amherst College. This segued into finding a photo of a statue on campus of, yup, you guessed it, Noah Webster. *Whaaat?* At the time, I simply found it strange since my only understanding of the man centered on Connecticut.

Anyway, Noah spent a lot of time getting the college up and running, especially when it came to fundraising. The college officially opened in September of 1821 with 47 students enrolled. As I dug into my research on Noah and his connection to Amherst College, I knew that I had to find the statue of him on campus. My wife and I were able to visit one January, and after some effort, found the *thing* among some of the older buildings dating back to Noah's time. I say *thing* because it's the oddest attempt at a glorifying statue I've ever seen. Noah looks like a Roman statesman sitting on a bench. His arms are extended in some sort of Jesus-on-the-cross pose. *The whole thing is quite odd, but I'm sure the pigeons enjoy it.*

Noah Webster on Amherst College, 1914 by Willard Paddock. Photo taken 2016

While Noah had allegedly been busy all this time with his dictionary, his proverbial stepping-off-the-cliff moment began when he sold the publishing rights to his *Blue-Backed Speller* to Hudson and

Company for $42,000 in 1816. What would be over a million dollars today was paid out to Noah over the next decade in smaller lump sums. For the first time, money was no longer an issue. Despite finding everything possible to distract him from the task at hand, he plodded through a significant chunk of the alphabet, and by the fall of 1821, he was researching and writing words beginning with the letter H.

Noah: He Went to Paris...

At this point, Noah decided on two things—one, it was time to return to New Haven, Connecticut, and two, to complete his research on the English language, he would need to travel to Europe.

In the summer of 1822, Noah moved back to New Haven and rented a house near the Yale campus. Initially alone, he hired a well-known architect to design a new house and oversaw the building of the project himself. It was a beautiful home for its time—so much so that Henry Ford eventually picked up the whole house and moved it to Dearborn, Michigan. It still sits there as part of a museum.

The beauty of designing and building one's own home is that you can build it to your own needs. In addition to the luxuries of the time on the first floor, designs on the second floor included an office where Noah could finish his dictionary. Double walls were installed to cut down any noise as well as a bed to take breaks. He was all in at this point. By the end of 1823, Noah closed in on the end of the alphabet.

To complete his second endeavor, Noah began plans for a working vacation in Europe in April 1824. Unlike today, with Amazon Prime and access to any resource with the click of a button, Noah needed to travel abroad to have access to any books outside the shores of the United States. In June, he and his son, William, set sail for France. They landed in Le Havre a month later and settled in Paris. Noah spent the next two months doing research at the Royal Library and continued plowing through his dictionary. In September, they set sail again for England and settled in at Cambridge. The rough draft of his dictionary was finally completed in January 1825.

In addition to writing till his hands bled, Noah also had the grand idea that he could convince the English that the two countries could be united under one language in terms of spelling and pronunciation. Of course, his dictionary would be the foundation. That idea fell on deaf ears. I can only imagine the roundtable talk at the local pub: "Who is this guy?" Regardless, with his research and dictionary complete and his grand dream totally snubbed, Noah and William returned home again in March of 1825.

Work immediately began on editing, which took another two years. The Sherman Converse Company was selected as the publisher. *The American Dictionary of the English Language* was finally published on November 26, 1828.

When you say that you're writing a book, that's one thing. But to say that you're writing a dictionary is in a totally different realm. It is, I suppose, like comparing running a half-marathon to climbing Mount Everest. It's tough to comprehend in numbers—the dictionary contained 70,000 words, 4,000 new scientific terms, and hundreds of words that were commonplace for the time but were now officially defined in writing. My own relationship with the work (other than my connection through lineage) was when I received an unabridged copy of the dictionary many Christmases ago from my parents. The book is massive; if someone threw it at you, it would kill you outright.

Beyond the abundance and sheer volume of words, Noah's work was distinctive in other ways. First, words were defined with far more depth than they had ever been before. Second, once England had given Noah the cold shoulder in terms of the focus on the English language, he'd reworked many definitions to reflect a more American vibe. Even with the sentences that were used to exemplify the definition of a word, he would use local, regional, and national places and names to give it an American feeling. Third, while of course it became a working resource for future misspellers and incorrect usages, the dictionary, in its totality, defined American culture.

With this last point, I totally agree with Noah Webster. Language, more than anything, distinguishes one group from another—and not just the difference between speaking French or German. I am constantly heckled by my southern friends for my usage of the word *wicked,* which has entrenched itself in the New England vernacular. Noah spent his lifetime trying to separate Americans from the English through his literary endeavors, and his dictionary truly embodied this sentiment.

To this day, the Merriam-Webster dictionary (Noah sold the rights to the dictionary to the Merriam publishing company in 1843) still adds new words every year. Additionally, Noah changed the spelling of many words. Theatre became theater, musick became music, and favour became favor. The list of word changes was extensive. In addition to simplifying the phonetics of words, Noah wanted to Americanize the English language.

Like Oliver Ellsworth, when Noah's final major work was published in 1828, he decided that his global traveling was over and he would finish his life in New Haven. He lived another fifteen years holding court as the father and grandfather of the house. But he, like Oliver, was not stagnant. With the help of his son-in-law, William Ellsworth, who was a newly elected U.S. representative in Congress from Connecticut, Noah was finally able to see a federal copyright law enacted. He would continue to write textbooks for schools into the 1830s. At some point during one of his stints in New Haven, he found God and became an active member of one of the churches there. He even dedicated his dictionary to God, and then in the early 1830s, he decided to rewrite the Bible in his own American vernacular. *Dude, really? Relax in your recliner and ask your grandkids to get you another beer from the fridge.* As always, he couldn't keep his nose out of politics, and he railed against the new Democratic party under Andrew

Jackson and Martin Van Buren through numerous op-ed pieces. Noah died peacefully in May of 1843 at the age of eighty-four.

Noah and Oliver: Two Patriots

I can't help but be in awe of the achievements of both men. And while I generally laugh at those who feel that their distant relatives have something to do with who they are today, I can't help but try to reflect on my two distant grandfathers' endeavors as they relate to mine. I am proud of their accomplishments, and I can only hope that I can live up to them to a certain degree.

Of course, after digging into the lives of my two most famous American ancestors, the real question is "Which of these men owned the desk?"

The simple answer is neither of them. *Whaaat?* To make matters worse, I realized that at some point while I was researching these two men. *Wait! Before you hurl this book across the room in disgust, let me justify my motive.*

The answer was always there in front of me, but once again, my stubbornness got in the way. While doing knee-deep research on these two men, I never gave a second look to the documents in the desk beyond organizing and filing them away. When I finally started reading said documents, it didn't take long for the reality of my idiocy to really set in. The name Seymour was plastered all over these documents beginning in the late 1700s and into the early 1900s. The Seymour desk as I knew it was named not for the manufacturer, but for the family who had it made and who owned it for almost 150 years. Rather than concentrating on the Websters and Ellsworths, I should have focused exclusively on the Seymour family, which, by all accounts, was as significant in Connecticut history as my relatives were and perhaps even more so.

While I could have left my two relatives in the dust at that point and moved on, I am now glad that I didn't. Truth be told, my ignorance specific to my desk did indeed push me to understand its secrets, but I also realized that I had equally limited knowledge of my own flesh and blood. Perhaps knowing the desk's true lineage from the beginning would have kept it that way.

At that point, the Seymour family and its connection to my desk was the next order of business. Who were these people? Did they have connections to my family during the time of Noah and Oliver or was it further down my family tree? Who owned the desk within the Seymour clan before it somehow wound up in my dad's hands? *Into another research rabbit hole I go.*

3

Suddenly Seymour

The contents of the Seymour desk were the key to everything, and my dad knew it. He'd written notes and questions that he had about specific documents accompanying the desk. I needed to retrace his steps and refocus my efforts. The first order of business was to finally go through the Seymour documents in the desk with a fine-toothed comb.

In addition to the notes and a few added materials from my dad, the primary sources in the desk fall into three categories: two letters dated 1797 and 1824, fifteen letters dated during the 1850s and 1860s, and over twenty-five letters from between 1903 and 1930. They all had some connection to this Seymour family. *But who are these people who wrote these letters?*

Coming to America

While the moment the Seymour family came to America wasn't as documented as my own ancestral roots in the New World (*for a white Anglo-Saxon male, you can't get much earlier or more prominent than the Pilgrims on the* Mayflower), they weren't far behind. For my purposes, the original Seymour was named Richard Seymour and he came to America in 1639 with his wife, Mercy. The couple initially settled in downtown Hartford (*don't get too excited*), bore four sons (Thomas, John, Zachariah, and Richard), and stayed there until 1651. Much like his descendants to follow him, Richard immediately stepped into the civic and political arena and was elected to a noteworthy position in those days—chimney viewer. *Oohhh, chimney viewer.* While it may not be a Supreme Court justice, it was important. Maybe more so.

The office of the chimney viewer was significant back in the day for two simple reasons—fireplaces and thatched roofs. The people of Hartford were required to check and clean their chimneys once a month, provide ladders, and make sure no tree limbs came within two feet of the top of the chimney. A fire during this period would be devastating to that family as well as the whole community. The office of chimney viewer carried the weight of enforcing these laws, and it came with a lot of perks—including a home provided by the town. While a publicly owned house on paper sounds great, owning your own home during the colonial era and beyond was the ultimate sign of prestige for many reasons, but most importantly when it came to providing for your descendants upon your death.

Richard and Mercy Seymour, looking to upgrade their standing, moved to Norwalk, Connecticut (southwest of Hartford along the coast), in 1651 to build a home and work on a new plantation that grew corn, barley, wheat, rye, and oats. It continued to expand to include livestock and flax, which was exported to Great Britain. By 1652, Richard and his family were again well established, and he was elected as a selectman in March 1655. His rise there did not last long, as he died six months later in September at the age of fifty. His wife, Mercy, wasted no time and remarried in November of the same year. *Different times, I guess.*

While Richard was no slouch, her new husband, Honorable John Steele, was one of eight magistrates appointed in 1636 to govern Connecticut by the Colony of Massachusetts Bay. He served in the Connecticut General Court as an elected Deputy of Hartford and then in Farmington (the town next to Hartford) until 1658. He also served in other capacities for both towns. Mercy's three boys, still under her care from the previous marriage, must have reaped the benefits of this new marriage. While the desire to go into public service may have started with their birth father, it clearly was further encouraged by their step-dad.

Richard and Mary's second son and first born in the New World was John Seymour. He was born in 1639 in Hartford, married Mary Watson in 1665, became a freeman or upstanding citizen in 1667, was a member of the Second Congregational Church of Hartford (East Hartford today), and lived in the same area until his death in 1712. His wife, Mary, died the same year. They had nine children, six of whom lived to adulthood. Their second son, Thomas, was again the key to my desk story. *Another freaking Thomas Seymour?* Not to be confused with the furniture maker Thomas Seymour. *Ugh. And it gets worse.*

This Thomas Seymour was born in 1669 in Hartford and married his first wife, Ruth Norton, in 1700. They produced three children (Mary, Thomas, and Ruth). Ruth Norton died in 1710, and Thomas remarried again in 1711 to Mary Waters. *Quick turnaround again.* They produced six more children.

Captain Thomas Seymour, as he was known, was a "prominent man of his day in Hartford," according to *A History of the Seymour Family: Descendants of Richard Seymour of Hartford, Connecticut, for Six Generations* by George Dudley Seymour and Donald Lines Jacobus in 1939. Thomas served in many capacities for the town of Hartford, including various town offices such as deputy to the Connecticut General Court and selectman. He also held a multitude of military posts and titles, ending with his appointment as captain in 1725. Upon his death, he willed most of vast properties in Hartford and other towns in Connecticut to his two eldest sons, Thomas and Bevil, by his second marriage. *Yes, another Thomas Seymour.*

Thomas, Jr., was born to Thomas, Sr.'s first wife in 1705 in Hartford, graduated from Yale in 1724, became a distinguished lawyer soon after, married Hephzibah Merrill in 1730, and died in March 1767. They had twelve children, seven of whom survived to adult-

hood. Thomas, Jr., like his father, served the town of Hartford extensively.

In addition to being a sought-after attorney, he served in the Connecticut General Assembly on multiple occasions, served in the military, and rose to the rank of captain. His biggest achievement was
being appointed to serve as the governor's and colony's personal attorney and representing the king of England in legal matters.

The First Mayor of Hartford

My story really begins with the birth of Thomas III, Thomas, Jr.,
and Hephzibah's fourth child, in 1735. He was the one who commissioned the creation of the desk, and he was its first owner—though it
is said that he had it made for his wife. Like many who had money,
he went to Yale and eventually graduated in 1755. He married Mary
Ledyard in the same year, and she produced seven children, six living
to adulthood.

They continued to live in the same house as Thomas's parents
in Hartford until 1767 when he inherited the house outright. Like
his ancestors before him and descendants after, Thomas III had an
illustrious career. In addition to being a prominent lawyer in his
own right, he represented Hartford in the new General Assembly between 1774 and 1793, was chosen as Speaker five times, and eventually
served in the Connecticut Senate between 1793 and 1803. Like his father, he was King's Attorney in 1767 and served in the same capacity
after the Revolution as the State's Attorney. He was Chief Judge of the
Court of Common Pleas for Hartford County between 1798 and 1803.
He also served in the local militia prior to the Revolution as captain
and lieutenant-colonel. During the revolution, he headed the Committee of Pay Table as its Paymaster.

Interesting but not confirmable was the fact that he probably
rubbed shoulders with Oliver Ellsworth, who served in a similar capacity on the same committee. Thomas also commanded three reg-

iments of Light Horse that supported the armies in New York. Following the war, he became the first mayor of Hartford (now incorporated) from 1784 to 1812 when he finally resigned at the ripe old age of seventy-seven. He would live for another seventeen years and die at the age of ninety-four in 1829.

Thomas and Mary Seymour, following their marriage in 1755 and the birth of seven children between 1757 and 1773, decided to move from his parents' home and build their own along the banks of the Little River on Arch Street in downtown Hartford. *Little River?* I, again, spent five years in the Hartford area and I never heard anything about the Little River. *Yeah, yeah. It was a little river. Duh.*

Digging deep on the web and now way off the beaten path, I discovered a few things. First, the only current reference to the Little River is a bar/restaurant called Little River Restoratives, which is slightly west of Arch Street on Capitol Avenue. Additionally, I found another bar named the Arch Street Tavern on the end of Arch Street to the east. *Hey, I like bars.* On the bar's website is a section about the history of the tavern and the street that it's located on. It reads,

> *In the 1600s, the founding residents settled at the junction of the Great River (Connecticut River) and the Little River (today the Whitehead Highway). Columbus Blvd. (Front St.) & Arch St. were among the earliest streets in Hartford. Known today as the "Father of Connecticut", Rev. Thomas Hooker resided on Arch Street (very near the Tavern's present site) alongside many other of Hartford's leading citizens. In those days, the Little River served as a watery highway on which barges ferried supplies into the heart of the young city. In 1895, the Hartford Brick Carriage Factory (now Arch Street Tavern) was built, where it manufactured buggies and carriages until the automobile caused its demise some 20 years later. The tavern has also served as a firehouse and a truck body shop before its opening in 1978.*

So, there it is. Whether you can trust the information on a tavern's website or not, it makes sense that Thomas Seymour III lived on

Arch Street and would have been considered one of "Hartford's leading citizens." Whatever the case, the river that flowed east into the Connecticut River was eventually diverted or dammed up, and the significant highway running parallel to Arch Street today was constructed.

Unfortunately, the original house built by Thomas III was torn down in 1870 and the property was eventually purchased by the George Lincoln Iron Foundry Company. Remnants of the company still exist in Connecticut today. While obviously the hub of activity through the 1800s, this section of town is now mostly concrete. *Time moves on, for good or bad.*

The Origin of a Desk

While I have no official documentation of when or by whom the Seymour desk was made, I do know that it was made for Mayor Thomas Seymour III, probably sometime between 1790 and 1800, for his wife, Mary Ledyard Seymour. I have multiple secondhand accounts of its origin as well as Thomas's will and testament to justify this proclamation. But who owned the desk following his death and prior to my family receiving it?

Through this whole process, I kept looking for that one smoking gun document that specifically stated that my new desk was the same desk that was built in 1790 by Thomas Seymour III. It doesn't exist. Nor should it. *It would have been nice if Thomas III had left a receipt with all the desk details tucked inside a drawer.*

Much of my research and eventual conclusions would need to be based on logical speculation and good old common sense. A major part of my circumstantial evidence was the contents of the desk that were passed along to me. Two of the letters in the desk were attributed to Mayor Thomas Seymour III. These two letters—battered, torn, and deeply faded—do nothing to clearly indicate that my desk is the same one that was manufactured for Mayor Thomas Seymour. But they do strengthen my case.

The first letter is dated July 19, 1797, from a gentleman named Joseph Isham, responding to a bill sent by Thomas for legal work done on a case referred to as *Caleb Chapman vs. Charles Williams*. No surprise here. Thomas was a prominent lawyer in Hartford. Again, though it is interesting from a novelty perspective and it confirms Thomas III's role as a lawyer, it serves no function in terms of the desk other than connecting it to the Seymours. But for my purposes, the date is significant. If the letter was written in 1797, then logic dictates that it would have been put into the desk after it was built and not before. Whatever the case, this style of desk was popular in the 1790s through the early 1800s, meaning it was probably built for the Seymours in the early 1790s and remained in his home for another fifty years.

The second letter, much more personal to the story, is a letter from Thomas III to his granddaughter, Mary Eliza, in 1824. At that point, Thomas was eighty-nine (he died four years later), and his granddaughter was twenty-five and living in New York City. He spends the first half of the letter talking about his impending death (*a little early for that, sir*) and his deep desire to meet his maker and rejoin his wife again. Mary Eliza was the daughter of Mary Juliana Seymour Chenevard, Thomas's only daughter. Thomas refers to a cousin living in the New York area, an Aunt Betsey who's not doing well, and he mentions that he's looking forward to seeing Mary Eliza soon. He ends it with "your affectionate GrandPa" and apologizes for the ink blots.

Nothing earth shattering there, other than confirming that the desk was in his hands into the early 1800s. *Or does it?* While the first lawyer letter makes perfect sense in terms of being in the desk, the second one does not. If Mayor Thomas Seymour sent the letter to his granddaughter, how did it wind up back in the desk and now in my possession? As a matter of fact, why did these two specific letters end up here and not any of the other hundreds that he must have received or sent, especially as a lawyer? These questions about the desk's letters would nag me through the whole process. As Elsa says, "Let it go!" *Ya, right!*

The Will

The death of Mayor Thomas Seymour in 1829 created a bit of confusion for my purposes. His first will was written in 1807 when his wife, Mary Ledyard Seymour, was still alive, and it was amended again slightly in 1821 following her death years before. Interestingly but not surprisingly, my dad left me a hard copy of the will among his other notes and assorted paperwork. It, like most wills of the time, was straightforward. Everything did not go to Thomas's wife following his death but rather was distributed among their descendants. This was quite normal. It reads, "I give unto my Dearly beloved Wife Mary, the entire use and improvement of my Homestead, mansion House, & out Houses thereon–also, the use of all my household goods & furniture–a good Cow & Horse, & pasturing the same–& the sum of two hundred dollars, to be paid to her annually by my Executor." As I said, his wife had passed years before he did, so this part of the will was null and void. The executor in this case was his son, Henry, and it basically asks Henry to take care of his wife if he preceded her in death.

To his two eldest sons (Thomas Youngs and William), he left nothing significant since he provided for them greatly while he was alive. To his third son, Edward, he left a different estate from the home on Arch Street, which was near the "Great Bridge" where he and his family had been already living and running a store. Edward retained all of that. It's when he's addressing his only daughter, Mary Juliana, that things get complicated. It reads,

I give to my dear & only Daughter, Mary Juliana Chenevard, all the Household Goods, furniture & plate, remaining in my House, upon the demise of her dear mother, excepting thereout, the Portraits of her Parents, & my Mahogany Desk & Book Case—and I also give to her one thousand dollars, to be paid to her by my Executor hereafter named, within six months after my decease, which I advise her to put upon Interest, for her own use.

To my novice eyes, it seems clear enough and fits nicely into my story. Mary Juliana got all the furniture and such upon her mother's death EXCEPT for the portraits, a bookcase, and a mahogany desk—which I can only assume is the same one that I now sit at. But when scouring over the book *A History of the Seymour Family* by George Dudley Seymour and Donald Lines Jacobus, I found a picture of a desk with the heading *The First Mayor's "Mahogany Desk and Book Case."* Initially taken aback because the picture looks nothing like the desk that I now own, I began to get a little red under the collar when I read the caption underneath. It reads, "This is a superb piece of cabinet work by Samuel Prince of New York, and is owned by a descendant of Mary Juliana Chenevard. This is the only piece of furniture specified in the First Mayor's will." While I have no doubt that Mary Juliana received the beautiful cabinet pictured in the book, I believe that the author was wrong about the desk in question being in the will. His version doesn't fit with the language of the will.

The "mahogany desk" did not go to Mary but to her older brother, Henry. Henry's section of the will reads, "I do give & bequeath unto my Son Henry Seymour, & to his heirs forever after the demise of his dear mother, my House & Homestead, containing about three Acres, together with all the rest, residue and remainder of my Estate, real & personal, not before given & devised." The last line is significant because I would assume that the portraits, desk, and bookcase are the "not before given and devised," as well as the rest of the estate. Whatever the case, either Mr. Dudley was wrong (*my vote*) or there were two mahogany desks (*boo!*). But I do know through multiple reliable sources that my mahogany desk started with Thomas III and was passed down the line from there. Everything else is mere chatter in the background.

One final note on the will. The youngest son, Ledyard, did not fare so well; apparently Mayor Thomas was not happy with his son's efforts in life. It reads, "and whereas I have paid & advanced considerable sums of money for my youngest Son Ledyard Seymour, who has been unfortunate in Business—therefore it is my will, not to give him any further at present, but to leave it to the discretion and affection of his Brother, my Executor hereafter named, to assist him, as far as he may judge it to be just & proper." *Ouch!!! And he left Henry to do the dirty work.*

Home Away From Home

Henry Seymour was born in 1764 in Hartford. He spent his early adult years in Philadelphia as a trading merchant; then he served the American Army by transporting money and supply vouchers between Philadelphia and upstate New York, and eventually lived in New York City until 1784 when he moved back to Hartford. He, like his older brother Thomas Youngs Seymour IV served as a major in the Governor's Horse Guards between 1803 and 1807. He married Jane Ellery in 1804, and they produced three children—Mary Ellery, Thomas Hart, and William Ellery. The Seymour desk remained in his possession on Arch Street until his death in 1846, I would assume, or perhaps as late as 1851 when his wife passed. While Henry clearly inherited the Seymour desk that I now own, I wasn't entirely sure who made the desk and when and who got the desk officially upon Henry's and Jane's deaths. I knew that I had to take the next step.

The next step usually meant finding primary sources from these individuals, but most people don't hang on to the piles of paperwork that we all generate over our lifetimes. Or, when we let our descendants deal with them, they usually just trash them. But I was hopeful, since I already had primary sources from some of these people.

For those who may have spent a lifetime avoiding the library, the major difference between primary sources and secondary sources is who wrote them. A primary source is usually a document, letter, diary or such from a person, whereas a secondary source is someone's account of those said primary sources—usually a book or article.

But where to start. On an educated whim, I checked the database of Connecticut's historical society, known as the Connecticut Museum of Culture and History, and hit the jackpot. No, more like the Megabucks. Most of these bigger organizations have extensive digital and hard copy collections with tons of primary sources. Thankfully and somewhat surprisingly, there were hundreds of primary resources relating to these Seymours. Most deal with Thomas Seymour III's grandson, Thomas Hart Seymour. *Yup. Another one. And how did the museum come by all of these documents?*

I contacted the Connecticut Museum of Culture and History in Hartford and planned a visit. All well and good, but we were still in the depths of Covid hell, and the visit and research would be difficult (masks, vaccination cards, limited time, etc.). The staff there was wonderful and had the boxes of Mayor Thomas Seymour's and Henry Seymour's life on paper, ready and waiting for me. Little did I know at that point that I would visit the museum time and time again over the next three years. *My home away from home.*

To be honest, while I had done a lot of book research for both my undergraduate and graduate work, I'd never had to wade through countless primary sources dealing with one person. When I finally sat down and opened said boxes, I was amazed at the extent and volume of the paperwork regarding the Seymour family through the middle of the 1800s. *At what point does someone realize that they should save all records for posterity's sake? Hell, I throw out tax records that are more than seven years old.*

I spent close to two hours wading through the Seymour materials without much to show for it. While I found a lot of neat stuff, I was really looking for some sort of official record of the purchase of the desk or a receipt of some kind. Of course, I was thinking in a 21st-century mindset where we get printed receipts for everything—not in an 18th-century one.

As I previously said, if I'm to believe Thomas III's will and comments made by others, my desk was passed on to Henry, Thomas's fourth son. Unlike his father, as well as his oldest son, Thomas Hart Seymour, there appears to be little in the way of personal documents attributed to Henry in the museum. But from all that I can deduce through general logic, Henry appears to have been closest to his father. One, Henry served as executor of his father's will. Two, he retained his father's house and specific articles of furniture, including the desk. Though he did not have it long; he would only outlive his father by seventeen years.

In addition to missing documentation proving the desk's origin, I did not find anything close to a will for Major Henry Seymour. But logic dictates that it would have passed to one of three children—Mary Ellery Seymour, Thomas Hart Seymour, or William Ellery Seymour. But which one? Here, the desk itself helps clarify things. Perhaps.

In addition to the two letters written to Mayor Thomas Seymour that were in the desk, there were also fifteen diverse letters to Thomas Hart Seymour during the latter part of his life. Again, it seems only logical that he would not have personal and professional letters in a desk that he did not own.

Added to this qualifier is the fact that his older sister, Mary, lived with him her entire adult life and never married nor had children. In theory, I guess that she could have owned the desk, but there are no letters specifically to her in its drawers. Additionally, their younger brother, William, had moved to New Orleans in his late teens and never officially returned to the Hartford area. William would have been in New Orleans at the time of his father, Henry's, death in 1846. So, it was doubtful that any of Henry and Jane Seymour's possessions were sent south following their deaths. Shipping goods across the country was no easy task at the time, and U-Hauls were not even a glimmer in someone's fantasy in the 1850s. For the sake of my inheritance and this book, this was a good thing. A desk shipped to New Orleans would probably not have made it past the Mason-Dixon line again. *But who was Thomas Hart Seymour? An amazing man, actually.*

4

When Andy Met Harry...

Much like my journey through the lives of Oliver Ellsworth and Noah Webster, I was awed at the dedication of service that Thomas Hart Seymour gave to his state and country. Obviously, my ignorance of his résumé is a bit more justified than that of my own flesh and blood, but learning about all these historical figures gives you a new appreciation for the sacrifices that many made over a long history of sacrifices without recognition. On the National Governors Association website (*a real yawner*), Thomas Seymour's brief professional biography reads:

> *THOMAS H. SEYMOUR was born in Hartford, Connecticut, on September 29, 1807. He graduated from Captain Alden Partridge's Military Institute in Middletown, studied law, and was admitted to the bar in 1833. Seymour had an illustrious military career. He served during the Mexican War, earning the rank of colonel due to his courageous leadership at the Battle of Chapultepec. Seymour also served as a probate judge from 1836 to 1838, was the editor of the Jeffersonian, a leading Democratic newspaper, from 1837 to 1838, and he served in the U.S. House of Representatives from 1843 to 1845. He ran unsuccessfully in the 1849 gubernatorial election, but won the following year by a legislative vote of 122 to 108. He was reelected to the governor's office the next three years. During his tenure, the General Assembly challenged the Compromise of 1850, which addressed the issue of fugitive slaves; however, its constitutionality was upheld by the 1851 De-*

mocratic convention. Seymour also served as an 1852 presidential elector, endorsing Franklin Pierce and, in return for his support, Seymour was appointed to serve as minister to Russia. He resigned from the governorship on October 13, 1853, and spent the next four years in Russia, where he built a warm and ongoing alliance with the Czar Nicholas and his son. After returning home, Seymour ran again for the governor's office, but was unsuccessful in both his 1860 and 1863 bids. He headed the Connecticut Peace Democrats, and at the 1864 Democratic National Convention he received 38 votes, on the first ballot, for president of the United States. Governor Thomas H. Seymour died on September 3, 1868, and is buried at the Cedar Hill Cemetery in Hartford.

Great stuff, Harrison, but what about the desk at this point?

Thomas Henry Seymour, date unknown

Have Desk, Will Travel

In terms of the desk's location between roughly 1850 and 1890, simplicity and logic rule the day. Henry Seymour inherited Thomas III's house on Arch Street in downtown Hartford upon his father's death in 1829. The Seymour desk would remain there until Henry's and his wife's deaths in 1846 and 1851, respectively. While I don't have the will to prove it, the desk was given to their oldest son, Thomas

Hart Seymour. It would move with him when he and his sister, Mary, moved to a home on Governor Street in East Hartford, just across the Connecticut River. *Did Governor Street get its name because of its now famous inhabitant, or was it mere coincidence? No clue.*

When did Thomas Seymour and his sister, Mary, move to their house in East Hartford and out of the family home on Arch Street? I'm not 100% sure, but census reports are helpful. According to the 1850 census, the Seymours were listed as dwelling at Number 1370 (*Whaaat? No street names?*), including their mother, Jane Ellery Seymour, Thomas, Mary, and a servant. I can only assume that the dwelling is the original home on Arch Street. According to the 1860 census, Jane is not listed (now long since dead), and the dwelling number is now 815. *Ugh. Still no street names.*

I can only suppose that Thomas and Mary Seymour, listed in the census along with two servants, were living at a new house on Governor Street in East Hartford. Of course, because the census for Hartford in both 1850 and 1860 used dwelling numbers without street names, I am not sure about anything. *Ugh.* As a working logical assumption, Thomas moved to East Hartford while he was the governor (in the early 1850s) and before becoming minister to Russia (in the late 1850s).

But where was the desk located upon the move to East Hartford? I can only surmise that it moved to their new home along with the other family possessions. But was Thomas's office while he was governor in his home or someplace else? *But seriously, folks. Whoever really documents the furniture in their house or office for posterity's sake?* Before I delve into said hearsay, I was stuck in another time warp of idiocy: Where did the governor of Connecticut work in the middle 1800s? The Old State House.

The center of Connecticut's government during that period was the Old State House located in downtown Hartford. It was built in 1796 and remained the center of government until 1878 when a new legislative building was built and occupied. Therefore, my next question became: Did Thomas use the desk at the Old State House or at his house in East Hartford? Another field trip was in order to find an answer.

Cathy and I headed down the road to Hartford to tour the Old State House. By this point, in late October 2023, I had made several trips to the Hartford area for some variation of research. This was no different. Once we parked and paid our entrance fees, we started with the two congressional halls—Senate and House, like the federal government. I browsed information in each and pondered the fact that Oliver Ellsworth and his son, William Wolcott Ellsworth, spent time in either or both halls. I also spent time admiring the beauty of both, but I needed to find the governor's office and someone who knew something about how it all worked at the time.

That person was Heidi Adams, a docent for the building. We quickly went through the pleasantries and a history of the governor's usage of the building. Then I posed my burning question: "Did governors bring in their own furniture, or did they use the furniture that went with the office?"

I half expected her to say, "How the hell would I know that, and who really cares?" But she quickly responded, "Probably not." Her rationale made sense. Heidi explained that because Connecticut governors at the time served one-year terms, they probably didn't bring in their own furniture. Her curiosity now piqued, she asked why I would need such information. I gave her my five-minute dog and pony show. When I got to the Oliver Ellsworth piece, she quickly blurted out, "Hey, we're cousins." She's related to the Ellsworths from Windsor, but her branch veers off before Oliver's lineage. *Small world.*

We finished our tour by checking out the governor's office, which now serves as the "Kid Governor's Office." Very cool, but it didn't give me the nostalgic feeling of the other rooms in the Old State House. *Oh well!*

So, in theory, the desk moved from Thomas's inherited house on Arch Street to his newly purchased home on Governor Street in East

Hartford without spending any time in the Old State House. I did wonder, was the house purchased while Thomas was still in the States and after his mother died (roughly 1851-54) or after his return from Russia in 1858? I'm not sure. It seems slightly unlikely that Mary Seymour would have purchased their new home on her own. *Not a statement of my prejudice, but a reflection of the times.*

The Letters

Wherever the desk resided during Thomas's life, I do know where it ended up. And, as I previously mentioned, I was awed at the diversity of the written materials connected to Thomas that came with the desk. These written artifacts ultimately drove me deeper into his life. Without them, I probably would have given him a brief mention and moved on to the next owner of the desk. But the contents belonging to Thomas intrigued me to the point of a dog battling its owner over a chew toy. I couldn't move on until I'd given this man the same research autopsy I'd done with my own relatives.

The Thomas Seymour materials that came with the desk were extensive. They included a book of calling cards (*more on that*), a brief report of Thomas's role in the Mexican War, and a series of letters from a variety of different people dating from 1850 to the mid-1860s. I am not sure whether Thomas put them in the desk himself or if they were deposited later by someone else. No matter. I was hooked and ready for another research coaster ride.

Again, Thomas Hart Seymour was born in Hartford in 1807. Curiously, his name appears as both Thomas Henry and Thomas Hart in multiple sources. It seems that he was born and baptized as Thomas Henry after his grandfather and father, respectively, but later he would refer to himself as Thomas Hart Seymour. I am not sure if there was a problem with his father, but it does beg the question. Added to the mix was the fact that his friends and relatives called him Harry, as seen on a ton of letters addressed to him.

Thomas Hart Seymour was educated at the local public school in Hartford, and he moved on to a military academy where he graduated in 1829. He then studied law while writing for a local paper and passed the bar in 1833. While law and the military attracted him, his first love became politics, and he was elected to the United States House of Representatives for a term of 1843 to 1845. Representatives to the U.S. Congress serve two-year terms, so he only served one. Whether he saw the writing on the wall with problems with Mexico or he was disenchanted with the role as a representative, he did not run again for that office and opted for the military and a trip to Mexico soon after.

The Making of a War Hero

For those who missed the lesson about the Mexican War between April 1846 and February 1848, you didn't miss much. In probably one of the United States' lowest points of diplomatic history, our government manufactured a justification to go to war against Mexico while the real reason was to acquire more land. With the Treaty of Guadalupe Hidalgo in February 1848, the U.S. Government "negotiated" a treaty with the Mexican government that gave us all the land west of Texas to California.

To understand the basis for the Mexican War, one must start with Texas. Without traveling too far down the rabbit hole, Texas colonists fought and eventually defeated Mexican forces in April 1836 to gain their independence and became an independent country. *Remember the Alamo, Pee-wee Herman, and all that.* While Mexico never officially acknowledged Texan independence, the United States' government surely did, with the hope of adding Texan territory to its fold. It didn't take long. Annexation became official in 1845, which complicated matters because Mexico never considered Texas to be independent. Of course, James Polk, the president at the time, wasn't satisfied with just Texas, and he sent a representative to Mexico to negotiate the purchase of the land all the way to California. Needless to say, the Mexican government scoffed at the idea.

Against the backdrop of manifest destiny and the concept that it was God's will that we possess all land between the oceans, Polk would not be deterred. After all attempts to negotiate a sale failed and the U.S. negotiator was abruptly sent home, Polk moved to Plan B and sent troops to the Rio Grande in Texas. To see this move as anything but a stick poking a hornet's nest would be naive since the Mexican government believed the disputed area between the northern Nueces River and southern Rio Grande was technically Mexico. In response, Mexican forces attacked and crushed a small American detachment along the Rio Grande in April 1846, which was probably what Polk wanted in the first place. War was declared in May 1846, but not without opposition from many in Congress and the public. The ruse was that apparent.

Thomas Seymour, for his part, was commissioned in the spring of 1847 as a major of the Connecticut infantry and then a month later commissioned by the U.S. Infantry. As wars go, the defeat of Mexico did not take very long. There were war fronts on all sides—California to the northwest, Texas to the north, and coastal Mexico to the east. It became clear that the Mexicans would not concede until the whole country was taken, and thus, Winfield Scott, the U.S. commander of military forces on the east coast at Veracruz, decided to slowly move into the heart of the country and take its capital city, Mexico City. Because the defense of the direct western route was sturdy, Scott decided to move his armies to the southwest before marching straight north into the capital. Mexico is not a flat country, and Mexico City is more than 7000 feet in elevation. Scott was wise in his choice to move his forces straight north (a much more gradual ascent), but it would be no picnic.

The U.S. Army and Marines' final obstacle would be capturing the historical Chapultepec Castle that served as the Mexican academy for aspiring officers. It was a direct stepping stone to the siege on Mexico City. *Stepping stone, my ass!* The U.S. forces would have to literally scale a 150-foot wall using only ladders and sheer willpower to take a well-defended castle wall. *Next time you're on the ladder of your house ascending to the roof line, think about a hostile Mexican pointing a rifle down at you.*

According to a variety of sources, the two regiments from the 9th and 15th infantry, including forty marines (*From the Halls of Montezuma...*) and totaling 250 men, scaled the walls. The 9th's commanding officer, Colonel Truman Ransom, led the attack but was killed in battle. Major Thomas Seymour took over, led his charges over the precipice, and the rest, as they say, is history. Seymour became known as the "Hero of Chapultepec." He honorably mustered out of the military in the summer of 1848 as a colonel and was welcomed home to Connecticut with great fanfare. *Noah Webster and Oliver Ellsworth can't hold a candle to that.*

One of the more unique items in my desk is a three-and-a-half-page essay, written and typed around 1916 on onion skin paper, about Seymour's efforts in Mexico. *For those of you from the baby boomer era, you remember the days of onion skin paper, crappy typewriters, and Wite-Out in liquid form.* Anyway, the essay is titled "Seymour and Chapultepec," but it has no name or time reference (other than a comment about being written sixty-eight years after the event in Mexico and forty-eight years after Thomas's death). It clearly was a brief, lauding, biographical piece of Thomas Seymour's life about his special efforts during the Mexican War. The author writes,

> *Their [Hartford citizens back during his time] interest then was insatiable, for a favorite son of Hartford, Thomas Hart Seymour, was in that famous battle [Chapultepec] and led the first American regiment to enter that was then supposed to be an impregnable stronghold. This fact is well remembered by the older citizens of Hartford, who saw day by day "Tom" Seymour, as he was familiarly called, democratic war horse and ex-governor mingling among them until his death forty-eight years ago.*

The glowing piece goes on from there. My questions were many. Who wrote this and why? Was this some kid's paper from school or something written for a newspaper? And, finally, how did it wind up with all the other materials, most of which were collected while he was alive? Keep in mind, it was written well after Thomas had passed away. My initial thought was that Thomas's niece Helen or nephew William Henry (he went by Henry) wrote it—his younger brother William's kids—but the timing doesn't work. They both would have been in their sixties in 1916. Even Thomas's four grandnieces and grandnephews (Henry's kids) were a stretch. *Who knows?* I did get the gist that the essay writer was local to the Hartford area, based on the continual reference to it. *Whatever. Add another item to the list of artifacts that pose more questions than they answer.*

The Making of a Governor

There is a long history of American military heroes who use their fame to propel them into political office, and Colonel Thomas Seymour was no different. Though he ran for governor of Connecticut in 1849 and lost, his Democratic Party made major headway from the previous year. Thomas ran for governor again in 1850, won by a wide margin, and served in that capacity through 1853. He would have probably continued in that role if newly elected President Franklin Pierce hadn't appointed him as U.S. Minister to Russia.

There were a handful of letters written to Governor Seymour during this time frame. The first is a letter written in May 1850 from a gentleman named Milledge Bonham who happened to be his superior officer during the war. In a letter written a few years later, Bonham, who was from South Carolina, is trying to cajole the new governor to support the South and its stance on the expansion of slavery in the Union. *Good luck, sir.*

Another letter, even more abstract and dated May 1852, was supposed to be delivered to the czar of Russia by Thomas, given that he was appointed as the new minister there. The letter is from a company called American Electromagnetic Printing Telegraph Company, and they were hoping to persuade the czar to use their company for an upgraded telegraph system in Russia. *Think an old-fashioned T-Mobile commercial.* I'm not sure, but I don't think anything came of this since the letter wound up in the desk.

The next three letters were a bit more interesting. *Or juicier, for want of a better term.* Each was mailed in a similar small envelope measuring roughly two-and-a-half inches by four-and-a-half inches. One originates from Veracruz, Mexico, passing through Mobile, Alabama, before eventually reaching Thomas Seymour in Hartford. It's dated June 1850, when he was governor. The other two are dated February 13 and 14, but with no year listed (*ugh*) and both have a Hartford postmark. Perhaps one arrived a day after the other, or perhaps a year apart. I'm not sure. While all three letters include poems, the June 1850 letter also contains a lock of brown hair. There is nothing written to explain the lock of hair other than a poem. All have very small and meticulous handwriting.

The two letters with no year contain poems and dates around Valentine's Day; these are love poems. A lengthy poem in the letter dated February 14 clearly laments the inability of the writer to put their feelings into words and simply ends with:

And now I'm duller than before
  The "flash" begins by thoughts to close
  So I will say and write no more
  "I love you" in the plainest prose

The six-stanza poem is signed only by "Valentine" at the end. I cannot find any reference to it on the web, so I assume that it was written by the sender or the original author.

The February 13 letter again contains a poem and nothing more, but it carries a different tone. It reads:

You may beckon to one, one may flirt with another
  And swear to a third, she is dearer than all!
  You may win over the father, or cousen [sic] the mother
  Of each fairy lass at play, concert, or ball.
  But why take the trouble these triumphs to gain,
  And earn the repute of a treacherous elf
  Since the whole is so clear to deny it were vain,
  That your whole adoration is centered in self.

Ouch. I may have to hold on to this. As I read this, I found myself singing Justin Bieber's song, "Love Yourself." Again, I could find no reference to these two stanzas online, but no matter—the intent is clear.

The third poem is the creepiest in my mind, though it may again be a 21st-century thing. If I had sent my wife, Cathy, a lock of my hair when we were dating many years ago, we might not be married now. It, like the others, contains a poem. The poem from June 1850 reads:

Go, forget me, why sorrows bring
  O'er thy brows shadows fling?
  Go, forget me, and to-morrow
  Brightly smile and sweetly sing.

  My heart is so full, I can only say.
  God bless you, dear Harry, forever.

I did find the source of the first part. It's the first stanza of a poem written by Charles Wolfe in the early 1800s. While the lover does not appear scorned, the vibe is clearly a breakup of some kind.

In terms of the lock of hair, it was not unusual to send locks of hair to someone in this period. But usually, especially in the Victorian era, it was in memory of a loved one who had died. But further digging also tells me that it was a sign of love and devotion. Indeed, this lock of hair was woven quite elegantly with a dried flower and a bow.

Whatever the case, it appears that someone was smitten with Thomas Seymour directly after his time in Mexico (the late 1840s) and up to his time as governor (the early 1850s). In terms of the Mexican War, Veracruz hugs the eastern coast of Mexico and the Gulf of Mexico, and it was the main jumping-off point for American soldiers entering the country. Colonel Seymour surely spent time there.

It wasn't lost on me that Thomas Seymour—nor his sister, for that matter—never married. This was well before women asked men out on dates or led the marriage parade, so sister Mary being single is not such a shock—especially if no man ever broached the issue. However, it seems strange for a man of the time to never marry, especially a catch like Governor Seymour. But clearly from these letters in and around the early 1850s, there was someone whom Thomas Seymour knew beyond the average acquaintance.

My gut feeling is that this person was someone whom Thomas Seymour met during the Mexican War (like many soldiers do during wars) and a romance was kindled. I can only assume by the tone of some of the poems that their relationship did not continue. Why not, I'm not sure. Thomas Seymour remained a bachelor his whole life, which in a sense, is a blessing. A married man would have been more likely to bring children into the world, and the desk would have never passed my way.

The Making of a Russian Minister

Thomas Hart Seymour's time as Connecticut's governor was short and sweet (May 1850 to October 1853), but not because he was an unpopular governor. Far from it. In the fall of 1853, Thomas Seymour was nominated to be the next minister to Russia by the newly elected president, Franklin Pierce. *Franklin Pierce?*

Franklin Pierce, the United States' 14th president, was a contemporary of Thomas Seymour, and they became political allies as well as friends. Thomas Seymour, then governor, supported his New England neighbor throughout his campaign, and in 1853, as a reward for his support, President Franklin Pierce nominated Thomas Seymour as minister of Russia. Thomas resigned his post as governor of Connecticut and served in Russia for the next five years.

The Blues

While I do have a few letters (one in French) to Thomas Seymour while he was serving as minister to Russia, none of them gave me an idea of his day-to-day workings there. Keep in mind that most of what I received along with the desk were letters to him rather than from him. Thankfully, one of the things that did come my way via the Connecticut Museum of Culture and History was a portion of his personal journal from the fall of 1855 to the fall of 1857.

There appear to be several consistent strands in Thomas Seymour's journaling. One is the standard detailing of his day, with the usual weather and health comments, woes of his salary in a government position, meetings with the bigwigs in Saint Petersburg, and comments on the news of the day. While I was a little apprehensive about delving into another man's journal for many reasons and the general day-to-day minutiae were—for lack of a better term—freaking boring, it did serve as a valuable tool in deciphering the next letter in my chronological sequence. Additionally, while the specifics were mundane, the generalities of a man serving his country in the middle of winter in Russia were telling. I began to wonder: If he had to do it all again, would he have politely declined his friend Franklin Pierce and remained in Connecticut as governor?

First, there were constant references to the cold temperatures and harsh conditions. According to first-hand accounts, the winter of 1855-56 in the United States was one of the worst at that time, with record low temperatures and snow. One can only assume that Saint Petersburg, Russia, fared similarly. While there are daily accounts of the weather, they progressively get more depressing as he moves into the winter months. One entry in particular sticks out. On December 4, 1855, he wrote:

> *The weather here [is] still cold: hard to keep the rooms warm; my blood is not what it was this time twelve months ago. I am not what I was then either. I am of no account; I can't accomplish anything. Why is it? Alas I don't know. I have more letters unanswered than I know how to get along with. Terrible.*

I am no psychologist, but it seems that he was dealing with a bit of winter blues that were creeping in on depression. Anyone living in a New England state like myself totally gets it. Weather can be tough and long in this part of the world, and I can only imagine that it was compounded significantly in Russia in 1855.

In addition to a quick introduction about the weather in every entry, Thomas Seymour continually refers to letters written and received every day (though from the previous quote, he was clearly having a hard time keeping up on December 4) and those he called on or visited and those who called on him. I initially thought that he was an overly personable guy, but it dawned on me that this was the nature of society in general and his job specifically. It is hard to envision a world without phones, email, and texts, but people indeed wrote letters to each other all the time, and when possible, they visited others personally.

In one of my other Thomas Seymour artifacts, I have a book of calling cards and such from people who visited him at his home in Hartford. People would come calling and give others their personal calling card (which looks like a business card). Further research tells me that a calling card or visiting card was sent to another as a request for a visit and the invitation was then granted when a second card was returned. *A little drawn out, but no different than a text like "Hey, I got a new ride. Is this a good time to swing by?"* Anyway, Thomas Seymour spent much of his time writing and visiting others. Along that line, there seemed to be a core group of friends whom he visited and dined with quite often.

How Was Your Trip, Dear?

One of the most eye-opening letters, dated November 22, 1855, from Paris, France, was from a gentleman named Augustus Erving. I was able to surmise that Thomas Seymour and Augustus worked together in Saint Petersburg until the fall of 1855 and that Augustus was making his way out of Europe to eventually head back to the States. Augustus's wife was to meet him in Paris (she was coming from the States), and they would both do some traveling before returning home. The first part of the letter describes Augustus's travels to Paris spanning several weeks.

The letter then details the arrival of his wife from the States, which was quite an ordeal, due primarily to the nature of sea travel in those days. Once he'd finally gotten his wife ashore, Augustus writes, "The passage was a rough one and she had been extremely ill, never having once during the trip been able to appear at the table. For a week, she did not take a mouthful of food, and at times, vomited clear blood." *And people complain about an hour delay on a flight.*

One forgets the problems that many have with motion sickness (if that was her ailment), but today one or two pills seem to do the trick. The rest of the November letter serves as nothing more than the normal fluff between friends and colleagues, and I was left to assume that Mr. and Mrs. Erving would travel back to the States at some later point. Mrs. Erving most likely assumed that her return trip couldn't get any worse. *Or could it?*

Unfortunately, Augustus's name begins to pop up again in early spring 1856 in Thomas Seymour's journal, well after he and his wife should have officially left for the United States. On March 15, 1856, the journal states, "Nothing of the unfortunate Pacific. God only knows what has become of poor Erving and his wife- a sad business truly. The steamer has gone for 36 days and no tidings of her." *Whaaaat?* I dug further. On March 18, 1856, it reads, "No news of the Pacific." On March 21, 1856: "No news of the Pacific—nearly 40 days out." On April 2, 1856: "Explorers fear that Mr. Erving and wife are lost; sad, sad, business; my heart is oppressed with grief." The last reference is on April 3: "No news of the Pacific."

Now I was beyond intrigued, and off to Google I went. I typed in something like *"Erving lost Pacific 1856,"* thinking that the couple was lost traveling somewhere on the Pacific Ocean—which in hindsight made little sense, since getting to the Pacific Ocean from Paris seems highly unlikely. But Google bailed me out. References to a "famous" lost steamer called the *SS Pacific* immediately popped up. It departed from Liverpool, England, on January 23, 1856, and was never seen again. My heart was racing. *Could it be possible that I had one of the last letters written by a man who eventually died at sea?* Among the references to the lost ship was a link to a short documentary about the event. Of course I clicked on it. In the documentary, the researcher and creator, Thomas Lynskey, describes one of maritime travel's "great" mysteries—the loss of the *SS Pacific.* But before we go there, it might be important to briefly discuss the nature of ocean travel in the 1850s.

As with car companies, or better yet, airline companies, competition was fierce between ocean liner companies for clientele during this time period. While nothing like it is today, there were many who traveled to Europe and other places who had money. While comfort of accommodations was important, speed of travel was the major issue in the 1850s. Mrs. Erving could attest to that.

The faster you could get from England to the States and back, the more attractive a company was. And the U.S. Collins Line Company, which owned the *SS Pacific,* was no different. The U.S. Collins Line, known for shipping cotton, wanted to encroach on the personal travel and mail service business of English companies. *Mail service? Of course, mail service, Harrison.* It's always all about communication. Letters were it, and just like today, expediency was paramount.

Subsequently, four ships, named the *Atlantic, Arctic, Baltic*, and, of course, *Pacific*, were commissioned and built in the late 1840s with the financial assistance of the U.S. government. Again, competition was fierce, and the only way to make a dent was to increase speed of travel. Unfortunately, as it has been stated, speed kills. Disaster struck in 1854 when the *SS Arctic* ran into another boat due to heavy fog off the coast of Newfoundland, Canada. Then the *SS Pacific* followed suit in January 1856, but in that case, there's no record of when or where it sank. The only hint of its demise came two years later when a note in a sealed bottle washed up on the shore of a remote Scottish island. *I can hear Sting singing in my head.* Part of it read,

> *On board the Pacific from Liverpool to N.Y. - Ship going down. Confusion on board - icebergs around us on every side. I know I cannot escape. I write that the cause of our loss is that friends may not live in suspense. The finder will please get it published. W.M. GRAHAM.*

While a relatively small passenger load (forty-five) compared to the crew (141) was lost, it seems that two of those were Mr. and Mrs. Erving. Their deaths were apparently due to speed as the *Pacific* tried to maneuver quickly among the icebergs in late January. Records show that it was a very cold winter in 1855-56, which would have compounded the iceberg issue. *Story sound familiar?*

Anyway, while I was pretty sure that the Ervings were on the fateful trip, I did a search on Ancestry.com, using the key date of January 23, 1856 as a marker—and bingo. There he was, Augustus Erving and his wife, Anna Wyman Erving. I even found a picture of their tombstone in a Hartford cemetery that had a mention of the *SS Pacific* on it. My last confirmation was connecting with Thomas Lynskey via email to see if he had access to the passenger list. He quickly passed on the information, and sure enough, there was Erving, Mr. A., and wife on the list with everyone else. *Mystery solved.*

Poor Anna Erving made the trip to visit her husband during his last days in Europe on a voyage from hell only to sail again two months later with an even worse fate on the return trip. This was all because the standards of travel back in the day required maximum speed at all costs, simply to get the mail into the right hands. *Today, we simply send a nasty emoji when someone doesn't text back within a few minutes.*

The Making of a Rabble Rouser

Thomas Seymour's term as minister to Russia ended in 1857 with the inauguration of a new Democrat president, James Buchanan, and a new administration that would appoint new ministers to other countries, including Russia. Thomas did not return home immediately and spent another year or so traveling throughout Europe.

Thomas Seymour returned to his home city of Hartford in 1858, and he received a hero's welcome with a parade, an honor guard, and a massive crowd. At that point, he was considered the most popular man in Connecticut. That would change.

The fanfare and his popularity soon ended with the Civil War on the horizon; he quickly lost favor among the masses due to his position on the war and his apparent support of slave-owning states. His support of slavery in the South may have been an oversimplification, but his stance against a war and invasion of the South was not. He became politically active again upon his return—trying initially to stop the advent of war and then to end hostilities while it raged. His stance was not taken lightly at home. In 1862, in the middle of the war, Orville Platt, a member of the Connecticut Lower House, turned Thomas's governor portrait toward the wall, where it remained until the war's end in 1865. *Life sucks and then your portrait is turned around.*

The bulk of the letters to Thomas Seymour in my possession were from this ten-year period, roughly 1858-1868, and most were nothing of significance. Two of the letters were in relation to gaining support for his reelection as governor—one of those letters was to his buddy and former president, Franklin Pierce. Thomas was not successful in his new governorship campaign, primarily since by 1860, the Democratic Party had split into two factions. This paved the way to Lincoln's first election and the eventual impetus for the Civil War. The Republican Party had swept every state in New England. Thomas Seymour would never hold office or a significant post again.

The other remaining nondescript letters include one detailing an upcoming David Watkinson trust meeting for the creation and funding of a new library in Hartford. Ironically, this same trust created the Watkinson School, a private school in Hartford that was started in the 1880s. It was also my first place of employment as a teacher in 1983. There are two letters from Thomas's sister-in-law in New Orleans and a close cousin in New York City from the early 1860s, though these have no envelopes, so no official dates. Finally, there is a letter dated December 10, 1862, discussing a bill for attorney work that Thomas had done. I tend to forget that Thomas was a lawyer when he was not working for the government. Following his stint in Europe and failed attempts to get back into state and federal politics, he hung up his shingle again. There were bills to be paid.

That's Crazy!

The last chronological letter in the desk is probably the most unique of them all. It is dated January 22, 1866, and at first glance it seems mundane, but it soon becomes a story in itself. The first clue of something slightly amiss is the heading:

"Conn. State Prison, Wethersfield." *Whaaat?*

The letter then reads:

Dear Sir,

Willard Clark formerly of New Haven (but at present confined here, some time) since asked permission to cut for you the accompanying block [I assume that the block was mailed with the letter]. It is as you will see cut from a solid piece of wood and is the result of patient persevering toil outside of his regular hours of labor and is similar to those cut by the same man for Misters Huntington and Hart who have on two occasions given the convicts very fine concerts.

Respectfully your obedient servant, Mr. Willard-Warden

Quick research tells me that there was indeed a prison in Wethersfield from 1827 to 1963, and there was a warden at that time named William Willard—which initially was confusing, since the wood-cutter was also named Willard. One can only surmise that Mr. Willard Clark was trying to make some extra money on the side and the warden was helping him out. I looked up Willard Clark in Ancestry.com under the census link in Wethersfield, Connecticut, in 1870, and sure enough, he was still serving time there. Hmmmm. What did he do? *I know, I know. Let it go, Andy.* The census report listed him as a Rule Maker under occupation, which I found quite ironic since he apparently was a Rule Breaker or he wouldn't be there. A few clicks later, I determined that Rule Makers were people who made wooden rulers. These were significant at the time, given that other measuring devices did not exist. Okay, so Willard wanted to sell rulers to Thomas and sent him a prototype. But who was this Willard Clark and what was he in for? *Don't do it, Andy!* That's when things got crazy—in the true sense of the word.

I started with an Ancestry.com search of Willard Clark in New Haven in and around the date of 1866 but only got a hit in 1850. *Interesting.* I backtracked on a simple Google search with something like "Willard Clark New Haven 1850," and bingo. *Or more likely, holy shit!*

It seems that my Willard Clark was serving a life sentence for a heinous and quite strange murder of a Mr. Richard Wight. Apparently, Willard walked into a Mrs. Bogart's house (Mr. Wight's mother-in-law) unannounced, and without any prior provocation, he asked Mr. Wight to join him in the front parlor away from the others (Mrs. Bogart and her daughter, Mrs. Nettie Bogart Wight). There, he put a gun to Wight's head, shot him once, and walked out. Of course, at this point, the criminal justice and forensic science part of me took over. *I was now in with both feet.*

The first written account of a Willard Clark was in 1840 when he was twelve years old and living in New Haven, Connecticut. He was working for a minister named Reverend Harry Croswell at the Trinity Episcopal Church. Based on an article, "Journal of Insanity. Trial of Willard Clark," from the *American Journal of Psychiatry*, Willard Clark worked for the reverend for three years. While Willard, according to the reverend, was being of "good character: kind and amiable," he did begin to show signs of "exceedingly sensitive, easily exasperated, and had periods of depression." He later worked as a grocery clerk in New Haven until the age of eighteen (1846), when, for no apparent reason, he pulled stakes and moved to Chicopee, Massachusetts—a good hour north of New Haven.

There, in 1847, he fell madly in love with a girl who is referred to as Miss Scott in court records. He had every intention of marrying her, until she, abruptly, left to visit friends in Maine and never returned. *Serious red flag.* Willard eventually learned that she had fallen in love with someone and married soon after. Not believing the story, he traveled to Maine to investigate, only to discover that it was indeed true. According to a lengthy description of the case on a website called Psychiatry Online, the event hit Willard hard and sent him into a serious depth of depression. Whether there was anything between Willard and Miss Scott in the first place or whether her trip to Maine was a way to get away from this would-be stalker, it does shed light on events yet to come. Willard eventually moved back to New Haven in the fall of 1848 and began working at the same grocery store as before. He thrived and eventually took possession of the grocery store and lived there as well.

Trouble began when in 1849 he became infatuated with a twelve-year-old girl named Nettie Bogart whom he saw walking to school each day as she passed his store. He did not push the issue until she was fourteen. According to her testimony, she was reluctant to engage in any courting process, but because these were different times, her mom agreed to the marriage after constant pressure from Willard. Unfortunately for Willard, a gentleman named Richard Wight, who was Willard's age, had moved into the Bogarts' home as a renter. Nettie began to fall in love with Richard—perhaps to escape Willard. *All of this is cringe-worthy, but it was a very different time with different standards.*

As if it wasn't bad enough to be scorned again by a woman who fell in love with another man, Willard was also, by all accounts, losing his mind. In 1854, Nettie broke off the engagement with Willard, stating that she had fallen out of love with him and that her interests had moved elsewhere—namely to Richard Wight. Nettie and Richard married in March of 1855. While this ultimately was the trigger that led to Richard's murder, court testimony from multiple individuals stated that Willard's facilities were slowly diminishing well before that day. According to a trial testimony of a Mrs. Mary Woodward:

I have known Willard Clark for about four years. Have traded there daily. Have noticed, through the past winter, that he has been unusually abstracted, and neglected his business, and has played on musical instruments when there were a half-dozen customers waiting in his store. Once he was in his room, and at another time in his store. I have asked him for articles; he would stare at me with a wild countenance, take up one thing and lay it down, and take up another, until I had twice called his attention to what I had come after. This was through the winter. I was in the store, and, instead of getting what I wanted, he looked at me with an unpleasantly wild countenance.

His descent into madness continued through the winter of 1855 until a month after the Wight marriage, when he borrowed a gun from a friend claiming to need it to get rid of a feral cat. On the day in question, he visited Mrs. Bogart (Nettie's mom) at her home with the gun tucked away and asked where the newly married couple was, only to be told that they were out. Mrs. Bogart did her best to dissuade

Willard from returning after she saw how upset he was. She later reported that Willard went on a rant about the couple's marriage and claimed that Nettie loved him more and that Richard would treat her poorly. Of course, Mrs. Bogart's attempts were in vain. Willard did return, and he murdered Richard in cold blood and, for all intents and purposes, in the first degree. Following the murder, he calmly walked out and returned the gun to its owner, saying only, "I shot a two-legged cat." He was promptly arrested.

At the trial several months later, many witnesses and most importantly a court psychologist and a priest spoke of his mental illness prior to the event and up to the murder itself. But the most influential testimony came from several doctors and preachers who spoke with Willard extensively prior to the trial. For the most part, they all said the same things. At the time of the murder and perhaps leading up to it, Willard believed that Richard was an evil man, that he had some evil power over Nettie, and that she truly loved Willard far more than Richard. Willard commented extensively that he was doing the world a service by killing Richard as if he was a "feral cat." In his delusional mind, these were facts, but there was no truth to any of it. In conclusion, the jury found the defendant "Not guilty, on the sole ground of insanity," and he was sent to the Retreat of the Insane in Hartford. The case appears in many legal writings as one of the first credible examples of an insanity defense.

I am not sure whether Thomas Seymour knew the mental state or the crime committed by his Rule Maker, Willard Clark, but it seems that the warden of Wethersfield Prison spoke highly of him. On that note, only after researching the murder and final sentencing did it dawn on me that Willard may have been sentenced to the Retreat of the Insane in Hartford in 1855, but he didn't remain there. At the time of the letter in 1866, he had been moved to Wethersfield. A quick check of the 1860 census informed me that he was housed in the New Haven state prison and moved to Wethersfield at some point prior to 1866. Amazingly, the judge who presided over the important case was none other than William Wolcott Ellsworth, my great, great, great, great-grandfather, Oliver's son and Noah's son-in-law.

No Stone Unturned

With this last letter, my collection of all things Thomas H. Seymour was complete and stashed back in its own drawer in the desk. But I still felt there had to be more information out there, especially primary documents from him rather than ones sent to him. Knowing that I should leave well enough alone and move on down the line, I decided to continue this branch of research that had given me a few interesting side stories but not much about the desk per se. Perhaps I can blame it on good historical and literary practice. Or maybe the need to leave no stone unturned was my cross to bear. All true—I was intrigued by this man and I felt that I needed more depth than what my pile of letters gave to me. I trudged on back to the Connecticut Museum of Culture and History.

My initial trip to the museum was spent purely looking for documentation about the desk's origin as well as additional wills to show a clear lineage. Though unsuccessful on both accounts, I did get a magnitude of materials connected to the Seymours in general and Thomas Hart specifically. Now, I was on a different mission and ready to dig harder into that magnitude. I figured that one additional trip would do the trick. It took three. It simply came down to the massive number of personal and professional letters attributed to Thomas Hart Seymour that were housed at the museum. Again, I was nagged with the question: *Who donated all of these letters to the museum?* I set to work!

The materials came in some serious boxes made specifically for holding legal size manila folders. Each box contained somewhere between 15 and 25 manila folders, and each folder was organized chronologically—sometimes holding a month's worth of paperwork and sometimes spanning several months. In Thomas Hart Seymour's case, there were fourteen boxes dedicated to his life. I concentrated on the first ten. Like a well-oiled machine, the staff would move one box to my cart off a whole cart of boxes dedicated to my research. I was only supposed to take three folders from the box (I cheated a few times) and return to my table. Then I moved methodically through each folder—jotting down notes and taking pictures of the letters that I felt I needed to read in detail later. *Easy, right? NOT!*

Each box probably contained 350 letters each—some more and some less. And if my math is correct, I roughly moved through more than 3000 letters over the course of three days. It was long and arduous work, especially when I had to document along the way. I knew that I had to come up with a system that would minimize the work or I would be there for weeks rather than days. *No stone unturned be damned!*

Initial perceptions ruled the day. There were a lot of letters from lots of different people. I really wasn't sure whether Thomas Seymour was a very popular guy or whether he was just the norm. Letters ranged between personal and professional and spanned decades—even after he was out of office following his stint as minister to Russia. Was it normal to save these many letters back in the day, or was he just a pack rat? *My wife, Cathy, can be accused of saving lots of paperwork—much to the disdain of her husband—but this was crazy.* Of course, one needs to consider that Thomas Seymour was a man deeply embedded in the politics of the day, so perhaps the professional letters and such were a matter of course. But why save all the personal letters as well? How did these letters wind up at the museum, and why did I wind up with a handful of similar letters in the desk while the bulk went elsewhere? Most importantly, when I finally came to grips with the work in front of me, how could I simplify the process without losing the scope of my purpose—or my mind as well?

The last question became the first mission, but before that, I needed to define the mission. What did I hope to gain? All I could think about was the old adage KISS, or Keep It Simple, Stupid. The book was about the desk, the descendants who had gotten it after his death, and then the connection to my relatives. Could I wade through these letters quickly, stopping only to document those critical to my research but still get a relative idea of this man? I hoped so. Crazily enough, in the middle of the process, I started to envision writing another book about this guy, which meant going back and reading every handwritten and often severely faded letter for content. I quickly put that thought aside. *Damn, Harrison, focus!*

My working process was simple over the three days: any letter with something like "Dear Sir" or "Gov. Seymour" or even "My Dearest H" (a moniker continuously used by a close friend from New Haven, Connecticut, who sent perhaps hundreds of letters over the course of several decades) I ignored—though I usually gave even these a quick once-over. While I worried that I would probably let something slip through the cracks, I really needed to focus on the topic at hand. Thomas Seymour's family. There were hundreds of familial letters, and most were from or to his sister, Mary, his brother, William, and his two nieces and nephews.

I ignored most of these *friendly* letters that were in the described boxes, set aside for a later chapter the ones from the inner core of the Seymour family, and focused on a few that really piqued my interest. Those just happened to be from some of the unique characters already mentioned.

Love Letters, A Fatal Voyage, and More Crazy Talk

First, there were several more letters from Thomas Seymour's secret admirer, but unlike those in the desk, they were not restricted to the post-Mexican War era. The first (love) letter in poem form is dated February 14, 1843. There are two other letters dated February 14, 1850—one a poem and the other a lengthy letter.

They were all much like the previous letters documented from my desk. Sappy by today's standards but perhaps not back in the day. No matter. As mentioned previously, nothing came of it, since he remained a bachelor until his death.

A far different letter from the somewhat humorous love poems and letters in the collection quickly caught my attention based on the handwriting and date—and not in a good way. The letter is dated January 1855 from Liverpool, England, to Minister Seymour in Saint Petersburg, Moscow, from his ill-fated friend, Augustus Erving. While my personal copy of an Erving letter is quite eerie, considering its time just prior to the downfall of the *SS Pacific*, this letter was far worse. It was mailed a day or two before the ship set sail. It appears that this new letter is probably the last letter ever mailed between them, based on the date and the origin. It, like mine, details the travels of Augustus Erving and his wife throughout Europe and eventually England. Most of the letter is meaningless (for my purposes), but one sentence near the end of the six-page letter is creepy beyond belief. It reads, "We are to sail on Wednesday the 23th [January] in the *Pacific* and, Providence permitting, I shall soon find myself on my native soil again, - after an absence of about 27 months." *Sigh! Providence be damned!*

While I photographed dozens and dozens of letters from relatives of Thomas Seymour (almost forty from his brother William alone) and eventually used them to round out a later chapter, there were still others from people of note. These were either between people I was already aware of (Franklin Pierce, the Watkinson Board), or some I wasn't (such as Samuel Morse, the Morse code guy). The most eye-catching letter in this three-day study-fest was from our insane friend, Willard Clark.

As I already stated, I had a letter dated 1866 from a warden selling Mr. Clark's wares to the then-retired Thomas Seymour, which led me down a side track story of insanity. I never really thought there was any other connection between Willard Clark and Thomas Seymour beyond that. *Wrong again, Harrison.*

On August 4, 1861, Willard Clark (and not the warden) wrote a lengthy letter to Mr. Seymour. I almost ignored it based on its introduction, *Dear Mr. Thomas H. Seymour,* but next to the date was a heading, New Haven County Jail. I quickly put on the brakes, leafed to the end, and there it was. "Truly Yours, Willard Clark." *What the hell! This was well before the Rule Maker letter.* I quickly went back to my notes and reminded myself that Willard had spent some time in the Retreat of the Insane in Hartford following his conviction in 1855, but he was moved to the New Haven jail sometime before 1860 when the census was taken. *Why was he writing to Thomas Seymour?*

After reading the first couple of paragraphs, I knew my answer. The guy was still quite nuts. Again, in the summer of 1861, Thomas Seymour was in the political mix as an adamant opponent of the Civil War, and the first battle of Bull Run had been fought two weeks before. Willard Clark, who had plenty of time on his hands, felt that he should use Thomas Seymour as his sounding board for his thoughts on the war.

It is important to consider that most people diagnosed as clinically insane are not blubbering and foaming at the mouth idiots but rather seem as normal as the next person. That is, until one takes the time to listen to their view of the world, or in Willard Clark's case, his rationale for ridding the world of a "feral cat." In this letter to Thomas Seymour, I got a glimpse of Willard's view of the world at a time when the world—at least on this side of the Atlantic—was turned upside down. I could try to paraphrase the four-page letter, but perhaps one paragraph will do. In a small section of a paragraph on page two, Willard writes,

> *I desire to see a revival of democratic philosophy. I believe the republican party, as at present organized, has received a wound at the battle of stone bridge (Bull Run) from which it will not recover and that an opposition party will triumph. But will that party be democratic and understand and reinaugurate the philosophy of Equality? It is pretty evident that it can-*

THE SEYMOUR DESK | 103

*not be. The world has passed the era of its greatest enlightenment, freedom,
and prosperity, and is now on the march toward superstition and despotism again—not backwards as we sometimes say, but forward. Reason and
faith founded instinct, are ever in antagonism; the one leading to atheism
and anarchy—a state of impossible freedom, the other leading to superstition and despotism...*

Yup. Whackadoodle. The paragraph continues for another two
pages. It, as well as the rest of the letter, is much the same. I get similar
writings from students. Well, maybe not as articulate, but in their
case, they're trying to awe or baffle me with bullshit. In Mr. Clark's
case, I truly believe that he felt his lengthy letter was as plain as the
nose on his face. *Nope, sir. You are bat-shit crazy.*

I am not sure what Thomas Seymour thought of this letter or
why he kept it. He didn't have the luxury of googling the guy, but
the heading of New Haven County Jail should have been a clue. On
the other hand, Thomas Seymour was in Russia during the murder and trial that put Willard Clark in jail, so who knows whether
Thomas Seymour was cognizant of his condition. Of course, it does
shed light on Willard's request in 1866. *Nah, thanks anyway. I'll get my
wooden rulers from someone else.* As to why Willard Clark sought out
Thomas Seymour specifically, he comments in the last paragraph that
Willard's brother, George, served under Thomas during the Mexican
War. *Aaahhhh!*

I'm Honored

Thomas Seymour died on September 3, 1868, at the age of sixty
from typhoid fever. I am not sure how long his ailment lasted before
he succumbed to it, but it usually wasn't long if left untreated, and at
that point, there was no cure. *My point?* I have found no record of a
will for him—or his sister Mary, for that matter. I did find it strange
considering that death was right around the corner, even for the

healthiest of people. All people of wealth and means in the mid-1800s seemed to need a will, especially someone like Thomas Seymour. After all, he was not married, had no children, had material wealth and a home, and was a lawyer. Added to that was the fact that his sister, Mary, outlived him by almost twenty years. I can only guess that all of Thomas's possessions stayed put on Governor Street, which most likely facilitated the desk moving on to my family. At that point, I still wasn't sure how it had, but I was determined to find out.

In the end, a man I knew nothing about prior to the heritance of the Seymour desk came to be a true blessing on my part—and not only because of said desk. Thomas Seymour was indeed a true red-blooded American patriot—a representative in Washington, a military hero, a state governor, a Russian minister, a lawyer, and a political busybody. While his views of slavery in the South and the Civil War may be very different from mine, he clearly was a sought-out mind during those times. Additionally, he was a highly respected man in his home state of Connecticut. Most importantly, based on all the letters that I read, he was a beloved family man.

Obviously, his résumé doesn't quite match that of either Oliver Ellsworth or Noah Webster, but while they were—as previously discussed ad nauseam—amazing men, they didn't leave me a desk. Their descendants did, though, which begs the question: How did a desk built in the 1790s for Thomas Seymour III, passed to son Henry and then grandson Thomas, wind up in my family? A family that I thought I knew at least more than Noah Webster and Oliver Ellsworth.

Nope. The idiot rises again and I thought I was doing so well.

5

Sweet Home Esperanza

I don't know about the reader, but I needed a break from the Seymour train. I had beaten the proverbial dead horse and decided to move back to my own family tree and fill in the branches.

My sister, Gwyn, created a family tree on paper while she was in high school (*always the overachiever*), and it turned out to be an amazing piece of work. Not simply because of the thoroughness that went into it, but because it was created well before the advent of the internet when we didn't have information at the click of a button. Gwyn created it through diligent and painstaking work and with the help of our grandmother Carlotta. The thought of all those circles and squares penciled in by hand baffles me today. *Looks like one of those rolls of parchments from years past.* I knew that there had to be a better way unless I had a football field at my disposal to roll the sucker out. *Thank God for* Ancestry.com.

In my sister's case, she, I believe, felt a need to understand herself through her past (in addition to completing a homework assignment). I was in the same mindset, though there was an additional goal that I hoped to achieve: find a connection between two families—the Seymours and the Ellsworths. I hoped that my own extended Harrison tree would answer that.

Using family tree websites like Ancestry.com or even genetic websites like 23 and Me is nothing new, and millions of people have used them to not only connect with their past but perhaps find relatives that they didn't know existed. While I was interested in the same, my initial mission was different. I needed to create a Harrison family tree to hopefully find some connection to the Seymours and a reason for why the desk would change families. Were we related somehow?

Ancestry.com became my BFF from this point on. Time and time again I went back to fill in huge holes of missing information. The website allows you to create a family tree using rudimentary search techniques. While I'm not a computer guru by any means, I do know my way around a computer program, especially when given enough time. Since most programs like these are built for the lowest common denominator, Ancestry.com was no problem for me. *Very user friendly.* The key is knowing your input information (full name, date of birth, marriage, death, living locations, etc.). With that information alone, you can find anyone.

Another perk of Ancestry.com is that it gives you access to others' family trees that may contain the person or persons you seek. In a perfect world, those users have made their work public so you have free access. If not, then you can ask for permission through the website to use their information. Lucky for me, my initial search for everything Harrison on Ancestry.com started with myself (*hey, I'm vain like everyone else—maybe more so*), and bingo. My cousin had already created a family tree. I quickly asked for permission and I, in due time, was in business. I moved her information into a tree that I had started and had the framework, or trunk, of a new family tree. I now needed to fill in the branches, twigs, and leaves. It took some time. *Think Alexa on steroids.* While I was more interested in the horizontal growth of my tree and, in theory, finding a logical link to the Seymours, I learned a few things through the vertical lineage as well.

First, seeing the direct line south to north through Noah Webster and Oliver Ellsworth gave my initial research some validity. Having spent months researching these two gentlemen and putting their lives down on paper gave me pause when I scrolled up through a relatively few generations to see their names. I'm not sure whether Gwyn got the same sensation looking at her creation of the football grid.

I also began to see commonalities in names that I didn't know about before. For instance, I always assumed that my brother Brad (Bradford) was named after William Bradford, a passenger on the *Mayflower* and the former governor of the Plymouth Bay Colony. Perhaps. But closer to home was Bradford Ellsworth who was my father's great-uncle. *Minor idiot moment.* All good until my own name came into question. The names that caught my attention were two women named Margaret Sinclair Creevey, who was my great-great-great-grandmother (1807-1887) and Carlotta Sinclair Creevey, who was my dad's cousin. She is apparently still alive and living in New Hartford, Connecticut. My middle name is Sinclair. For the longest time, I just assumed it was a connection to my dad's paternal side of the family and a link to a Scottish clan who lived in the northwestern part of the country. While there is validity to the clan connection ("*devote thy work to God*" *is their motto*), I was apparently named for these women. *Yup. Idiot!* Additionally, I discovered that the Sinclairs may have started in Scotland, but my lineage through the clan was based in Ireland. *Damn. If my mom—a staunch English patriot and hater of the Irish—had known that, I might have had Cumberbatch as my middle name rather than Sinclair.*

Anyway. Once I filled in the blanks south to north on my family tree, I began to move east to west, or basically adding families that married into the Ellsworth and Webster lineage. It was a daunting task, but I ultimately found no real connection between the Seymours and the Ellsworths. *Ugh!* Thankfully, I was left with an impressive family tree that would come into play time and time again as I began to piece the bigger puzzle together. But who actually were these people who had merely been names occasionally mentioned by my dad and who were now circles and squares on my tree?

A Family I Barely Knew

As I already mentioned, the melding of the Noah Webster and Oliver Ellsworth families is a simple one. Noah's eldest daughter, Emily Scholton Webster (born in 1790 and died in 1861), married Oliver's son William Wolcott (born in 1791 and died in 1868) in September 1813. The first of several Webster rural Amherst, Massachusetts, weddings. *Please remove the cow dung from your shoes as you enter the chapel.*

William Ellsworth and his twin brother, Henry, were seventeen when their father, Oliver, died in 1808. They both graduated from Yale in 1810 and both continued with their studies to get law degrees. William, in addition to working as a prominent lawyer in Connecticut throughout his life, represented Connecticut in the United States Congress from 1829 to 1834 (this is when he worked with his father-in-law, Noah Webster, to finally get a federal copyright law passed), served as governor of Connecticut from 1838 to 1842 (so he and Thomas Seymour sat in the same office ten years apart), and served as an associate justice to the Connecticut Supreme Court from 1847 to 1861. *A fine résumé, indeed.*

Emily Webster met William while he was attending Yale and she was living in New Haven. As pointed out earlier, Emily was none too happy with her father's plans to move from cosmopolitan New Haven to the middle of nowhere Amherst in 1812, especially since she and William were hot and heavy at that point. According to one account, he took her to Yale's junior ball in 1809 when she was almost eighteen years old and he was almost seventeen. He supposedly asked for her hand in marriage right after the dance. They would have been betrothed for more than three years by 1812—which is when Noah abruptly announced that he was moving the family to the country. I can only imagine William's response when his soon-to-be bride mentioned that she was moving to Amherst. *You're moving where?*

Nevertheless, they were married the following year and produced six children, five of whom survived to adulthood. For my purposes, their fourth child and second son, Oliver II—who was born in 1820 and died in 1878—was my next direct lineage. He was my great-great-great-grandfather. He married his first wife, Caroline Cleveland Smith, in 1854. Together, they had one child, William Webster Ellsworth, in 1855. Caroline died in 1866, and Oliver remarried in 1868 to Mary Wolcott Janvrin. She and their only son, Oliver, both died during childbirth in 1870. Oliver was married again a year and a half later to Mary's older sister, Orah. *Didn't see that one coming.* They had two children. Oliver, in addition to his multiple marriages and unlike his forefathers who were lawyers and politicians, worked as a merchant and a publisher and traveled the country and the world doing his job.

My great-great-grandfather and Oliver's first son, William Webster Ellsworth, was not totally unfamiliar to me. My father mentioned him with admiration often and, as with the desk, felt that I would especially appreciate his life story. And I, as with the desk, didn't pay much attention. *Wash, rinse, repeat.*

William was born in Hartford in 1855 and lived to 1936, nine years after my father was born in 1927. Unlike most of William's ancestors before him and his descendants after, he did not graduate from Yale—nor from any college, for that matter. WW Ellsworth (as he signed most things) went into publishing and became a writer and lecturer later in life. In a historical letter, my grandmother Carlotta writes,

> *W.W.E. was also a Hartford boy, but he spent most of his young years in and near Boston and at various boarding schools. He had been prepared to go to college but found that his mother's parents, Roswell Chamberlain and Lois Cleveland Cady Smith, were in ill health and needed his assistance. At the time Nellie (his future wife) and William met, he was in the insurance business, but soon after their marriage, he joined his mother's cousin, Roswell Smith, who was establishing what became the Century Company.*

In 1878, at the age of twenty-three, he joined the *Scribner's Monthly Magazine*, which would later become *Century Magazine* and eventually *The Forum*. The magazine was quite popular for about fifty years, between roughly 1875 and 1925. The magazine was based in New York City and covered a wide range of topics, including the Civil War and the period of Reconstruction (roughly 1865-1880), progressive issues of the time like women's suffrage, and the rise of socialism in the United States.

From 1891 to 1913, William served as the secretary of the Century Publishing Company and as its president from 1913 to 1915. Following his time with the publishing company, he began a career as a lecturer. According to many sources, including my dad, he introduced a slide projector with colored slides in his presentations, which was quite the innovation at that time. *Again, another noteworthy career.*

I am not sure of the exact details, but William and his eventual wife, Helen Smith (Nellie, as she is referred to), met in Hartford and courted each other until their marriage in 1878. Again, my grandmother bailed me out. She writes in the same letter mentioned above that William and Helen met at a New Year's party in January 1876.

Nellie Smith spent most of her childhood in Hartford with her two older sisters, Fanny and Lottie, and her younger one, Lucy. They lived a relatively normal life, though the absence of their father, Morris, over long stretches in New Orleans, would put a lot of stress on their mother, Julie. Schooling for young ladies at this time was tough to come by, but their broad education was important to the Smith family, and they had the resources. Not only were they well read, but all were accomplished musicians, especially Lottie (she worked for Steinway Piano Company during her lifetime), and all were trained in the appropriate aspects of culture for young women in the late 19th century.

Nellie, at the age of eighteen, would travel to Europe and stay there for another two years. I do not know whether Nellie knew of William Ellsworth prior to her exit to Europe or if she met him for the first time in January 1876 after her return. But it was clear that they were an item in the summer of 1876. They were engaged in December of 1877 and, like many after them, married at a quaint place called Esperanza in the summer of 1878. *Esperanza?*

I Am Not a "House Guy"

At this point, it might be wise to expound a bit about Esperanza. Esperanza, quite simply, is the name of an old and majestic home and vast property in New Hartford, Connecticut. It was the summer home for Morris and Julie Smith and their four girls beginning in the mid-1870s. It eventually become their only home in 1878, and has been passed through generations of Smiths and Ellsworths ever since. William Webster Ellsworth married into the estate and, I guess, the family that went with it. Little did I know at the time that the Esperanza family would consume my research efforts for months on end.

Esperanza, New Hartford, Connecticut, 2016.

Only on one occasion had I visited Esperanza. It resides in the sleepy Connecticut town of New Hartford just twenty miles northwest of Hartford. I went there with my parents when I was in high school and, for some reason, we were in that part of the world. At that point, the gorgeous house and estate was lived in by my great aunt, Eileen Creevey Hall, and her husband, Newman. Eileen was the younger sister of my paternal grandmother, Carlotta Creevey Harrison. I think that my parents assumed that because I loved history even in high school I would be intrigued by the deep history that the manse possessed. While I was quite intrigued by the two unique people who lived there, I am generally not a house kind of guy. I am not a car guy either. To me, they are simply tools to a more convenient lifestyle. Of course, now that I'm older and perhaps wiser, I have a little more respect for the manse in New Hartford and the history of the people who lived there. *Wash. Rinse. Repeat.*

My second trip to Esperanza was pure happenstance. Very early in my book adventure, I convinced Cathy to travel south to the Ellsworth estate in Windsor, Connecticut. As previously mentioned, I did have a fleeting thought that I would donate the desk to the Ellsworth estate—this was when I assumed that the desk came from one or the other of my founding fathers. With that in mind, I reached out to one of the guides of the Ellsworth estate and museum who just so happened to be another relative of mine. *Of course, this makes far more sense than a random docent at Old State House.* We went back and forth via email, I sent her pictures of my desk, and we came up with a mutual date.

Once there, in October of 2021, Cathy and I got a tour of the house and talked shop, as well as the possibility of a monetary donation for a continuing renovation of the estate. There was a big push for new windows. *Hell, I was offering them a 1790 heirloom from the Big Guy Ellsworth who lived there and now they wanted money?* I brought up the issue of the desk, but the guide really didn't seem interested—though she could not speak for the other board members. Years later, I'm obviously glad nothing came of it, since it never belonged to Oliver Ellsworth anyway.

As our guide and I got down to the nitty gritty of who was related to whom in this huge Ellsworth tree—based on a descendants book I purchased there—I mentioned my (and her) direct Ellsworth relative living in New Hartford. Surprisingly, the guide had no idea that these relatives lived in the area and had heard nothing of the Esperanza home. *I tried not to show disdain, but I'm not a good poker player.* I had to spend some time bringing her up to speed. I used the newly purchased book to help my cause and eventually hit the road again headed north. *Or not.*

The conversation about Esperanza at the Ellsworth Estate prompted me to suggest to Cathy that we swing by the old Ellsworth and Smith homestead in the same trip, not really knowing what we might find. In fact, I really wasn't sure about anything Esperanza-related at that point because I wasn't sure who'd bought the house when Newman and Eileen Hall had passed away. I was fairly sure where the house was in New Hartford—*thank you, Google Maps*—but I didn't want to be that creepy guy dropping by a huge estate uninvited, especially if I had no connection to anyone currently living there. I assured Cathy that I was somewhat confident that once we turned off the main drag into the property, I would have a lengthy driveway to do my creepy stalking bit without drawing much attention. *Oops, sorry! Must have made a wrong turn.* But as it happens far too often, I was wrong. Really wrong. *Wash. Rinse. Repeat.*

When we pulled into the drive, there wasn't a lengthy driveway to make our quick retreat but a huge open area. Basically, no driveway at all. In front of us was a huge working farm, a gorgeous house, and multiple outbuildings. My first thought was "Okay, a quick three-point turn and we can pretend this never happened." But then I noticed two individuals not far away working on a fence of a paddock that contained horses. They both stopped what they were doing and looked at us like, "What is this idiot doing?" *Yup, they got me!* I looked at Cathy and she gave me that more-than-three-decades of marriage glare that basically says, "Now what, Einstein?" So, I carefully got out of the truck and trekked toward the woman who was also moving to greet me. She had a "clearly I've got more important things to do here" look on her face. Not knowing what to do other than try the "let's not beat around the bush" approach, I stated, "My name is Andrew Harrison and that's my wife, Cathy, and you and I might be related." The woman's look went from "I've got work to do" to "Honey, please call the cops. We have a live one." But before she did so, I quickly explained that I was the son of Dirck Harrison, Eileen and Newman's nephew, and asked whether she was a relative of Eileen and Newman Hall. Slightly relieved, she said that she was and that they were her grandparents. Crisis averted.

I continued, explaining our visit to the area and that I was looking into the history of the family. I didn't want to bury her with desk facts to scare her off so early in the process. But then she threw me a curve ball when she said, "You probably want to talk to my dad, Jamie, about any history." Now I was dumbfounded. *Why was the name Jamie so familiar?* Then I remembered: Eileen and Newman Hall had married in 1938 (much later than my grandmother and grandfather) and had two children in the early 1940s, Dr. James (Jamie) Creevey Hall and Elizabeth Arnold Hall. My dad—their cousin—was in his teens at that point. Jamie and his wife, Holly, had two children: John in 1978 and Anne in 1981. Anne—my second cousin who was two decades younger than I—was the person I was speaking with. I stifled my urge to say, "Jamie's still alive?" (Keep in mind that my dad had passed almost a year before this visit at the ripe old age of ninety-three.) Thankfully, I quickly realized that there would be no reason why he wouldn't be alive.

At this point, I expected to see an almost eighty-year-old geezer who would kindly introduce himself and send us on our way. When Anne got her dad on the phone (*it's a big property*), no geezer appeared but instead I met a man who was fairly spry and full of pep with his long hair pulled back in a ponytail—and he was hitting on a vape the whole time. And who was I kidding? This made absolute sense. I could picture my father at age eighty walking toward me. My dad, like his cousin, had a personality as big as life and was fairly agile until his legs finally gave out on him.

Once we got our pleasantries out of the way and Jamie gave his condolences for my dad's passing, he insisted on taking us inside to see the house. We didn't refuse.

The quick tour opened my eyes to a manse that could tell you lots of stories. From a front room with a beautiful fireplace and a Steinway piano to a kitchen that was rustic and modern at the same time, I knew that I would have to return at some point for a more planned adventure. The room that really caught my eye was the library and sitting room that had wall-to-wall bookshelves. The sight of the books prompted a thought.

I remembered a book (more like a pamphlet) written specifically about Esperanza during one of my deep searches about the place. You can find almost anything on Amazon.com, and sure enough, it was referenced on the website. Of course and not surprisingly, it stated in the right-hand corner, "Copies Temporarily Unavailable." *Damn. But perhaps now?*

I quickly asked, "Jamie, do you by chance have a copy of that Esperanza book by my great-grandmother?" Jamie quickly responded, "Of course," as he retreated to a closet and pulled out a copy of the tiny yellow book (ninety-six pages) named *The Story of Our Esperanza*. It was written by Lucy Morris Ellsworth Creevey (my great-grandmother) in 1956. Jamie responded, "We have a ton of these things. Keep it." While I was grateful for this resource to fill in some gaps—as well as augment an article from the *Hartford Courant* about the house—the value of this tiny book would extend well beyond a detailed history of the house and its inhabitants.

Esperanza, as it was referred to throughout my life, means Anchor of Life. Julia (Julie) Ann Palmer Smith, my great-great-great-grandmother, gave it that name upon its purchase in 1871. Julie was a prominent author of so-called romance novels, though none had the success of her contemporary, Harriet Beecher Stowe. Her husband, Morris Woodward Smith, ran a successful saddlery business in New Orleans, of all places, though the main saddlery shop was in Hartford (*think Yankee Candle from South Deerfield, Massachusetts, and its numerous outlets nationwide*). From what I can tell, the couple were wealthy enough for Morris to live as a boarder in New Orleans for most of the year and return to the Hartford area for the remainder of the year (for summer and, at times, the holidays). Again, the girls (Fanny, Carlotta/Lottie, Helen/Nellie, and Lucy) were born and raised in Hartford with Julie doing all of the childcare and such. *I could not see my wife, Cathy, agreeing to those circumstances, but it was a different time in the middle to late 1800s.*

Julie and Morris Smith, dates unknown

Though Julie first visited the area of New Hartford in the early 1860s, her search for a house began in earnest in the early 1870s. She and Morris eventually purchased a house in May 1871, only to have it burn down in November while work was being done on it. In turn, they purchased a house across the street from the ruins of the other house. The new house had been built in 1815 and, according to many sources, would have been hardly recognizable as what it is now. Through the remaining quarter of a century, Julie and Morris continued to work on the property—adding rooms to the main house, horse barns, and a boat house (they purchased a piece of land on the nearby West Hill Pond).

Ellsworths and Smiths Unite

According to the Esperanza book given to me by Jamie Hall, William Ellsworth first visited Esperanza in the summer of 1876 during his courtship of Nellie Smith. It reads,

> Will Ellsworth was beginning to come up often from Hartford (summer of 1876). He told me that when he first came up he would walk up from the station—fancy that! He would see his dear Nellie, standing behind the little hemlock trees that had been planted around in a semi-circle in front of the house. She would stand there, waiting for him, her head just a little higher than the little trees. He evidently became quite enraptured with Esperanza.

Very nice indeed. But it gets worse (or better) depending on your viewpoint on all things touchy-feely. In July 1876, William wrote a poem in their guest book. *No, Harrison, no!* It reads,

Esperanza, "hopeful anchor!"
　Fairest spot of Litchfield hills!
　Dear thy mem'ry dwells within me,
　　Dear thy name like music thrills
　All my heart, and brings remembrance
　Of thy days in pleasure passed,
　Of thy meadows and thy woodlands,
　In the mould of beauty cast.

There is another stanza, but it is much the same and I'd rather not vomit on the keyboard. *Anyways. It is amazing what men will do to impress a mate.*

After Nellie Smith and William Ellsworth married in the summer of 1878, they began a life in New York City—though they lived their parents' lifestyle by spending summers in Esperanza. The year 1878 was also significant because Julie and Morris Smith officially sold their house in Hartford and moved to Esperanza permanently; however, the New Orleans commute would continue for Morris Smith for another twenty years.

William and Nellie had four children between 1879 and 1892—Lucy, Bradford, Helen, and Elisabeth. The eldest, Lucy, was the next leg of the Ellsworth/Smith and Andrew Harrison lineage. Lucy, born in 1879, eventually married Dr. George Creevey in 1901. He and Lucy would also spend their child-bearing years in New York City where George became a prominent physician as an anesthesiologist. But like the previous two generations, they spent significant time in Esperanza and eventually retired there as well. Their story is a little bit more complicated.

Don't Stand, Don't Stand...

As many wealthy people did and still do, Nellie and William hired a governess to help with the four rambunctious children as they grew. In the summer of 1890, they sent the most recent governess packing and Nellie took on a more active role in raising the youngsters. But after Bradford tried to blow off his hand with gunpowder in a glass bottle, they decided to hire a tutor to corral the kids and educate them as well. His name was Mr. George Creevey, as he was referred to by the four Ellsworth kids.

Esperanza, c. 1929. Front Row, Left to Right-Barbara Harrison Mulhern (4), Nellie Smith Ellsworth (74), William Webster Ellsworth (74), Dirck Dey Harrison (2). Back Row, Left to Right- Carlotta Creevey Harrison (27), Dr. Francis French Harrison (31), Lucy Morris Ellsworth Creevey (50), Dr. George Mason Creevey (57).

George Creevey was only eighteen years old, but the kids adored him as something like a big brother figure. Pictures from the yellow Esperanza book confirmed their glorious time together during their summers at the estate. *Think Maria and the von Trapp crew here.* But the reference to a "Mr. Creevey" immediately sent my radar blaring. My Grandmother Carlotta's maiden name was Creevey, and even back in the day, it was not very common. Sure enough, I dug further into the book. Eighteen-year-old George Creevey must have been slightly smitten with twelve-year-old Lucy Ellsworth, as he came calling after he had graduated college and medical school. They married in 1901, ten years after their first summer encounter. She was twenty-one, and he was twenty-eight. Of course, the teacher in me cringed a little bit hearing this, but these were different times.

When I discovered this little gem, I, of course, had to share it with the family, including my Aunt Barbara. Her comment via email simply said, "I was wondering when you were going to mention that one." *Too funny!*

Who Wants It?

After Lucy and George Creevey married in 1901, they produced three children—Carlotta (my grandmother), Kennedy, and Eileen (whom I mentioned earlier). Lucy and George were tasked to care for Esperanza upon the death of Nellie Smith Ellsworth in 1945 (William Webster Ellsworth died in 1936). Dr. George Creevey ended up dying that same year, while Lucy Ellsworth Creevey would live until 1960. Eileen Creevey Hall (my great-aunt) and her husband, Newman, were given the reins of the Esperanza estate in the mid-1950s. They had lived in New Haven previously. By 2003, the care for the manse and themselves became too much, and they moved into an assisted living facility nearby. Their son, Jamie, and his wife, Holly, officially took over the estate. Eileen and Newman passed in 2006 and 2007, respectively.

Jamie and Holly moved from Vermont in 1982 so he could pursue a doctorate degree in geology. Holly, an art teacher in Vermont, continued teaching art in Connecticut until 2012, when she retired. She continues to paint. During our impromptu visit, Cathy and I saw her studio in one of the outbuildings on the property. *Gorgeous work.*

Following Jamie and Holly's move from Vermont, they built a small home across the street from Esperanza in 1987 and stayed there until 2003. The small house was eventually sold soon after. Anne Hall, Jamie's daughter, and her husband moved on to the estate in 2008.

She is now the trustee of the property and technically in charge of its upkeep as well as caring for her aging parents. *Gee, thanks, Dad!*

The sequence of events will probably repeat itself when Jamie and Holly need to move due to age and Anne will take over the main house. In terms of the property's future, Jamie alluded to the fact that it will pass to his two granddaughters from his other kid, John, who lives in Virginia. Beyond that, he doesn't know its future. Again, without any specific details, the estate is a money pit in terms of maintenance and heating, according to Jamie. *Maybe I'll start my own campaign fund.*

My trip down memory lane was a blessing for myself, though perhaps not for the reader. *What about the desk?* For a guy who has spent a lifetime intrigued by and sometimes teaching our nation's history and its significant players, I, up until this book, lacked the same knowledge of my own family. *Shameful!* What is the expression about a cobbler and his kid's shoes? But the reader is right. I needed to move back to the questions at hand—how did the desk wind up in my hands?

Ironically, Esperanza and its original inhabitants were the linchpin that connected the two families: the Ellsworths and Seymours. But one name kept rising to the top when it came to that connection: Helen Seymour, William Seymour's only daughter and Thomas and Mary Seymour's only niece. Her name was mentioned on numerous occasions by my father in his chicken-scratch notes. According to him, she lived in New Orleans all her life, never married, had some physical and mental health problems, had a connection to the desk, AND had a drug addiction. *Whaaat?*

6

Helen Seymour 1.0

Leaving Esperanza and my family behind—at least for the time being—I knew I needed to pick up the Seymour ball again. Ultimately, this was where the true story lay.

Just to review: The desk sat in East Hartford in the home of Thomas and Mary Seymour (brother and sister) from the early 1850s to 1868 when Thomas passed away. Since Mary never left the house until her passing in 1887, in theory, the desk (as well as everything else in the house) was hers by default for almost twenty years. *Wait! Isn't the chapter title clearly Helen Seymour and not Mary Seymour?*

Valid point. And I truly believed that Helen Seymour was the key to how the desk transferred from her family to mine. But somehow there had to be a connection between Mary Seymour and Helen Seymour—other than simple genetics—or the desk would have wound up elsewhere. *I hoped.*

Proud Mary

While I was logically safe in saying that the desk never left the Hartford area until Mary's death, I was completely wrong about Mary's whereabouts during her entire lifetime. Initially, my narrow-mindedness got the best of me. I knew that Mary and Thomas had lived together most of their lives, minus his time in Russia, and I assumed that if anyone did any traveling, it was him. I equally assumed that Mary, a spinster her whole life, must have spent her whole life as a homemaker in Hartford and East Hartford while her worldly brother was the social butterfly. Wrong. Based on multiple resources, Mary moved to New Orleans in the early 1850s to live with her brother William and his family while her brother Thomas worked in Russia. And who could blame her?

I can only assume that Mary, alone in East Hartford and with no one to talk to, decided to pull up stakes, move to New Orleans for several years, and stay with her younger brother, her sister-in-law, Mary, and their two young kids, Helen and Harry. Perhaps, this was the plan all along once Thomas got the appointment. She wrote numerous letters to her brother in Russia that were postmarked New Orleans.

But this was not her longest stay in New Orleans. Not by a long shot. My first inkling of a second significant stay came with a lengthy description of the movement of a Seymour antique clock—of all things—in the Seymour genealogy book mentioned earlier. *Book worthy, but not by this guy.* It seems that Mary Seymour pulled up stakes again in 1870, two years after her brother's death. She moved the furniture and such into the attic, including the antique clock and, presumably, my desk, rented out the place, and went to live with her brother William until 1885. *Homebody, indeed!*

As I began to look at Mary in a different light, I wondered what effect she may have had on her niece, Helen. If my math is correct, Mary lived with Helen in New Orleans through a big chunk of Helen's early years (one to four years old) and then again through her teenage to young adult years (roughly fifteen to thirty-two years old). She must have had some influence on her only niece, Helen.

Finally, Helen

Who was Helen Seymour? Nobody really. So much so that it is almost impossible to find information about her. Even worse, I have no pictures of her. In today's world of selfies and group shots, it seems unimaginable that cameras were just beginning to be a thing by the second half of the 19th century.

But the reality is that we all have a story to tell, and I was determined to at least try to tell hers. Additionally, it was at this point that I realized that my journey to uncover the movement of my desk was less about the desk itself and more about the people who owned it. While there is a lot of written history about those who owned the desk before Helen Seymour inherited it and obviously those after, I was again at a loss finding anything about her. *Ugh.* This one endeavor would take a lot of willpower and test my patience for months on end. *Helen Seymour, here I come!*

Helena (Helen) Ellery Seymour was born in 1853, though I have no official date of her birth. Strangely, all the census records say that she was born in Hartford, which initially made no sense—according to my limited information at the time, she spent her whole life in New Orleans. *Wrong again, Harrison.* Her brother, William, who went by Harry, was born a year later in Hartford as well. *Hmmmmm. Move on, Harrison.* According to the 1860-1880 censuses, the Seymours lived on 346 Carondelet Street, which was a few blocks away from their father's business in downtown New Orleans. The 1880 census proved significant. Not only were William Ellery Seymour and his wife, Mary Brooks Seymour, living there, but their two children, Helen (twenty-seven) and Harry (twenty-six), and William's older sister, Mary, were as well. Again, I often pondered the connection between Helen and Aunt Mary. Perhaps during this twenty-year period while both were in New Orleans, they grew close to each other. With that, I really had nothing more. *Back to home away from home.*

This lack of information triggered the need to travel back to the Connecticut Museum of Culture and History. Earlier, I mentioned that there were hundreds of letters to Thomas Hart Seymour in their records, mostly from friends and family. *Thank God.* These family letters would be my focus to hopefully add substance to the life of Helen Seymour.

Once I came to grips with the magnitude of information pertaining to Thomas Hart Seymour at the museum, I realized that the one day I had set aside to dig through letters would not be enough. It took me three. I simply confirmed a letter was from one of the direct Seymours and took photographs. Later, I culled through the hundreds of photos and organized them by name—while at the same time deleting any letter that I could not read. For example, Mary Seymour was notorious for writing paragraphs crosswise on previous written paragraphs, and her handwriting became almost illegible as she aged. I simply did not have the patience nor the energy to negotiate through some of her letters. But these letters, though for the most part unreadable, confirmed one thing. Mary was writing most of them from New Orleans during Thomas's time in Europe, watching and perhaps caring for Helen Seymour as she grew in her younger years.

Thomas Seymour's brother William's letters occupied the bulk of my collection, which made sense. He lived in New Orleans, and Thomas lived in Hartford—minus those five years in Russia. A couple things stuck out. William traveled north a lot, and usually with his family (Mary, Helen, and Harry). Perfectly logical. His childhood home and familial connections were in the Hartford area. I would find out later that he had business connections there as well.

In addition to the normal parental comments about their kids to a close brother who rarely saw them, there was a theme that continued throughout all the letters—sickness. Again, I am not sure whether it is consistent with the times, but Helen, and Harry for that matter, always seem to be battling something. As I stated earlier, my dad mentioned something about Helen's illnesses and their possible link to drug usage. Was there always something going on health-wise with Helen?

For example, in July 1860, William speaks of measles running through the house. A big deal back in the day, but nothing seems to come of it. But in December 1862, Helen was apparently quite sick.

Again, no details, but her illness is mentioned in separate letters, four days apart. She would have been nine-and-a-half at the time.

In a letter written from Canada in July 1867, William mentions that Helen had taken ill again. No details, but it was significant enough to be mentioned. Beyond that, William acknowledges that Helen and her brother seemed quite happy and did quite well at school. And when the kids were not in school, they traveled north with him.

In an October 1867 letter, William wrote from New York to his brother in East Hartford. I can only assume that he had been in the northeast since July, based on the previously mentioned letter. He finishes, "With much love to sister and the children, I am truly your affectionate." Young Helen and Henry were staying with their aunt and uncle in East Hartford while their father and perhaps their mother, Mary, were in New York City. No big deal here. I've left my kids with my brother Matt on multiple occasions. *Your point, Harrison?* Much like a lawyer building a case, I needed to establish a close relationship between Helen Seymour and her aunt and uncle. Unlike Mary, who stayed in New Orleans for years in some cases, I had no record of Thomas doing the same. Thus, Helen traveling to and staying in East Hartford was important to my story.

The most important group of additional letters in Thomas's collection were those from young Helen herself. These new letters represent a very small window of time—roughly from the age she could write (perhaps the late 1850s) to 1868 when Thomas passed away. There are only a mere handful of letters, and while some are not worth noting because of her young age, it does give me an initial glimpse of my mystery woman, Helen.

In general, I chose five letters to document that were written by Helen (she signs them all Helena). They were written between 1863 and 1867, or when she was ten to fourteen years old. All were written from New Orleans, except for one from Canada as her family made their way to the northeast. They apparently liked to take the scenic route—north upstream on the Mississippi River, east through the Great Lakes to the Niagara Falls area and into Canada, and south to Saratoga, New York (William's home office), Hartford, and New York City. Many of the letters were either a response to one of Thomas's letters to her or thank you letters in response to gifts that he most likely sent. Younger brother Harry sent similar letters.

In a letter dated only January 1863 (Helen was almost ten), she discusses new chickens that she and Harry just received, a lost family dog, and a photograph of a family friend, who interestingly lived in the Hartford area.

The next letter from Helen to Uncle Thomas is dated July 14, 1866, from St. Catharines, Canada. Again, this was their normal summer trek north. She mentions the lack of "girls" to play with, spending time writing, and a big fight in the dining area with plates and glasses being thrown. *Nice!* She ends with "Give my best love to Auntie."

In December 1867 (no date), she again wrote to Uncle "Henry." She comments about the abnormally warm weather for December in New Orleans and, of course, mentions that she will write to "Auntie" on New Year's Day, informing her of all the presents that she received for the holidays. I was able to cross reference a letter that Harry had written a few weeks later to get the relative date and month.

More than six months later, Helen sent another letter to Thomas, dated February 3, 1867, from New Orleans. She would have been almost fourteen years old. My first impression was the depth and breadth of the letter. She comes off as a very intelligent and maturing young lady. It is very different from the previous two letters I mentioned. She discusses going to the opera and wishing it was in English. *Amen, sister.* She discusses going to Sunday school that morning and then again for the evening service. Ugh.

The last letter from Helen to Uncle Thomas in his collection is dated March 3, 1867. She starts by thanking Uncle Thomas for a watch case that he sent her. In this letter, she politely writes about the lack of correspondence from her uncle and hopes for something soon. Again, she comments about "Auntie" (and asks Thomas to pass it along) and also writes about the warm weather, going to a glass blower, and Harry getting a new pet rabbit. She finishes with a comment about Valentine's Day. She writes, "I received a Valentine and I can guess/I know who it came from, though the Hartford could not be seen, for it was the only pretty one that I got." *Valentine? Aunt Mary? Somebody else?*

In terms of a general reflection on her letters to her uncle, there is a warm connection between the two, even though their interaction may have been limited to summer visits. More importantly, though, is the connection between Mary and Helen. Obviously, they spent time together in New Orleans during Helen's most formative ages—one to four. Helen also visited her in East Hartford, as mentioned earlier. Additionally, Helen always referenced Mary in her letters to Uncle Thomas. Unfortunately, though I do not have any letters between Helen and Mary, I would assume there were many. I truly believed that the two had grown close.

Helen's Strange Addiction

Beyond the Mary/Helen bond, there was the question of Helen's potential addiction. My dad was seemingly fixated on this issue, and I suppose that it might have been justified based on his overall perception of Helen Seymour. In his mind—as I learned through his notes—he perceived Helen as both a drug addict and an indigent living on the margins of society in New Orleans. I had no reason to initially disbelieve him since his information came from his mother, Carlotta Creevey Harrison, and she was a far more reliable conduit about the history of the desk and its owners. In his eyes, it seemed implausible for a woman like Helen to have a personal connection to the desk, especially if she never left New Orleans, and thus he decided that it wasn't worth in-depth research on the woman. All valid assumptions and questions, but I became more curious about the actual addiction part rather than the specific person addicted. At least for now. *Into another rabbit hole I went.*

Having spent a lifetime teaching in a high school classroom where most of my courses had some connection to drugs and alcohol, I consider myself—for better or worse—more knowledgeable than most about the two topics. But this is the 21st century in America and not the 19th century. Were substance abuse issues that much different then? No, as I would learn. In fact, the similarities between the rampant opioid use in the second half of the 19th century and the current issues of pain meds and high-test heroin use are eerie. *Another book, Harrison? SHHHHH!* I set to work.

I started by researching alcohol use in that period, knowing that it was probably a dead end. These were different times. I was not wrong. While there were probably many people who were alcoholics in the late 1800s, most of those were men. In fact, it was considered highly anti-social or even immoral for women to drink in public. *In public* is the key phrase here. Many women, excluding those of ill repute, drank out of sight of the general public. However, saloons were the norm back in the day and only men frequented them; thus alcoholism, through the conventional route, was exclusively for men.

There was one avenue that both men and women could travel, though—patent medicines. The name gives the impression that everything was on the up and up, but the words, "patent medicine" do not clearly convey what it actually meant. For some perspective, everyone my age remembers the rash of spaghetti westerns (called so because many of them were filmed in Italy) about some frontier town where some would-be car salesman sold the newest elixir that solved every ache and pain. The reality is that these individuals did exist, and their wares would have given a woman an avenue to getting alcohol. And these concoctions weren't just available via the traveling salesman—they were also sold in drugstores, which were open to all. Before you begin to judge these people for believing that these cure-alls were something more than a stiff drink, look at a NyQuil bottle that might be in your medicine cabinet right now.

While alcohol was a possible option, it didn't seem to fit Helen's family dynamics. Additionally, my father never mentioned an alcohol addiction but hinted at something more like opium. *Really, Harrison? Why didn't you start with that?*

Another valid question. But at that point, I really wasn't sold on the whole "Helen panhandling on the street to get her next fix" scenario, and I needed to eliminate all other possibilities.

Similarly, I questioned cocaine addiction as well, but for a different reason. Timing. Coca in leaf form has always been an option, but cocaine as a medicinal product didn't hit the market until 1884, as either cocaine-laced cigarettes, a solution used for injection, or a powder to be sniffed. At that point, it became as popular with doctors and pharmacists as opium-derived medications were. Given that questions about the addictive nature of opium and morphine were coming to light at the turn of the century, cocaine seemed heaven-sent. The upside to the use of cocaine-based products over opioid-based products was that cocaine didn't carry the same physical withdrawal symptoms as opium, morphine, or even alcohol. The downside was mental withdrawal, which could even be worse. The intense highs of cocaine carried equally intense downs and depression that drove many to continued use, simply to avoid such withdrawals.

Helen, born in 1853, would have been in her forties by the time cocaine was available to doctors as an alternative to opium and morphine. Unfortunately, Dirck only knew she had an addiction at some point, but he had no idea when that might have occurred in her life. So, the logical choice was opium or morphine.

Opium in powder form and morphine in liquid form were not a phenomenon that came out of the blue in the middle and late 1800s. There are records of usage during the middle and late 1700s, and furthermore, there was reported usage by both armies during the Revolutionary War. Interestingly, it was never prescribed to cure any ailment at this point. The only apparent use was to dull the pain, whatever that may be. No reports of widespread addiction occurred. Usage as a painkiller continued through the early 1800s and was usually referred to as laudanum (a liquid concoction of opium and alcohol).

However, matters began to change for the worse during the first half of the 19th century when doctors started to prescribe opium for more than pain relief. In the 1840s, 24,000 pounds of opium were imported into the United States. By 1872, that had risen to 416,864, and by 1897, it was 1,072,914 pounds. *Numbers don't lie.*

The only thing that eventually replaced opium as a cure-all was morphine—though they do have the same origins. Because morphine was a pure and consistent form in terms of potency, it became the go-to choice, especially for pain. It still is today. This was great news for those in severe pain, but not so great for those with common ailments who were now in greater danger of developing an addiction. Even with its increased benefits as a painkiller, morphine did not gain wide use until the 1860s and 1870s with the advent of hypodermic needles. To be sure, the use of opium and morphine increased between 1830 and 1860 and probably due to a series of epidemics during this time frame. Cholera, dysentery, and cholera again.

Keep in mind, there was no general cure or even known cause for such ailments at the time, but by golly, opium and/or morphine sure did ease the symptoms—at least before you died. The increase in opiates was compounded by another disease of sorts, in this case, war. The Civil War began in earnest in the summer of 1861 and so did the age of opium in pill form as a universal painkiller.

Following the war, the introduction of the hypodermic needle on a universal scale not only helped increase the number of addicts but also changed the shape of opioid addiction for the next half century. Before the use of the needle, medication came in one of two forms: pills or powder with opium and liquid with morphine. In all scenarios, it was ingested. In case you're wondering, I have purposely neglected the smoking aspect since it most likely did not apply to Helen Seymour.

Needless to say, the hypodermic needle became a quite popular option after its introduction. For all the wrong reasons. Popularity of the instrument grew through the 1870s, and by the 1880s, all physicians were using it. In most cases, it was for morphine exclusively. Injected morphine avoided some gastric side effects of ingested opiates, and more importantly, it was much stronger in its effect and much quicker. Doctors now had a more viable option for a patient in desperate need. There were three major problems with this, and not all were their fault.

One, the ability to deal with the pain was only temporary and only more morphine would maintain a level of comfort. It did not cure the real problem that was causing the pain.

Two, the real problem in my mind—and I'll give them a pass due to ignorance—was that opium and morphine were not simply used for chronic pain, but for almost everything that plagued patients. These may have included but were not limited to simple issues of chronic headaches, reoccurring hangovers (*great—adding one addiction to another*), insomnia, asthma, a multitude of infectious diseases of the day (malaria, chronic diarrhea, dysentery, and syphilis), masturbation (*whaaat?*), nymphomania, photophobia, and the ever-popular "female complaints," generally in the form of dysmenorrhea or menstrual cramps. Again, I'll give physicians a pass at this point in medical history simply because there weren't a lot of medicinal cures for anything. *Hey, try a shot of morphine and let me know how you feel.* Of course, I'm sure a lot of patients came back quite pleased and asked for more—regardless of whether or not it really had any effect on their ailing toe.

Third is the connection between the increased usage of opium-based products and long-term addiction. Most physicians were ignorant (or chose to be) of the long-term effects of continuous use of opiates, especially injected morphine, in the late 1800s. On the other hand, it is important to point out that not all who were prescribed morphine became addicted to it, much like not all who drink will always become addicted.

Again, without totally dismissing Dirck's adamancy—or my grandmother's for that matter—if Helen was addicted to opium, does it really matter? Maybe not. Maybe so. Addiction is a strange animal. Some people carry about their personal addictions without affecting all aspects of their lives, while others go off the deep end. In Helen's case, I have no clue. I only know that she lived until eighty-seven.

In conclusion, she may have used morphine and may have been addicted to it, but for what? What health condition did she have that would lead a doctor or pharmacist to prescribe such a medication? I have no medical records on this but only continual comments about her poor health from multiple sources. Could a doctor have prescribed opioids to deal with it? Absolutely. Could she have developed an addiction? Absolutely. Do I have other things to write about? Absolutely. *Moving on. Or was I?*

Back to the Future

Well before researching drug addiction in the second half of the 19th century but knee deep into the "Who the hell is Helen Seymour?" abyss, I knew that a trip to New Orleans might be in order. *The whole no stone unturned thing.* I had little-to-no actual concrete information about Helen Seymour and her movements throughout her lifetime—and especially her time in New Orleans—and maybe her home town could help. Additionally, I was intrigued my great-great-great-grandfather, Morris Smith, who worked his entire professional career in New Orleans, and he, I believed, was the connection between my family and Helen's. Of course, there was the fact that I had never visited New Orleans. *All work and no play...*

Unfortunately, like a lot of things in my life, the trip always found its way to the back burner for a good year. *Redoing the basement of our house is also back there.* Finally, I said enough is enough and set a date for early February 2025. I booked my flight, rental car, and lodging reservations for three days in the Crescent City. Enough time to do my research, enjoy a little down time away from the New England winter, and return home. Only when I tried to add on an extra day or two did the *idiot* moniker rear its ugly head once more. I could not understand why I couldn't find a reasonably priced motel room for the weekend. Mardi Gras wasn't for another month. And then it dawned on me. *Where was the Super Bowl this year?* Yup, New Orleans. *Sigh. Well, embrace the chaos, Harrison.*

I landed in New Orleans on Wednesday around noon, got my rental, and headed downtown—but not before I changed out of my blue jeans and into shorts. The upper 70s in New Orleans were a true blessing.

Travel downtown, on the other hand, was anything but. It was a freaking war zone. The fallout from a terrorist attack involving a nut job in a speeding vehicle weeks before and the build-up to the Super Bowl had necessitated all types of cops and armed soldiers stationed everywhere, as well as roadblocks all over the place. Helicopters hovering over constantly were just the icing on the cake. *What was I thinking?* Only after parking the rental, taking a short walk to the New Orleans Williams Research Center to investigate some documents relating to Helen Seymour, and finally getting situated did I finally find some sense of normalcy. But not before another gem fell from the sky.

As my dumb luck would have it, right down the road from the research center was the New Orleans Pharmacy Museum. *Hmmm.* I walked in and immediately knew that I had hit a gold mine. It was the exact location of New Orleans' first apothecary and first pharmacist, Louis J. Dulfilho, Jr. The pharmacy opened in the 1820s and remained a fixture for the downtown community until the 1870s. Could this pharmacy have served as an initial source of Helen's addiction during her original time in New Orleans? *Maybe.* Her home during this time (1853-1885) was less than a mile away, and her father's place of business was even less than that. My dumb luck continued when the museum attendant said that the only guided tours with a historian during the week were starting the next day at 10 a.m. *Hot dog!*

I got to the pharmacy museum a little before 10 a.m. the next day and hoped for a small tour group so I could really pick our guide's brain. My reality couldn't have been further from that scenario. There was a group of high school students joining me and a few other adults. *Ugh.* Quite hypocritical, I know, but I was on a mission here. All good in the end. The students were excellent, and my specific questions would just have to wait for another day via email.

Like I had done so many times before as I stumbled through this research process, I tried to view apothecaries or pharmacies in the 19th century with 21st-century eyes and failed miserably. When I delved into the realm of opioids in the second half of the 19th century, I assumed that someone like Helen Seymour, a young lady of relative means while she lived under her father's roof, would see a doctor for her ailments and her "prescriptions" as well. After listening to our tour guide, who was extremely well versed, I learned that Helen Seymour could have easily walked to the pharmacy that we were now standing in, explained her problems, and received the "appropriate" medication and/or advice.

Over the course of an hour, our guide led us through the various medical applications that could be found in a 19th-century pharmacy, focusing, of course, on the very absurd. Extremely interesting, but again, I was on a specific mission. Thankfully, about halfway through the tour, our guide centered the discussion on the use of opioids for almost everything. I was quickly shocked to learn—and I don't get shocked easily—that there were such things as opioid-soaked tampons and that the use of *a* hypodermic needle meant *one* hypodermic needle used over and over again. As our guide began to describe the types of patients and their symptoms, I realized that there was no reason why Helen Seymour wouldn't have been one of them. The big question mark, other than whether she saw a doctor exclusively for her treatment, was timing. This pharmacy closed sometime in the early 1870s. Another pharmacy opened, closer to her home, but not until the early 1880s. Basically a ten-year gap when Helen would have been in her twenties. *Ugh.* Just another question mark I couldn't answer.

As with much of my research, the visit to the pharmacy museum was fascinating, and it augmented what I already knew about addiction in the late 1800s. Assuming that my dad's comments were legit, I had to catalog the pharmacy angle as a definite maybe. *Moving on. Really.*

Home Again, Home Again...

Leaving the addiction as a possibility, I returned to the question of the close relationship between Helen Seymour and Mary Seymour. As detailed earlier, Mary Seymour had moved to New Orleans in 1870 to live with her younger brother, William, following the death of her other brother, Thomas. She would live there for another fifteen years, alongside her favorite niece, Helen, who was seventeen at the time. Mary returned to East Hartford in 1885 following the death of her brother, William, Sr., in 1883 at the age of seventy-three. As of 1885, Helen—then twenty-seven—was unmarried, still living at the house, and had no occupation listed for her.

At this point, a fleeting thought came to mind. When Aunt Mary moved out of the New Orleans house in 1885 and returned to East Hartford, did Helen go with her? By 1885, Aunt Mary would have been eighty years old and perhaps in need of care; Helen might have gone with her to serve as her caregiver. This would shed new light on the transition of the East Hartford Seymour wares three years later, when Mary Seymour had died in 1887. The 1890 census would have been really helpful, but I learned during my efforts that much of the written material of the 1890 census was lost in a fire on January 10, 1921, when the information was housed in a Department of Commerce building. This missing census would come back to haunt me time and time again. *Ugh.*

Mary Seymour died on April 6, 1887. Whether Helen Seymour was with her at the time, I do not know—though my gut tells me that she was. *Hey, it's my story!*

If we take a leap of faith and assume that Helen could have traveled north as early as 1885 when Aunt Mary returned home to East Hartford, where did she go after her death two years later? Did Helen return to New Orleans around that time? I'm not really sure, but two factors may help answer this. One, Mary Brooks Seymour, Helen's mother, also died in October, 1887. Two, like the East Hartford house, the New Orleans home sold in 1887. So, if Helen had moved north to be with Aunt Helen, then there wasn't much to move back to after her mother died and her house sold soon after.

The Desk

As documented in Chapter 1, selling one's house is one thing, but clearing out the same house is a whole other matter. My gut feeling tells me that Helen Seymour was around for both events sometime in 1887 or 1888. It is only a theory, but it was partially confirmed when I hit pay dirt learning about the process of moving the Seymour wares from the house in East Hartford.

My first epiphany moment came from the Seymour genealogy book that I previously referenced. While the detailed information in the Seymour book did not specifically discuss my desk, it did make it clear that "heirs" inherited Mary's possessions. On page 467, and in reference to the East Hartford house, the genealogy book reads, "The heirs who had the disposition of the property first removed from the house everything that was considered as of personal interest or as having special value." Again, while it doesn't mention my desk, I would put the Seymour desk into the "special value" category. Additionally, the author uses the term "heirs." I suppose taken broadly that could be anyone, but in terms of family, Mary did not have a lot of heirs. Helen would be on a short list.

The most telling artifact when documenting the desk's movements (which ultimately killed two birds with one stone) was buried in the bowels of the desk itself. *Two birds with one stone? Somewhat out of date expression today. How about bullying two people with one text?* It's a three-page memo written on October 9, 1930. *1930?* The note serves as proof of the desk's provenance, already discussed earlier, and its travels soon after. It reads:

This desk was the property of the Honorable Thomas Seymour

- *Born 1735*
- *Yale 1755*
- *Member of Assembly, king's attorney for the colony*
- *U.S. Attorney after the Revolution*
- *Member of the Council of Safety*
- *Judge of Common Pleas*
- *First Mayor of Hartford*
- *Married Mary Ledyard*

His son, Major Henry Seymour

- *Married Susan Ellery*

His son, Thomas Henry Seymour

- *Born 1807*
- *Colonel in Mexican War-1846*
- *Governor of Connecticut-1850-52*
- *Presidential elector-1852*
- *US Minister to Russia- 1853-1859*

This desk was taken by me from the Seymour House in Hartford when the Seymour estate was settled. I can swear to its authenticity.
Carlotta Norton Smith October 9th 1930

I was already quite familiar with everything up until the last sentence and the signature. In fact, it summarizes much of my work. But Carlotta Norton Smith? Lottie, as she was normally called, was my great-great-great-aunt—or Nellie Ellsworth's sister. While she and her sister, Fanny, would eventually settle in Esperanza permanently, Lottie was in New York City, working for the Steinway Piano Company, when the house was cleared out. At that point, Esperanza was still a summer destination of the Smith family, including Lottie. Why was she involved in the move to East Hartford if she lived in New York City? I'm not sure. But good friends have always helped each other move from one place to another. Were these two, Helen and Lottie, close friends? Apparently so. Was I beginning to get that tingly feeling that this was the Seymour/Ellsworth connection that I had been searching for? Absolutely.

If I'm reading this right, the desk was "taken" by my great-great-great-aunt Carlotta (Lottie) from Thomas and Mary's house sometime after 1887. If she took the desk from the Seymour house in East Hartford, where did she take it? New York City? Perhaps. But Esperanza would seem like the more logical place. Was Helen there at the time to help? As I stated before, I think so. Did everything else in the inheritance get moved to Esperanza (including the desk) at that time? Again, not unfathomable, but unfortunately, I have nothing to prove it. I have, based purely on logic, concluded that most of the inherited Seymour items—including the desk—spent some time at Esperanza after 1888. For how long? I don't know. But I was determined to find out.

Of course, Lottie's note does one other thing. *The stone thing, or text thing, if you will.* Mere acquaintances don't help move one's valued stuff without some strong basis for attachment. *Big rabbit hole.*

7

Linkage

I knew I needed to find a reason why the Seymour desk might have ended up at Esperanza in 1888. There had to be a connection between Helen Seymour and the Smiths of Esperanza, and I was bound and determined to find it. As I researched and documented earlier, there was no family connection between the Seymours and Smiths directly by marriage. I even checked the Seymour family tree, as I did with my own, to find some overlap. There was none. Period.

But sometimes the lack of a blood connection has an inner meaning. Consider this. While blood relatives tend to be tight, friendships outside of your family tend to be tighter. You pick your friends, but you really have no choice in terms of family. I knew my biggest hurdle yet was to find how these two families connected—and to enough of an extent to justify giving a significant family heirloom to a non-family member.

There had been nibbles up until that point. There was obviously the desk itself, given that Lottie Smith moved the desk from East Hartford to Esperanza, presumably. But, again, this only showed a connection and not how and why the connection was formed.

The first clue to this mystery came out of the blue, dropped from heaven, or any other metaphor you can think of from a seemingly unlikely source. It was Lucy Ellsworth Creevey's yellow Esperanza book that changed the whole focus of my research.

As I said, I got a copy of the book *The Story of Our Esperanza,* by Lucy Ellsworth Creevey (my great-grandmother), in the fall of 2021 from my dad's cousin, Jamie. But I never really picked it up until a year later. Why? At that point, I was in a different place in my research. I truly believed that the desk was owned by either Noah Webster or Oliver Ellsworth. But at the beginning of 2023, I began looking at the present-day Ellsworths and their connection to Esperanza, and this is when I began reading the Esperanza book more seriously.

Again, Esperanza was purchased and renovated by Morris and Julie Smith (my great great-great-grandparents) in December 1871 after their initial summer home in New Hartford burned to the ground. By the summer of 1874, Esperanza was close to completion and a hub for visitors far and wide. The manse has countless photos of famous writers of the time who visited, including Mark Twain and Walt Whitman.

Then, on page nine of the Esperanza book, there it was. In a letter written on August 18, 1874, to Nellie in Europe, Julia writes,

> *The house is nearly done. Next Saturday we expect to be all settled. The new chambers are very nice. The view from their windows is very fine indeed. I thought maybe my little Nell would like one for her own when she comes back to me. Helen Seymour is here and rooms with Fanny in Minnietrost [a name for one of the rooms].*

Boom. Linkage! While the name, Helen Seymour, is not that uncommon and there were several Helens on my side of the family, I really felt like I had finally hit pay dirt. I began my mental checklist. The ages of Helen and the four Smith girls (Fanny, Lottie, Nellie, and Lucy) made sense. Helen would have been twenty-one at the time, and Fanny, the oldest, was twenty-three. Fanny's younger sister, Carlotta, was born in 1853, the same year as Helen Seymour. Mere coincidence?

I kept reading, but now rather than reading for content, I was scanning for that name. The next mention of Helen Seymour was on page forty-seven. In 1902, my grandmother Carlotta was born, and it reads:

> *Baby Carlotta arrived at 4 P.M. on Saturday, September 13, 1902. One of my longer days [again her mother Lucy is speaking]. Aunt Helen Seymour, who was going to nurse me, arrived on the evening train. The next few days passed along pleasantly, until Friday evening, September 19. Aunt Helen was brushing my hair when mother called her to come downstairs quickly.*

Aunt? Wait a minute. Whaaaat? While I was indeed ecstatic, I was equally baffled. I had scoured Ancestry.com tirelessly looking for a connection between the two families but never found a thing linking them. The hair brushing incident refers to Morris passing out and eventually dying that same day. *I imagine that puts a damper on things.*

And, finally on page forty-nine, there's a reference to Helen in 1904. It reads:

> *I remember seeing Aunt Carlotta (Lottie) walking down the garden pathway with Aunt Helen Seymour. Aunt Carlotta had sparking dark eyes and black hair. Aunt Helen was a lovely blonde with immense blue eyes and golden hair: both women were tall and very slim. Aunt Helen came from New Orleans. She had a soft drawing speech, she would speak of the rustling palms (rhyming with lambs) or she would say— 'What a lovely calm evening.' It was a constant fascination to me and I adored her. She and the Smith daughters were life-long friends, Julie always considered her a part of her family of girls.*

This sentence settled it for me. The term aunt referred to nothing more than a close friend who assumed the title of aunt or uncle. Many people have such a person in their life. Ironically, I also had an *Uncle* Dan and *Aunt* Sarah who were very close friends of my parents. I have fond memories of my Uncle Dan teaching my brother Matt and I the best inside (though highly illegal) basketball moves in our driveway after he'd had a few cocktails. *As the adage goes in sports: If you ain't cheatin', you ain't tryin'!*

While this clearly closed one door—Helen Seymour knew my side of the family intimately—it blew open a huge gap in another. How were these girls connected if not by blood? One does not become an *Aunt* simply by happenstance.

At this point, I knew that I needed to reconnect with Jamie Hall, and I reached out via email. We both agreed that another visit to Esperanza would perhaps answer some of the questions that I had. After several messages back and forth, we settled on a late April 2023 visit.

In the meantime, I set to work trying to make some connection between the Seymours and New Hartford. In my mind, perhaps the "girls"—as referred to in Lucy Ellsworth's book—knew each other through long summers in New Hartford, starting in the early 1870s after Morris and Julie Smith bought Esperanza. I trudged on via Ancestry.com and indeed found some Seymours who were prominent in New Hartford in the 1800s and 1900s. Unfortunately, while Helen Seymour was related to the family of Seymours in New Hartford, it was at least four to five generations removed.

In hindsight, it made sense. While Helen's immediate family was strictly in New Orleans, the rest of her extended family were grounded in the Hartford area—but not necessarily in New Hartford. More importantly, based on the content from the Esperanza book, Helen and the Smith girls seemed intimately connected even before the property in New Hartford was purchased in 1871. I was clearly missing something. I planned my second trip to Esperanza, hoping for some concrete answers.

Jamie Hall aka Yoda

At 9 a.m. on Saturday, April 29, 2023, one of my closest friends and a former colleague headed down the road to visit Esperanza. Jeremy Robinson was born and raised in New Hartford, Connecticut, and had mentioned on many occasions that he would love to visit Esperanza since he had only heard about its history from afar and had only seen it from the outside. So off we went.

I must admit that I was a little nervous. Was I encroaching too much on this family that I barely knew, even though we were technically family? Would I find anything worthwhile? Would Jeremy have to stand around while I tried to squeeze information out of Jamie Hall? As I've told myself and others on many occasions: *You worry too much!* This was no different.

After we got a few pleasantries out of the way and did a quick purview of my needs, Jamie and I set to work while Motts (Jeremy's nickname) got the grand tour of the huge house from Jamie's wife, Holly. He was in heaven. Meanwhile, Jamie and I batted around a few questions I had. I learned that the Smiths lived in the area of Asylum Avenue and Albany Avenue (today, prominent thoroughfares) in the downtown area of Hartford. Later, I discovered through letters that the Smiths lived in two houses in Hartford before moving to Esperanza permanently. Jamie also informed me that Morris Smith ran a lucrative saddlery company in Hartford, but it also had branches in New Orleans, New York, and St. Louis. Although this was all very helpful information, it was one statement on his part that really hit home. "You need to stop focusing on Esperanza and focus on a connection in New Orleans."

It was a pivotal moment. I had visions of that famous scene from *All the President's Men* in the spooky dark parking garage where the associate director of the FBI, Mark Felt, aka Deep Throat (Hal Holbrook), tells the *Washington Post* reporter, Bob Woodward (Robert Redford), to "Follow the money!" In my case, I needed to garner the familial connection through New Orleans.

New Orleans was the key simply because Helen spent most of her early life there, and it was also where Morris Smith spent much of his professional career. And I knew this. The Esperanza book spells this out clearly. There were constant references up until the turn of the century of letters back and forth between Morris in New Orleans and Julie in Hartford and eventually New Hartford. Through much of the last quarter of the 19th century, Morris worked in New Orleans and would return at Christmas and in the summer. I assume that he worked at the Hartford office during the summer months since the saddlery business was centered there.

At some point, Jamie left the front room of the house and returned with a ratty-looking book. My eyes must have looked like saucers. In one of our back-and-forth emails, Jamie had mentioned that he had several guest books that date back to the time period in question. Now, he handed me one of the guest books and commented that he thought the dates were right for my research. Thank God, Motts was there tossing names and places back and forth relevant to New Hartford because I became totally engrossed in the book—and probably came off a bit rude because of it.

A quick explanation of the guest book. If you have visited a nice inn or something relatively upscale on Vrbo, it may have a guest book that allows guests to comment about their stay there. While this book had all that and much more This guest book covered from roughly the late 1800s through the middle of the 1900s, and it had countless comments, drawings, poems, and even a few black and white photos. After an initial quick perusal, I searched for one specific date: September 19, 1902—the date that *Aunt* Helen Seymour came to New Hartford to help my great-grandmother with the new baby (my grandmother Carlotta), according to the Esperanza book. Not that I didn't believe the book, but I needed some confirmation. After about five minutes of figuratively going back in time, I found it. On two pages dedicated to the birth of my grandmother, there was a de-tailed list of everyone staying at the house. At the bottom, it read, "Grandaunt Helen Seymour—Who didn't get here in time for the first greeting but who will doubtless get well acquainted with the little stranger before she leaves." What is amazing about this one entry is that Helen is listed with all the other relatives who were there at the time. Somehow, Helen Seymour—who had no direct blood relationship with the Smiths, Ellsworths, or Creeveys—had made the official cast list. *How the hell does this woman connect with my family?*

Of course, my next order of business was to go through the guest book page by page, looking for more Helen Seymour references. But I had no luck. Perhaps, her family connection was so significant that it didn't warrant a guest book reference each time she visited. Whatever the case, I was satisfied with this lone citation, because it did confirm Helen's relationship with the Esperanza family as an older woman (she would have been in her early fifties).

While I didn't see any other Helen Seymour references, I did find other entries that initially caught me off guard. My parents. After the initial shock, I quickly and quietly said to myself, *Of course, they would be in here!* As mentioned, the guest book went up through the mid-1950s, right in my dad's wheelhouse. The first reference was when he was two or three (1929-30) and had signed it as "D is for Dirck." *Wow!* It continued up through when my mom, Joyce, entered the picture. On November 17, 1957, my dad wrote, "Once again at Esperanza after too many years absent—almost unchanged." My mom wrote in her beautiful handwriting, "It is truly all that I heard about."

Two other entries of note. There is a picture that I've never seen of my dad when he was twelve years old sitting next to a pond (Creevey Pool) with his younger sister, Anne. His shirt was off, and he was goofing for the camera. The last reference was a visit from my dad between September 1 and 4, 1944. I can only guess that he was heading to Yale for his sophomore year—his last before entering the Navy. He must have left Cooperstown, New York, stayed in New Hartford, and then headed to New Haven. I am only guessing at this point, but the timing and travel direction fits. While it has nothing to do with my goal for this trip, it truly warmed my heart.

After a stress-free two-hour visit, Motts and I bid our farewells. Before heading out of town, we went to the family plot with Anne Hall as our guide and visited the gravestones of relatives whom I was slowly beginning to know by name. Four generations, starting with Morris and Julie Smith, their four girls, their grandkids, and finally ending with Eileen and Newman Hall, my great-aunt and -uncle. Little did I know how familiar I would become with these distant relatives.

Follow the Money

Follow the money—or in my case, focus on New Orleans. So I did. The first task was to get a true understanding of Morris Smith's business in Hartford and New Orleans. Thankfully, Jamie had steered me in the right direction in New Orleans, and more importantly, to Morris's business there—a saddlery company, as mentioned earlier. Again, whether it was pure stupidity or simple ignorance, I was really quite naive about the importance of saddlery outfitters back in the day prior to the advent of cars. *Think AutoZone.* Many people in the mid-1800s, and especially those of wealth, owned a horse as a means of travel. While trains were prevalent, especially after the Civil War, people needed horses to travel locally.

Morris Smith's saddlery business was started by his father, Normand Smith. On the company's website (yes, it is still active, and the longest-running saddlery company in the country), it reads,

> The Smith-Worthington Company was originally founded in 1794, in Hartford Connecticut, by Normand Smith. Smith started the business making saddles, harnesses, horseman's caps and holsters but soon expanded to include trunks, belts, bridles, stirrups, spurs, bits, and other horse related items. Smith's Company quickly grew to be the largest manufacturer of horse equipment in the United States and widely recognized throughout the world. The manufacturing center was located in Hartford Connecticut and had showrooms in New Orleans and New York City. It was in the 1840's that the manager of the New York City showroom, George Wor-

thington, became partner of the company and the name changed to The Smith-Worthington Company.

By the time Normand passed in 1860, Morris and his half-brothers were already running the company, and not just in Hartford. According to an article from the website ConnecticutHistory.org that was written by Patrick Skahill, "In the 1830s, Smith opened a shop in New Orleans, and by 1842 the company opened a satellite facility in New York City. The company changed partners and names many times and finally became Smith-Worthington when the Hartford and New York concerns merged in 1905." While that article, as well as one from the *Hartford Courant*, gives Normand credit for opening retail stores in New Orleans and then in New York City, Jamie informed me via follow-up emails that Morris became the name and face of the store in the South. *Focus on New Orleans.*

Initial research turned up nothing on a Smith-Worthington company in New Orleans, but I did get hits for *Smith and Brother.* Not very inventive, but it got far more complicated as I dug into the Smith extended family. Normand Smith married three times and clearly wasn't just making saddles. It seems that Normand had a big family—sixteen in all, with Morris and his younger brother, Jonathan, born last. Deeper research through census records confirmed Morris's blood brother, Jonathan, and his half-brothers, Thomas and Charles, all worked for the company as well. Jamie confirmed this with a simple note: "Morris did work with his brother and half-brothers from time to time—not always as smoothly or as satisfactorily as he might have been wanted!" I would later confirm through letters between Morris and his wife that the family had problems with the saddle company in the second half of the 19th century. *It wasn't pretty.*

So, Morris joined the subsidiary with his brothers in New Orleans and used Smith and Brother as the initial company there. In order to confirm this, I searched the name on Newspapers.com, and bingo. I found multiple advertisements in local New Orleans area newspapers at that time for Smith and Brother. *Listed in the newspaper? Strange? To-day, if you're listed extensively in newspapers, it's probably for the wrong reasons.*

Keep in mind that newspapers in the 1800s served as much more than news outlets—which is mostly how we perceive them today. They were the social media of their time. There were countless short notifications of residents' personal affairs, especially concerning travel. On one occasion, the paper mentions that "Mr. M.W. Smith" is staying at a certain hotel and on another that "Mrs. M.W. Smith" just arrived on such and such boat. *Nothing changes.* I'm sure as an en-trepreneur in a new area, Morris didn't mind at all. Free publicity.

Additionally, advertisements were more extensive in terms of the details of the merchandise available—but what other means were there to get the word out? Smith and Brother ran the same advertise-ment for weeks on end, but I did notice that they began waning after the Civil War ended in 1865. *More research.*

First off, as Jamie mentioned, the brothers' part in the company, at least in terms of New Orleans, had fallen exclusively to Morris by the late 1860s. According to the 1870 census, his half-brother Thomas Deacon Smith had "retired from the business." All references to the company were limited to M.W. Smith from that point on.

Once I had firmly established that Morris Smith was in New Or-leans from roughly 1850 to sometime before the turn of the century, I needed to do the same research for his counterpart—William Ellery Seymour, Helen's father.

Neighbors

William Seymour was born in 1810 and was the youngest of three Seymour children—Mary, Thomas Henry, and William. But unlike the other two who stayed in Hartford, he headed to New Orleans at the age of twenty and never left. Thankfully, my Seymour book gave some insight into this. It reads, "For more than 30 years, he [William

Ellery Seymour] was a member of the firm, Stevens and Seymour, wholesale, and during that period, bore the reputation of a pure, honest, and incorruptible man and merchant." *Damn. I'd take that on my tombstone.*

The Stevens stationery company existed in New Orleans several years before William Seymour joined in 1847 at the age of thirty-seven. Much like the saddlery business, it was well advertised in the local newspapers, and the company became Stevens and Seymour in 1860. A quick side note on stationery companies back in the day—stationery companies were nothing like the Hallmark stores of today and were perhaps closer to a Staples. Keep in mind that paper was the only means of communication. By the 1870s, the company diversified its inventory and ultimately began focusing on school textbooks.

I know … blah, blah, blah. What's the point of all this? Great question. I knew that Helen and the Smith girls were close—as the Esperanza book indicated—but I wanted to know how that was possible, given that they were living 1000 miles apart. I truly felt that it had to start with the two businessmen running their respective companies at relatively the same time and place. I was not wrong.

While they may have done business with each other (with Seymour selling his stationery products to the saddlery rather than the reverse), I focused more on their business addresses. The Stevens and Seymour business was located on Common Street the entire time that William worked for the company. Until 1865, it was located in the lower 50s of Common Street (this varied over a twenty-year period), and after that, it was located at 96 and 98 Common Street up until William's death in 1883. I learned later that the business did not move, rather the address numbers changed. Common Street ran directly into the port—prime location for any business that needed goods from the outside world.

Next, the Smith Saddlery Company. This was when I immediately knew I'd hit the mark. Between 1846 and roughly 1855, Morris Smith's saddlery shop was right across the street from William Seymour's stationery business on Common Street (50 and 52 and 51 and 53 respectively). Keep in mind that New Orleans was not a New York City or even a Boston in the mid-1800s, so I imagine there had to be some intimacy between shop owners in the area. These two had to have known each other, and perhaps they were close friends because of location, vocation, and family. Both William Seymour and Morris Smith had their kids in the early 1850s. Perhaps over morning coffee, they discussed their kids—as all parents do. And both had significant roots in the Hartford area.

In 1855, Morris's business moved to 79 Canal Street and stayed there until he retired in the 1890s. While the two businesses were now on different streets, those streets literally ran side by side until joining at the Mississippi River. Basically walking distance. At that point, I truly believed that the connection between the Seymours and Smiths began with the fathers, William and Morris, and that they were business associates and eventually close friends. Now I just needed to prove it. I needed to see it first-hand.

Brunch With the Ghost of Morris

One of my goals for a delayed trip to New Orleans was to find the relative location of Morris's and William's businesses in downtown New Orleans. Another stroke of luck came with a picture from the New Orleans Williams Research Center digital archives dated 1849 that showed the local businesses on the corner of Common Street and Magazine Street (a major thoroughfare today), and the saddlery shop was on it.

New Orleans, 1849, Corner of Common Street and Magazine Street, Smith Saddlery on the far left.

After my work at the Williams Research Center and my impromptu visit to the pharmacy museum on my first day in New Orleans, I hiked about a half mile out of the French Quarter and into the business district due west. To my surprise, there was a fancy hotel and a restaurant now located at the very spot of my great-great-great-grandfather's business on Common Street. The restaurant was called the Ruby Slipper CBD (Central Business District), and it specialized in brunch fare. *Hmmm.* My next day's itinerary was definitely filling up. Before heading back to my car, I quickly looked across the street from the Ruby Slipper to see where William Seymour's business may have stood. Unfortunately, it had not served it as well as the saddlery shop's eventual destiny. Brick walls and padlocked doors. On the other hand, it was a very narrow street, used only for one-way traffic. These two could have spoken to each other from the respective shops.

The next morning and after my tour of the pharmacy, I back-tracked toward the business district again. I had an amazing brunch at the Ruby Slipper, again the very location of Morris Smith's saddlery shop. I wanted to dazzle my waiter with this fun fact, but he seemed a little bit too frazzled to give a damn. Of course, the place could have been empty and he probably wouldn't have cared. I sat, enjoyed my omelet and grits, and pondered the significance of this place. Assuming that these two local merchants had to have known each other based on mere proximity of their businesses over several years, I needed more.

The Smith Letters

Thankfully, Jamie Hall came to my rescue again. According to Jamie, there were a lot of letters between my great-great-great-grand-parents, Morris and Julie Smith, while Morris was working in New Orleans and Julie was living in Hartford. *More written letters?* I don't know whether my face gave me away (*damn, bad poker face*), but all I could think about was all the primary documents—most in the form of handwritten letters—that I had waded through for the last year and a half. Jamie must have seen my non-poker face of obvious discomfort and quickly followed up with the fact that my grandmother Carlotta had transposed and typed all the written letters, and they were now in PDF files. I was elated. Jamie said he would upload the files to a thumb drive and mail it my way.

The thumb drive contained two huge digital folders—one from roughly 1846, when Julie and Morris Smith began dating, to the early 1860s; and the second that covered the period up until Julie's untimely death in 1883. The files within each folder were divided up by year and contained numerous typed letters. These were usually between Morris and Julie, but they eventually included their four girls and other significant friends and family. Everything was well organized and easy to follow. The time and energy that my grandmother exerted to read and reread each sentence, rewrite each letter, and finally have them typed was mind boggling. Again, this was in the 1970s and without the advantage of a word processor where you can type and fix as you go. Having worked through countless letters myself at this point, I knew how draining it was. Additionally, there was a synopsis of the letters by year at the beginning, serving much like an outline of a book, and editorial notes at the end of the letters explaining new people and book references, as well as her personal input. *Amazing!*

While I credit my thoroughness and organizational skills to my mom—especially concerning my academic pursuits—I now know that I was blessed with these skills from both sides of the tree. Of course, looking back at my paternal grandmother, based on our rare encounters, I shouldn't be surprised. She was an avid collector of seashells. She had boxes and boxes of various shells from across the world and all were organized, identified, and labeled. Even for an adolescent boy who only cared about sports, it was pretty cool. *Back to the grindstone.*

As mentioned earlier, Morris and Julie Smith started their Esperanza existence in the early 1870s and the homestead has remained in the family ever since. But their lives together began well before that. They met in New York City in 1845, when he was seventeen and she was twenty-seven. *Scandalous.* They married five years later. While he tried his damnedest to stay out of the family saddlery business, he was eventually sent to New Orleans to work at the retail store there. For the record, all the leather work was done in the Hartford factory, and it was only retail outlets in New York, New Orleans, and St. Louis. Though Morris constantly remarked to Julie that he wanted to leave the business and move permanently back north, he never did. He stayed in the business until he retired in the mid-1890s and even after Julie's death in 1883.

As I stated above, the Smiths' general routine was that Morris stayed in New Orleans between the fall and spring of each year while Julie stayed in Hartford and New Hartford raising their four girls. For almost thirty-five years, the two existed in a long-distance relation-ship. I can't even imagine.

Without telephones, texting, or Zoom, they were left to write to each other tirelessly. Their relentless correspondence, I hoped, would shed some light on the connection between their family and the Sey-mours. If the Smith girls were as close to Helen Seymour as it was suggested in the Esperanza book, then it must be at least alluded to in the letters that were now in my possession. I was excited about finally making a true connection between them, but that excitement quickly waned when I came to grips with the sheer number of the letters be-tween Morris and Julie Smith.

While the two are probably outliers in terms of their prowess as letter writers, I had to remind myself that I was looking at their situ-ation from a 21st-century viewpoint. I should have been prepared for the volume, especially after wading through Thomas Seymour's let-ters. This was how people communicated back in the day. You didn't pick up the phone to tell your wife how your day was on a business trip. You didn't text someone with obnoxious acronyms and little pic-tures. You didn't have a Zoom meeting. You wrote to each other. And these two wrote extensively. Especially Julie—she had one handwrit-ten letter that was forty-four pages long. *I love Cathy a great deal, but...*

As I said, the files were divided up by years, and each letter was la-beled in terms of the author, the month, the rough day(s), and most importantly, from where it was written. But here was the problem: Because these were free-flowing letters written over several days at times, I never knew when or if there was a mention of a "Seymour." For days on end, I went through each letter, looking for some ref-erence to either Helen Seymour or her father, William. It was the proverbial needle in a haystack. But the references were there—espe-cially for William. As I began to develop a pattern for my own sanity, I moved through each paragraph looking for the telltale name and pay-ing far more attention to letters coming from Morris than those from

Julie, since I believed the connection between the two families had to come from New Orleans rather than from Hartford. *Thank you, Jamie.*

Though pressured by time and my ultimate goal, I couldn't help but become familiar with the day-to-day dialogue of this married couple who happened to be my distant relatives. Julie spent much of her time detailing the maintenance of a home, care of the girls, and contacts that she had since her previous letter. Morris, on the other hand, spent a lot of his time discussing business, contacts of his own in New Orleans, and his future return to the Hartford area. It was amazing how loyal each was to the other in terms of their respective circumstances. There were always issues about money, kids, and family, but they always fell back on their love for each other and their four girls. I was able to watch the two parents and their daughters grow as individuals and as a family through these letters. I felt slightly creepy to read their most intimate thoughts and challenges, but research was research.

Beyond my grandmother's meticulous organizational skills, I added another layer of order—letters pre-Esperanza and post-Esperanza. I knew that Helen Seymour and the girls knew each other intimately when they summered and eventually lived at Esperanza together in the early 1870s, but I really had no solid connection prior to that other than assumptions. I hoped that the first group of letters would answer my questions.

More Than Neighbors

Between 1852, when I found the first reference to a "Mrs. Seymour" (William's wife, Mary), and 1872, the date of Helen's first trip to Esperanza, there were more than fifteen different accounts of some connection to the Seymours. Keep in mind that I most likely missed a few along the way, and many of the references are merely comments in passing. Much like when Cathy and I are debriefing about our days in our respective living room locations (she on *her* leather chair, and

I on *my* couch). *"Hey, when I was at the store today, I saw so-and-so and they said hi."*

While William Seymour and Morris Smith were never in business together officially, they obviously ran with the same crowd in New Orleans. There were references to dinners together and games of cribbage, along with countless overlapping business matters. Unfortunately, there was only one reference to Helen. On November 13, 1863, Morris writes to Julie: "Last night I was at Wm Seymour's house—and took with me the card pictures of our children—to show Miss Helen (11 years)—and told her about Mr. Curtis' school, played cribbage for 3 hours with Mr. S." *Was this the first time that Helen had ever seen his girls, or was he showing her the picture because she already knew them? Does one reference a Miss Helen without knowing her intimately?* I did not know, but I was also nagged by a bigger question.

While it makes perfect sense that Morris and William's relationship grew steadily over the years, how did all the girls meet if the Smith girls were in Hartford through their early childhood? Then it dawned on me that perhaps Jamie's "Focus on New Orleans" mantra was slightly off. I already knew, based on previous research, that the Seymours also traveled to Hartford in the summer. This must have been where the girls first met.

If the fathers were quite close, why wouldn't they continue their *bromance* in Hartford, where it would inevitably involve the girls? Unfortunately, the letters, although vital to my research, didn't help in this case because there were no letters between Julie and Morris in the summer months. No need to write to each other if they were finally living together under the same roof. If Helen and the Smith girls became acquainted in the Hartford area due to their dads' connection in New Orleans, I had no way to know.

Additionally, the Stevens and Seymour stationery business in New Orleans was much like the Smith Saddlery business in terms of the Hartford hub. In this case, the main base was in Saratoga, New York. E.R. Stevens (Seymour's business partner) did not spend a lot of time in New Orleans. William Seymour, like Morris Smith, ran the business there, and he probably used the summer months to tidy things up on the home base in Saratoga, which is 150 miles from Hartford. Again, this is pure speculation, but it serves as another piece of the puzzle for keeping the Seymour family in the northeast for an extended period of time.

Leaving the "how and when" the girls became close friends as a relative gray area, I decided to concentrate on their friendship after the Smiths had bought and refurbished Esperanza in the early 1870s. In this case, the letters between Julie and Morris—and now the older girls as well—did not disappoint. In the winter of 1872-73, Fanny Smith, then twenty-one years old, stayed in New Orleans, and in the winter of 1873-74, Lottie Smith, also twenty-one, did the same. Prior to this, Julie writes to Lottie, "I think there is no doubt about your going to New Orleans next winter, and I feel as if you would have a regal good time with Helen Seymour." While Lottie was in New Orleans in the winter of 1874, she asked her mother if Helen Seymour could visit Esperanza that same summer. Julie responded on March 11, 1874:

> *Of course I want Helen. Give my Love to her, and tell her I must have her all summer. She is one of my own girls, and her home is Esperanza forever and ever. Now be sure and bring her on with you. If we are not settled, she won't mind because she is one of us.*

In my mind, this says it all. Julie clearly feels that Helen is part of the family. So much so that she's willing to have her for the whole summer, even though construction projects were still going on. At that point (the early 1870s), all five girls would have been in their twenties, and they clearly had a well-established friendship. As my mom would say, "They were joined at the hip." Again, I can only guess that the friendship started much earlier while Helen was visiting the Hartford area with her dad.

References to Helen continue through the 1870s. All are nothing more than casual comments about her and her family—except for a few notes that caught me off guard. This was when Helen's potential chemical dependency resurfaced, which might have been because of a physical or mental health problem. I don't know what I was expecting in these countless letters, but I was hoping to read something that clearly spoke to Helen's problems, such as when they started and to what extent. Then it dawned on me that if we're tight-lipped about mental disorders and depression in the 21st century, it was probably that much worse in the late 19th century. Though I never read any comments on her specific mental state or her medical care, I did find a few comments that may be enough. In January 1878, Morris comments that Helen is "not well" and nothing more. She was twenty-five at the time. It seems to me that if it was something like a broken leg or the flu or even a disease that was rampant in the south in the 1800s (i.e. malaria), then he would have said so. To me, it's what's *not* said that makes this poignant. An equally telling comment that raised my eyebrows was from Julie to Nellie in January 1879.

At that point, Nellie Smith Ellsworth and William Webster Ellsworth were living in New York, and Nellie was pregnant with their first child. My great-grandmother, Lucy Morris Ellsworth, was born in April of that year. Julie writes, "Helen Seymour's doctor told her nothing could be worse for her than the motion of the street cars—as the jarring is very trying, for that reason I hope you have ceased your visits to Brooklyn—by this time." *Whaaat?* I had so many questions once I read this. Given that the roads in New York City were probably horrible, was Julie telling her daughter to stop riding the streetcars so as not to hurt the baby? Apparently, Helen's doctor told her not to ride them in New Orleans.

Then my mind went to the dark side. Was Helen also pregnant in 1879? Did she give up her child? *No way!* But it would answer so many other questions. Helen would have been twenty-five at the time. If she was pregnant and unmarried, it could explain her issues with her health and prescription opioids. It could answer her marriage status. And it could answer why she left New Orleans. On a whim, I doubled downed on my research. In this case, looking for births around this time, using Seymour as a guide. Nothing. Of course, a young lady of relative means with a new child who was given up for adoption might not have been reported through the normal channels. Pregnant or not, Helen was obviously seeing a doctor or a pharmacist for some sort of issue that warranted some weird advice in New Orleans. *Take two tablespoons of laudanum every four hours and don't ride the streetcars!*

While I might not have any clear answers about Helen's health conditions or even an unwanted pregnancy, I did feel that I was solidifying a friendship between the Smith girls and Helen based on Morris and Julie's letters. Unfortunately, Julie Smith died unexpectedly in 1883 from a horse accident at Esperanza, and so with her went the typed letters compiled by my grandmother between her and Morris. The Smith girls and Helen Seymour would have been in their twenties still.

It's unfathomable to think that Morris, who would continue to work in New Orleans for another decade and a half after his wife's death, would stop writing to his daughters and they to him. Thankfully, with a parting note, Carlotta mentions letters that did in fact postdate 1883, but she didn't type them up. So where were they?

Off to the Home of Baseball

I quickly emailed Jamie, and he confirmed that there were far more letters than the transcribed letters in my possession. *Yeaaah!* But he did not have them. *Booo!* In fact, he did not have the originals that Carlotta had typed up either. He and I only had the scanned copies. I was perplexed. I thought that there were boxes and boxes of the stuff in some attic somewhere on the Esperanza property. But according to Jamie in a follow-up email, my grandmother Carlotta scooped up everything in the late 1960s and took them off to Cooperstown, New York (home of baseball), to do her thing. She then donated the whole lot to the Fenimore Art Museum in Cooperstown in the late 1970s.

Now, I was really perplexed, and, according to Jamie, Carlotta's sister Eileen and brother Kennedy were also beyond perplexed. *Pissed may be the better word.* I guess that it was assumed that all the Smith and Ellsworth letters would return to Esperanza once Carlotta was finished with them. Of course, these Ellsworth and Creevey family politics were meaningless to me—other than that they gave me a new direction. A quick Google search here, a few clicks there, and voilà, I confirmed that the mother lode was in the bowels of the Fenimore Art Museum in Cooperstown. I quickly sent out an email inquiry, and in due time, another road trip was planned.

Bright and early on Monday, June 12, 2023, I headed down the road to Cooperstown, a three-hour drive. I found the museum easily enough. The staff politely directed me to a separate building that served as their library. Much like my work at the Connecticut Museum of Culture and History, there was strict protocol when it came to examining historical documents (drinks on a separate table, pencils only, view one folder at a time, etc.), which immediately indicated the enormity of the situation. I felt like a real historian.

The warm fuzzy feeling ended when the librarian rolled out a cart with three large boxes. I opened the first box. Not only were there dozens of folders in each box, but each folder contained countless numbers of letters—all handwritten. Looking at the first letter, I realized that there was no way I was going to be able to read all of this in the two days that I had allotted myself. So, as I had with the typed letters, I simply started looking for any reference to Helen Seymour. But therein lay the problem. Some letters were extremely difficult to read, simply because the handwriting was atrocious (Fanny's was the worst). So, again, I quickly photographed each letter as best as I could, paying closer attention to those letters coming out of New Orleans. I would deal with the content later. I got through the first two boxes in two hours and took a required break when the library shut down for an hour. Then it was time for lunch with my aunt, by design.

My Aunt Barbara and I met at her beautiful home in the rolling hills in Cooperstown. Driving to her house, about fifteen minutes from the library, I couldn't understand why I felt unnaturally nervous. As aunts and uncles go, I can count them one hand—three, and all aunts. My mom had one sister, Jean, an identical twin. And whereas many twins who live in different parts of the world begin to act and look slightly different, my mom and Jean remained identical up to their deaths, even though they lived in different towns (Glens Falls, New York, and Scituate, Massachusetts). When Aunt Jean came to visit or we visited them, it was like having two moms around. They would even finish each other's sentences when I was getting reprimanded for something.

My Aunt Anne, Dirck and Barbara's younger sister, lived in the Buffalo-Rochester area for as long as I knew her. An amazing woman: a medical doctor in the field of pediatrics when women didn't do such things. But we were never close.

So, Barbara had big shoes to fill. She did not disappoint, even though up until my work on this book, we'd only spoken on rare occasions. But she's one of those people whom I can instantly pick up a conversation with as if we talk in person daily. She's an excellent listener. Interestingly enough, my father's death and my decision to take on this project have increased our communication and thus our connection. When I didn't have my father to bounce questions off, Barbara stepped up mightily over the last three years.

After some soul searching, I believed that my nervousness was based on my father's last year or two. He was in and out of the hospital as his body began to really fail, and perhaps I feared to find the same when I walked into Barbara's house for lunch—especially given that she was turning ninety-eight in the upcoming October.

Thankfully, while she had a bit of trouble getting around and needed a cane for a few moments, she moved pretty darn well for a woman who was ninety-seven-and-a-half. Her mind was razor sharp.

Knowing that I only had a small amount of time, we got to it. She wanted the details of my research at the Fenimore Museum, especially as it related to the Ellsworth connection. We discussed Helen Seymour as a potential addict, the time in her life that was unaccounted for, and her ever-elusive connection to my family.

I knew that I had a long day still ahead of me—though I could have stayed at Barbara's all day. Before I left, she said that she wanted to show me her new toy in the garage. I assumed it was a new car of some sort, but it was even better—the most bad-ass golf cart I've ever seen. She smiled with a grin. "I love to tool around the grounds [there's a lot of acreage on her property]. If you had stayed longer, we could have gone for a spin."

The rest of my afternoon was a long three hours—wading through letter after letter (some with horrific handwriting) and taking photos as I went. By 4:30 p.m., I was back on the highway for another three-hour drive. In the middle of that drive, I caught myself inwardly whining about the havoc that the day had wreaked on my body, then remembered that my almost centenarian aunt had made a similar retort six hours earlier. "Let me tell you, Andy. Getting old is for the birds!" *You think?* I put my inner monologue about my aches and pains away for a while.

Elementary, My Dear Andrew

Once back at my desk, I set to work deciphering the photographed letters that had some reference to Helen Seymour. It was torture. I can't imagine my grandmother doing this same thing with the hundreds of letters that she went through. While I had the luxury of a new Samsung tablet with a zoom function for troublesome words, I assume that Carlotta was left to the ol' magnifying glass. *A regular Sherlock Holmes.*

In the end, I was left with ten letters or so that had some reference to Helen Seymour. The first few held nothing earth shattering. Much of the same as from my previous work. There was reference to the Seymours traveling north in 1869, another referencing an 1874 holiday show in New Orleans that Lottie participated in, and finally, a comment by Morris about bringing Helen with him when he traveled north. I hit the lottery on the final two sets of letters.

The first letter was from Morris to Fanny in May 1888 from New Orleans. Morris writes, "Helen Seymour's house was sold today for $3200 and when expenses are deducted, she will get above $2900. This with the proceeds of the Hartford House and other possessions will gain her about $500 for her own of which she has promised to keep for her, Harry's children, and help."

This is a very telling paragraph. First, in today's standards, $2900 and $500 would be equal to about $110,000. Not bad. Of course, I'm not sure—depending on how you read this—if she received $3200 or $500. Big difference. If it was only $500, then what happened to the rest? Not sure. What struck me as odd is the tone of Morris's letter. He seems to have taken on a surrogate father role (Helen's dad had died in 1883), which gives special significance to the last line. *She has promised?* I'm not sure whether he served as the negotiator of the sale of the house(s), but since he had intimate details of both sales, it wouldn't surprise me if he had unofficially taken her under his wing. Keep in mind that she was thirty-five and single at the time and perhaps adrift. Was he also concerned about how she would use her new resources? The final note seems to allude to this point. While times may be finally improving for women trying to make it on their own today, I can't imagine someone like Helen Seymour doing so back then. Perhaps Morris's concerns were justified and he was clearly more than just an interested party. But he did have good practice. He was also the single father of two single but well-established daughters, Fanny and Lottie.

As for the connection between the Seymours and the Smiths, there was no need for assumptions anymore. I had plenty of evidence to show that Helen Seymour was extremely close to the girls from their teenage years onward.

But I still felt that I had missed something in terms of Helen Seymour. There must be something to her other than being a woman who'd spent her whole life in New Orleans, who had some sort of physical and mental condition that warranted opioids, who might have traveled to East Hartford with her aunt, and who became friends with a family that I'm descended from. And, of course, there was the desk.

Back to the grind.

8

Helen Seymour 2.0

At this point, I didn't have anything really solid to work with in terms of Helen's life—only assumptions. Was her life that meaningless? Did she return to New Orleans? Did she stay at Esperanza? I was a bit perplexed, but a little voice in my head kept saying, "There is more to this woman than initially perceived. Keep digging." So I did.

The first crack in my mystery came from a known source. There is a sequence of letters from Morris that were written between March and April of 1902 to his daughters Lottie and Fanny that were in the collection at the museum in Cooperstown. In 1902, Morris, now very retired and living permanently in New Hartford, wrote a series of letters referencing Helen to his daughters from the Oak Hall Hotel in Tryon, North Carolina. *Tryon, North Carolina?*

Tryon sits on the border between western North Carolina and South Carolina, halfway between Charlotte and Asheville. Middle of nowhere. Based on the letterhead Morris was using, he, then seventy-four, and Helen, almost fifty, stayed at the Oak Hall Hotel. I quickly looked up the Oak Hall Hotel and found that it was built in 1882. It became a go-to place for the rich and famous in the first half of the 20th century—including F. Scott Fitzgerald. *Go figure?* Of course, I suppose that Morris might fall into that category. But Helen? There were five letters in all, and each made some reference to Helen. That was the good news.

All of these letters carried the same theme. Morris was staying at the hotel in some sort of convalescence stint and Helen was serving as a sort of nurse while he was there. There is some discussion of paying her for her care ($3 a day) for the next several weeks in his first letter to Fanny on March 27, 1902. In this same conversation, he writes, "I could fix it with her nursery now...." Unfortunately, the rest is unreadable. But that little voice in my head was getting louder. Did she have a job somewhere in a nursery? Was she a nurse? While this was a relatively new development in my research of her life, this was not the first time I had read comments about Helen's role as a quasi-nurse. The most notable one, of course, was the reference to Helen traveling to Esperanza in September 1902 to serve as a nurse to Lucy Creevey and her newborn, Carlotta. Initially, I thought she was just another body to help out with the new baby, but perhaps it was far more than that. On top of that was the comment that Helen was summoned when Morris suffered a heart attack around the same time.

Was Helen a trained nurse? *I'm such an idiot. It was all there from the beginning.*

A Regular Florence Nightingale

The next four letters from Tryon are much the same. On March 31, Morris wrote to Fanny, "I am doing well. Weak in my joints and short breath. Clear head... Helen is a great comfort. We take a short walk every day to the Episcopal Church where I rest on the steps." On April 3, he wrote to Lottie, "I have trouble in writing, but I depended on Helen to keep you advised—will do better here after." Later in the letter he wrote, "Will send Helen home at the end of next week." *Home? Where's home?*

On April 4, Morris again comments about Helen to Lottie: "Lucky for us that Helen is so competent." Helen then writes her own personal note at the bottom of Morris's letter. It reads, "Dear Lotty—Don't do anything about my rent until you hear from me—it is not do [sic] yet—will write later. Yours, Helen." This little note is quite telling, because clearly Lottie was going to pay some sort of rent for Helen but not quite yet. *Rent? Where?* Ugh.

Finally, on April 27, Morris wrote to Lottie, "Helen Seymour left last evening. She will stop a day in Washington and carry for [sic] the Sunday for Philadelphia. She will tell you that I am perfectly well." Morris continues, "Will send Helen home at the end of the week," which would have been the 13th at the latest. Did she leave and come back or continue to stay until the 26th? Where is "home"? Washington? Philadelphia? New Orleans? *Now the little voice in my head was screaming!*

I went back to that one-line sentence in April 1902 where Helen told Lottie not to worry about helping her with rent for now. To put this into perspective, and if I have my facts straight, Helen might have been living in the mid-Atlantic in 1902, but she helped Morris in Tryon, North Carolina, that year, and then traveled to New Hartford, Connecticut, in the fall to help with the newborn baby. A little unorthodox, but clearly much easier than traveling from New Orleans for both events.

But where was Helen between the late 1880s and the early 1900s? I was slowly beginning to see her in a whole different light—other than as a wandering drug addict with health issues. On a whim (and a gut feeling), I checked the major city directories in the 1890s in the mid-Atlantic for Helen's name and I hit the jackpot.

A quick note about city directories. They are a fickle sort. For those in the baby boomer crowd, they were precursors to the telephone books of yesteryear—but they contained only addresses and occupation. Both of these categories would serve me well. The fickle part was the name used. I found references to Helena Seymour, Helen Seymour, Helena E. Seymour, H. E. Seymour, and finally Miss Helen Seymour. All of them were the same person. Over time, I got a knack for the subtleties of the city directory program of Ancestry.com and headed into "find the nurse" mode.

In 1892, a "Helen E. Seymour" was listed as a head nurse in Washington Children's Hospital in Washington, D.C. This hospital opened in the 1860s and is now known as Children's National Hospital. According to its website, universities started sending medical students to the hospital in 1887 and a nursing school began on-site in 1888. From the little information that city directories provide, it appears that Helen stayed in the Washington, D.C., area until 1902. Could she have been in the capital prior to 1892? Perhaps. The fact that she's listed as a head nurse in 1892 begs the question of whether she started as early as 1888, though I found no record of that. I really was beginning to see this woman for who she really was—a single, motivated, trained nurse trying to make ends meet and having difficulty doing so. If nursing is still considered a female-heavy career today, then it was much more so in the 1890s, and I'm sure the pay was horrible.

This Washington connection was a breakthrough, and it was all beginning to make everything else seem plausible. Helen, by all accounts, was working at a nursery in the spring of 1902, based on Morris Smith's Tryon letters. Probably in Washington. Probably in the nursery floor of the same hospital. Then she took a train to New Hartford in the fall of 1902, a few days after my grandmother's birth. I assumed that she returned to Washington after that. Unfortunately, I have nothing in writing and no information through city directories to verify where she was or what she was doing until 1904. In 1904, a letter in my possession was sent to Helen from a woman named Anna Crocker. That letter was addressed to Little Compton, Rhode Island.

Wait. Who? Anna Crocker? And Little Compton, Rhode Island? You can't be doing this crap this far into the book, Harrison. I totally agree, so perhaps a little explanation is necessary. Well, maybe not so little.

The Crockers

The largest collection of primary sources in the Seymour desk were letters from Anna and Frank Crocker to Helen Seymour. While all previous Seymour materials—both inside the desk and found through subsequent research—made sense since the desk belonged to the Seymour family, the Crocker letters made no sense at all. *Who the hell were Anna and Frank Crocker?*

I went through these letters quickly to get a feel for their contents, hoping that something would jump out to give me context about the connection between Helen Seymour and the Crockers. But the reality is that no one writes a letter as if they're writing a book—explaining and re-explaining the context of the parties' relationships. Unfortunately, my initial perusal of these letters gave me nothing definitive to work with. *I needed to full-court press this thing.*

The Crocker letters can be divided into two separate groups. One is the letters written from Anna Crocker to Helen Seymour between 1904 and 1922. The larger group of letters is from Frank Crocker, dating from 1928 to 1930. An added piece to this was that all the letters were one-sided. Meaning, I don't have similar letters from Helen—and based on the content of the Crocker letters, they did exist. It was like listening to someone's lengthy one-sided conversation on the phone and trying to get a gist of the whole story. *Tough sledding.*

While my head truly ached trying to fit this into the bigger picture, three main conclusions arose. Helen Seymour and the Crockers knew each other quite well. Anna Crocker and Helen Seymour were somehow related. And the Crockers held on to the Seymour desk for her for almost thirty years. *Whaaat?* But before I could totally come to grips with the fact that some people named Crocker "owned" my desk for almost thirty years, I needed to find out who these people were. *Ancestry.com yet again.*

Much like my work on the Harrison family tree—which was now quite full—I set to work on a new family tree for the Seymours. I initially focused on the Thomas/Henry/Thomas/Mary/Helen Seymour line, because ultimately that was the same lineage of the desk. I went through the same process as before. I sought out other Seymour family trees on Ancestry.com. Thankfully there were several, and most were public. Eventually, I had a rough framework of the Seymour family documented earlier in the book. No Crocker. *Ugh.* Like the Harrison tree, I needed to move east and west to find some connection.

The amount of material was daunting. Back in the day, people had lots of kids and those kids had lots of kids. *You get the idea.* But I was bound and determined to find the connection between the two.

I spent a good day and a half, hour upon hour, more fully filling in the Seymour family tree that I had started. Thankfully, there were several public Ancestry trees from which to continually add names, then add names from those names, and then once more. Practice, as they say, makes perfect, and I became quite adept at pulling a bit of information that I didn't have from one tree, plugging the little tidbit into mine, and ignoring the majority of the other material as redundant. It was some of the most meticulous and time-consuming work I have ever done—and this coming from a man who gets immense personal pleasure out of the process rather than the result. But finally, it paid off. Anna Crocker's full name was Anna Elizabeth Phelps Crocker, and *Phelps* was the link between the two—though it was quite a remote link.

Trying to explain to someone the moment when I determined that Anna Crocker was a relative of Helen Seymour is quite humorous and scary at the same time. Picture a sixty-ish, 6'5" man sitting alone at the very desk that he's writing about after spending hours grinding away, looking for a connection, and finally finding it. I jumped out of my chair and did my best Tiger Woods fist pump. I screamed a guttural noise at the top of my lungs. Something similar to the scream accompanying a massive spike from Rob Gronkowski after he caught a twenty-yard pass, shed two angry tacklers, and dragged two more with him into the end zone. It was an amazing feeling.

The simple answer to the connection—without totally burdening you with a bunch of new names—is that Anna Phelps Crocker and Helen Seymour's direct common relatives were Mayor Thomas Seymour III and his wife, Mary. As a reminder, they were Helen and Anna's great grandparents and the original owners of the Seymour desk. If my math is correct, Helen and Anna were second cousins once removed, meaning that Anna was one generation later than Helen, even though they were only six years apart. Helen was born in 1853, and Anna Crocker in 1859. Well within an age range to know each other intimately.

Quite satisfied with myself—though Cathy failed to see the significance of my discovery when she came home from a full day of *real* work—I needed to seal the deal and make the connection between the two in terms of time and location. Context is key. While I was pretty sure there weren't a lot of Anna Phelps Crockers in the United States at that time, it wouldn't make much sense if Anna moved to California early in her life and never returned. Anna and her husband, Frank, had to have some connection to Connecticut in general and Hartford/East Hartford specifically. Otherwise, it wouldn't make sense. A deeper glance to the Crockers was in order.

My first intimation that Anna and Helen were more than acquaintances was the fact that Anna was born in East Hartford, Connecticut, in 1859. *Thank you again, Ancestry.com.* Her father and mother are listed in the 1860 census as dwelling at number 329 in East Hartford, while Thomas and Mary Seymour were at 815. Of course, this tells me nothing in terms of location, only that there were close to 500 documented dwellings between them. *Booo! No street names!* The Phelpses were also in East Hartford in 1870 (Anna was eleven at the time), but while the Phelpses were still in East Hartford in the 1880 census, Anna Phelps was not. She was living with her older sister in Maine. *No bother.* The initial context was made. Was it plausible that the Phelpses of East Hartford had connections with Thomas and Mary Seymour of East Hartford, especially if they were family? Of course, but the letters between Anna and Helen were the key to this relationship.

The letters between the two (though one-sided) were not simply cordial. These were letters sharing family information from the heart, heavy with personal concern for the other. *What's your point, Harrison?* My point is that Helen Seymour's home was in New Orleans throughout her childhood. How did a clear bond develop between the two if they lived 1500 miles apart? Easy. They connected much like the Smith girls did with Helen. During her summer trips to East Hartford.

Picture this. All kids need to play, and back in the day, that meant outdoors. Hanging with Uncle Thomas and Aunt Mary was cool, but the kids down the way were much cooler AND they were related. Again, the letters in my position between Anna Crocker and Helen Seymour show that these two—even as adults—truly cared for each other deeply and carried on conversations as if they saw each other every day. With the Anna and Helen connection somewhat solved, I moved on to Anna's husband, Frank.

Charles Frances Crocker was born in 1857 in Rhode Island, and except for a few gaps of other employment, he was a salesman by trade for the majority of his life (mainly shoes). I found nothing else on him as a young man until the time period that Anna and Frank became a pair. Today, we encourage our children and students not to put their world out there on the World Wide Web for everyone to see. I had the opposite problem with Frank. No digital footprint. All I know is that Anna and Frank married in 1881 in East Hartford, but I have no idea how and when they met. *Hey, my name is Frank. You want to get married tomorrow? I sell shoes.* Not willing to let sleeping dogs lie, I did some more digging.

Finding people today based on their profession is child's play, but in this case, we were talking about almost 150 years ago. *Good luck.* Amazingly, I did find some references to a shoe salesman named Frank Crocker in the Boston area in the 1880s. What I eventually did learn was that the Crockers spent a significant amount of time outside of New England. In Washington, D.C. Between 1891 and 1906-7. Roughly the same time that Helen Seymour was in Washington. *The voice in my head was now doing the same Gronk guttural scream mentioned earlier.*

Straight out of Little Compton

All the Crocker letters, but especially those from Anna, were like the countless letters that I read over the entirety of my research—lengthy and detailed. In the age of hieroglyphic text messages, letter writing is indeed a lost art. In the Crocker letters, there is endless flow, again one-sided, about Anna's family minutiae and personal circumstances. While her mindless dribble didn't really help me in my desk quest, it did give me insight into the two families in question. Thankfully, the creation of the Seymour family tree, including Anna's branches, was quite helpful as she frequently used common acquaintances whom I could then immediately find on the family tree for perspective. And rightfully so. Why wouldn't two close family friends write about their common acquaintances? But this also solidified my deduction that Helen must have spent significant time as a young person in the Hartford area. Why would Anna keep talking about immediate family members all initially from Hartford if Helen didn't have her own frame of reference with these people?

The first letter in this series from Anna Crocker to Helena Ellery Seymour is dated September 21, 1904. The name and mailing address is Miss Helen, care of H.W. Goodrich, Seaconnect Point, Little Compton, Rhode Island. I had so many questions at this point that my head was spinning. *Seaconnect Point, Little Compton? Goodrich? Why was Helen even there? What happened to her nursing gig in Washington? And, of course, where was the desk?*

The first question was easy enough. Little Compton sits on a little spit of land off the coast of Rhode Island. *Google map it, folks. I'll wait!* Much like most of the Maine coast, Rhode Island looks like a bunch of fingers jutting into the ocean, though on a much smaller scale. Seaconnect Point is simply a smaller but far richer area of Little Compton. Much like its neighbor to the northwest, Newport, Seaconnect Point became a hot spot for the wealthy to build huge summer mansions during the late 1800s. The Goodrich family was one such family.

After extensive research, I was able to piece together a plausible reason why Helen Seymour might have been in Little Compton in the summer of 1904. Mrs. Madeleine Goodrich was actually Madeleine Lloyd prior to her marriage. The Lloyds (two sisters and a brother) were an extremely wealthy and connected family originating in Chicago. Again, like many with means in the late 1800s, they built a huge summer manse off the coast of Little Compton. In addition to being über-rich, they were equally socially motivated to help the less fortunate. The manse was referred to as the Watch House or the "House without a key," and the family was known to invite all walks of life to stay there. Given that, I assumed that Helen's stay had something to do with her perceived "down and out" lifestyle. That was, until I learned that she was a trained and well-experienced nurse. Could Helen have been in Little Compton on a professional basis? I was leaning that way. I started digging. Again.

Were there young children at the Little Compton Lloyd/Goodrich summer homes? The answer is yes. In fact, there were three grandchildren born around the time. I am not sure whether Helen was there for specific pediatric care, but it does make better sense than the idea that she was vacationing or in some sort of 19th-century rehab program. On the other side of the spectrum, perhaps she was providing elder care during her stay. I began to ponder the idea that she was a nurse for hire (Tryon, Esperanza, and Little Compton), and I realized that I was looking at this from a 21st-century perspective again. If we have problems concerning our very young ones or our very old ones, we call 911. What would someone of wealth—like those in Little Compton—do in an emergency? The advent of 911, with ambulances minutes away and a hospital right around the corner, was a long way off. But in the three circumstances mentioned (Tryon, Esperanza, and

Little Compton), the money needed to hire a nurse like Helen Seymour was not a major issue.

With Helen's location clarified in the summer of 1904, as well as the summers preceding and post-ceding 1904 (based on previous comments from Anna Crocker), I wondered where she was during the rest of the year. I was pretty confident that she was in Washington through the end of 1902 but unsure about anything beyond that. There are no city directory listings for her in Washington after 1902. Was she still there while she was doing the summer thing in Little Compton? I'm not sure her employer in Washington would be co-pacetic with that arrangement. *Hey. Heading to my summer manse for three months. Don't wait up.* Could she have been doing a full-time gig with the same Little Compton family? Plausible, and helped by the fact that the Goodrichs lived in New Jersey. Unfortunately, I turned up nothing to confirm that. But I did find one curious bit of information during my new search.

Using the city directories again, I began playing with the variables, changing from year to year, starting in 1903 (if 1902 was the last date that Helen was in Washington, D.C.). Amazingly, I got a hit: Gloucester, Massachusetts. *Whaaat?* Gloucester is about an hour north of Boston and has a long history as a fishing community. Helen's name appears twice in 1903 and 1905. She's listed as a nurse at the Addison Gilbert Hospital and as a boarder at a house in town with other nurses. How she connected to the Lloyds and Goodrichs of Little Compton from there made little sense, but it made far more sense that she would travel to Little Compton from Massachusetts rather than from New Orleans or even Washington, D.C. Whether this is the same Helen Seymour, I am not sure.

Who's Got the Desk?

Having somewhat pieced together Helen's movements between 1887 (when her aunt died and the house sold in East Hartford) and

1905 (when she may have been working as a nurse in Gloucester, Massachusetts), I was left with one last question from my list above. Where was the desk all this time? Again, the 1904 letter is helpful. Sort of.

Beyond the normal conversations that would be consistent with any letter between two close family friends (status of the Crockers' lives, updates on relatives and friends they both knew, the weather, etc.), two things stick out in Anna's letters to Helen. First, there are the issues with Helen's health and, of course, Helen's inheritance—including the desk. The 1904 letter is no different. Anna writes, "Your things are all safe & I hope it will be a long time before I turn them over to your niece on account of anything happening to you, as you wrote of. I hope instead you may have a place for them yourself. But until you do I shall be happy to keep them for you." While the desk is not mentioned, I would assume that it is among "your things." This is confirmed in future letters between the two. But before I moved in that direction, a nagging question was in my craw. Did Helen ever physically possess the desk? The simple answer is yes.

I strongly suspect that the Seymour desk followed Helen from East Hartford to Esperanza to Washington. It's the only thing that fits. Helen, at some point, took up a position in Washington, D.C., at the Children's Hospital. The earliest listing I located through the city directory is in 1892 as a head nurse. Did she start as a head nurse right off the bat or progress into that role after some time there? I am not sure, but there could be a situation where Helen cleared out her aunt's home in 1888, moved everything to Esperanza for a short time (with the help of Lottie), and then moved almost everything with her when she took up residence in the nation's capital sometime before 1892. Let's say 1890. Of course, the 1890 census data would be really, really helpful here. *Ugh.*

Helen worked and lived in Washington for the next thirteen years or so until she moved to Gloucester, Massachusetts, to work as a nurse at the local hospital. Additionally, she spent her summers around this time serving in some professional capacity in Little Compton, Rhode Island. Unfortunately, she felt that she couldn't bring her inherited possessions to that position and left them with Anna and Frank Crocker. Why the Crockers? One, Anna Crocker was one of her trusted and closest family friends, and she would understand the historical value of these items. Two, conveniently, the Crockers also lived in Washington, D.C. An easy move. Finally, this career change for Helen was only temporary and she would be back in the near future to recollect her possessions. *Right? Wrong!*

Moving in Opposite Directions

The next letters in my possession from Anna Crocker are dated various months in 1911. There are four of them. Again, all of them carry the same good-family-friend tone. But a lot of things had changed by that point. Helen was in New Orleans again and had been there for five years or so. Anna and Frank Crocker were living in Springfield, Massachusetts, and the desk was still with them. *So much to tell.*

At some point, Helen moved back to New Orleans, though I wasn't sure when based solely on the 1911 letters. Again, city directories were a great help. The first reference to Helen in New Orleans is in 1906 in a city directory where she's listed as a nurse and living at 3201 Coliseum Street, probably as a boarder. For the next five years, there is no other city directory with updated information. Additionally, I found no reference to Helen in the 1910 census. *Ugh.* Without solid information, I can only assume that she remained at the Coliseum address until 1911. In the city directory for that year, and for 1912 as well, Helen lists 1320 Josephine Street as her residence and nurse as her occupation. *Josephine Street? Why did that sound familiar? Some census report?* Maybe. On a whim, I found Helen's brother, William, conveniently on the same page of the city directory and indeed at the same address. *Aha!* Curious, I went back to the 1910 census, and he, his wife, Frances, and his youngest son, Carl, are listed as residents of the same address. Helen was not. Why did Helen move ⹂nto her brother's home in 1911? Money? How long did she stay? Agair., not sure. There were no more city directories for Helen until 1918. But for now, I had her moving from Coliseum Street to Josephine Street sometime between 1906 and 11, though probably after the 1910 census was taken.

While Helen was reestablishing herself in New Orleans, the Crockers were packing up and moving north after living in Washington, D.C., for about fifteen years. At some point, between the 1904 letter and the 1911 letters, Frank sold his shoe business in Washington, D.C., and went into a new business working for a family friend who sold art. It never paid the money that he thought it would, and Frank eventually took a job with the Lynn Shoe Company in the Boston area sometime around 1906 or 1907. The couple moved back to New England and settled into a house on the coast of Massachusetts, just north of Boston. Serving as a traveling salesman, Frank spent a lot of time away from home. Not good, according to Anna. After a stint with two different shoe companies, they again pulled up stakes.

Anna's sister, Nellie Day, who, according to Anna, was quite successful in business, needed a partner in the Springfield, Massachusetts, area. Frank and Anna moved to Springfield in October 1909, and Frank assumed that role. Additionally, Anna and Frank moved into the Day home and stayed there for another ten years. It seems logical that the desk was there during that time. Amazingly, I found a local article—including pictures of the house—on a website that focuses on the history of some of the older homes in the area. Sure enough, there is mention of the Crockers and Days in the article. *Mini road trip?*

Since Springfield, Massachusetts, is only forty-five minutes from our home in Northfield, Cathy and I went for it. *She's such a good soul.* We found the house easily enough, and it appeared just as it did in the photos in the article. It still is a beautiful home and well taken care of—we even saw a gentleman mowing the lawn. I got out to take pictures and had thoughts of pulling an Esperanza move. *Hey, you don't mind if I take a look inside your beautiful house, right? I had a desk that was in the house at one point.* In the end, the mower guy was part of a hired company, and I didn't go any further. But I did realize that this was the first location (other than Esperanza) where I knew the desk existed before it moved permanently to my side of the family. Its two main locations in Hartford and East Hartford had been torn down.

Fish or Cut Bait

It was time to look at the next batch of Crocker letters from 1911. The first letter in the group is dated January 16, 1911, almost six and a half years after the last 1904 letter. These gaps are the norm. Anna, after getting family matters out of the way, discusses the furniture being held for Helen. Keep in mind that the Crockers have perhaps held on to to her inherited possessions for almost ten years (and maybe more), and there is the subtle sense that Anna would like Helen to either "fish or cut bait," as my dad would say. In hindsight, having moved twice over the five years (Washington, D.C., to Lynn to Springfield) and bringing along Helen's belongings probably wasn't sitting well with the transient couple. Anna thanks Helen for "giving me the chair," but proceeds to offer to buy the rest of the furniture and other possessions. Old plates and glass cologne bottles are mentioned. With the artifacts in mind, Anna alludes to her father, Samuel G. Phelps, Governor Thomas Seymour, and his sister, Mary. She writes, "You know perhaps that my father loved and revered your uncle, the governor and from a little child I was told of him as a man whom I was to honor. Then I remember well the gentle lady Miss Mary Seymour." She offers to pay for the whole lot and then adds, "Would you be willing for me to pay you part now and part in six months?" *There it is.* Obviously, nothing came of this offer and the many that came later.

Accompanying this letter is a list of items. I can only deduce that Helen must have asked for such a list and Anna followed through. The list is extensive (normal knickknacks and such) and does not include the bigger furniture pieces, including the desk. Based on other letters from Anna, most of these items would remain with her and were never shipped to New Orleans. Nothing initially caught my eye until I noticed the third item from the bottom: "1 framed picture of man—I think you told me it was Julie P. Smith's husband or a relative of hers." *Wait? Julie P. Smith?* It couldn't be a coincidence. The portrait must be of Helen's surrogate father and my relative, Morris Smith. In 1911, he would have been dead for almost ten years. It makes no sense if one assumes that it was part of the Seymour inheritance from East Hartford. But I had another more logical explanation. If Helen had spent time in Esperanza after Morris's death, maybe she asked for the portrait in remembrance of him.

The next letter, dated mid-February 1911, discusses the desk after a lengthy discussion of Frank's own health issues. Formalities aside, Anna states,

> *How I wish I could see you and talk about your things. The desk in particular. I shall hate to part with it as I wrote you. But I feel that you ought to get all you can for it and that may be more than I can afford to pay. Will you not write to that Mr. Seymour and see what he will pay for it? Then let me know and if I can I will pay the same. But if you find he will give a big price for it (and I find that I cannot reach it) then I feel it must go to him; for I would not feel right to pay you less than you can get for it as much as I prize it. The lowboy not having the history connected to it.*

If I am reading between the lines here, Anna is hoping that Helen would take whatever price she could offer. Of course that never happened. The other issue is the mysterious "Mr. Seymour." *It would have been nice if there was a first name.* I spent several hours trying to come up with a real name, but there were too many male Seymours to choose from. While "that Mr. Seymour" intrigues me, I know that the desk never winds up in his hands and he is never mentioned again other than this letter. *Moving on!*

In the same letter, Anna continues, "I think you told me it was made for the first wife of Thos. Seymour. I feel I can pay you as much for that as anyone." Again, another reference to the desk's age and lineage. Anna then goes on to discuss the other possessions listed in a previous letter and alludes to Helen's willingness to divide the items between the two. She writes, "But please state in your next [letter] just what you value most and they shall be ready for you whenever you send for them." One can only assume that Helen had responded to the list of possessions that Anna had made for her. Then comes a quote that seems to put future communication (or lack of communication) into context. Anna writes, "Your letter says that if anything happened to you before they are sent I am to keep them all. I can't tell you how deeply this has touched me and how much I appreciate your wish that I should have your treasured keep sakes." *Wow!!!* Of course, she quickly follows with the necessary comment that Helen's demise is well in the future so no need for this train of thought. Ironically, Helen outlives Anna by more than ten years. The bone of contention—especially for Frank, further down the road—is the fact that Helen goes dark time and time again and, in many cases, for years. They, and perhaps rightfully so, fear the worst and that Helen has passed. Given the note quoted, it would lead Anna and Frank to believe that they are to do what they will with Helen's possessions, assuming that she has passed.

Anna continues, "Will you please send the history of the desk (and sign your name to it) just as you wrote it in my letter so that I may keep it in the desk or if I am to part with it, I will put it in one of the drawers for the Mr. Seymour who buys it." Obviously, the lineage is key to this story. It has been stated multiple times that the desk was built for Mayor Thomas Seymour's wife, Mary, around 1790, passed on to Henry Seymour, then Governor Thomas Seymour, then sister Mary Seymour, and then finally to Helen. But to adequately appraise the desk, the lineage needs to be in writing. *Basically, my mission in a nutshell—but I do tend to elaborate a bit.* Trying not to put Anna in a bad light, a clear and detailed account of the desk's provenance would surely add value to it if it were sold to the highest bidder.

In another letter, dated May 7, 1911, Anna starts, "I was very glad to get your letter and will answer at once as I know you want to decide about the desk." Again, this letter is the first letter to reference the Seymour desk specifically, and based on the tone, it appears that Helen is willing to sell it. I really wish I had Helen's responses to Anna's inquiries. It always seems that I am trying to make solid interpretations with only half the information. Was Helen just tired of the whole thing and selling to a friend and family member would solve the problem? Was money a significant issue in Helen's life? Not sure. Thankfully (at least for my purposes), Anna says that she cannot afford the piece and writes, "It is a valuable heirloom and only people of means can afford to buy such." Anna continues, suggesting that they sell it to the Atheneum (now known as the Wadsworth Atheneum Museum of Art) in Hartford, a newly created museum. She mentions that selling it to the Atheneum would be more cost-effective than shipping it to New Orleans. She then states, "It seems to me that a desk belonging to the first mayor of the city, used also by a governor well-beloved and honored in his day, would be a relic the Hartford people would prize." She then backs off slightly by mentioning that it is only a suggestion and that she would be happy to crate it and ship it once she has a reliable address. Anna follows up with the price of a lowboy and dressing table and quickly reminds Helen that these are "not hard wood." *No interpretation needed here.*

The next letter is actually a postcard dated August 31, 1911. Short and sweet. The postcard is of the Springfield Armory in Springfield, Massachusetts. Anna is again concerned about Helen's health since she hasn't heard from her in a while. She writes, "Hoping that your silence is only on account of your being too busy to write." It must have been gut wrenching for Anna, who clearly worries about her close friend and her lack of constant communication—at least by early 1900s standards. Today, with communication so immediate, we can usually get to the root of a relative lack of communication within a day or two. *Sorry. My phone crapped the bed. Just got a new one.* In Anna's case, we're talking months and even years of silence. At this point, she's assuming the worst. There is no mention of the desk or any of the Seymour-inherited artifacts on the postcard. Anna simply wants to know if her friend is still alive.

Alive and Well

Helen was, in fact, quite alive, though her life mission apparently shifted significantly as she moved from nursing to working at institutes for children and women living on the fringes of society. Multiple city directories listed her as the matron of Protestant Orphans Home on Magazine Street in 1918 through 1922. The 1920 census confirms this as well. These homes or asylums were commonplace from the mid-1800s to the mid-1900s, especially for children. New Orleans was continually plagued with periods of rampant malaria and yellow fever, which killed thousands. By default, there were many orphaned children, and this ultimately spurred a need for housing. So-called asylums, though they have a different connotation today, were locations for homeless children and women. The Protestant Orphans Home was one such place, and Helen Seymour would serve as its supervisor—as well as two other asylums—over a span of twenty years. In 1918, she would have been sixty-five years old. *Ugh.*

In 1922, again based on city directories, Helen moved from the Protestant Orphans Home to the Milne Home for Destitute Girls, where she served as superintendent. It was with this job that I hit pay dirt. In one of my deep searches, I found a website called Milne Developmental Services, and it had an extensive historical document of the agency embedded within it. As I scrolled through the document, I came across the following paragraph:

The fall of 1921 brought about an opportunity to purchase the Mioton property at 1913 Gentilly Road for the sum of $60,000. After negotiating a loan for this purpose, Milne Home was moved from Kenner to a site on Gentilly Boulevard by April 1922. That same month Miss Helen Seymour, a graduate nurse with ten years' experience as head of the Seventh Street Orphan Asylum, became the superintendent.

Holy Sugar Pops! I let out such a major snort from my couch upon reading this that Cathy looked up from her own laptop and asked if I was okay. This sense of accomplishment was not to the same extent as finding a connection between Helen Seymour and Anna Crocker, but it was close.

This one paragraph clarified two things. First, Helen Seymour was indeed a trained nurse, as I had strongly suspected earlier. Second, the gap of time between 1912 and 1918 was filled. She served as a matron at the Protestant Orphans Home between 1912 and April 1922 and was then hired by the Milne Home and started in 1923. An added gem to this epiphany was a photo a few paragraphs later. It is of a group of young kids with a few adults among them. While I couldn't be sure, it seems likely that Helen Seymour is one of the adults among the young girls in the photo. The date, December 1923, fits within the chronology.

For whatever reason, Helen left that location. I found nothing in the referenced document explaining why. *I don't like unanswered whys.*

The Milne

While Helen's work at the Milne Home for Destitute Women and her abrupt departure puzzled me, it was my efforts on the Williams Research Center website that brought the delayed trip to New Orleans forward again from the back burner. Researching Helen's jobs in New Orleans, I fell upon the mother lode of material, including photos. It is within this collection that I found a reference to Helen Seymour's hiring that I documented earlier.

But now, it was the photos that enticed me. I had spent countless hours piecing together this woman's life, but I still had no idea what she looked like. As I mentioned, I found a digital group photo from the Milne digital collection around the appropriate time period, but I still wasn't sure that Helen was in it. It was at this point that I decided a quick jaunt to New Orleans and some time at the Williams Research Center was in order. *Wait. You're traveling to New Orleans from Northfield, Massachusetts, solely to find a photo of this mystery woman?* Ummmm. Yeah.

The Williams Research Center, as part of the Historic New Orleans Collection, lies in the historic French Quarter on Chartres Street, just two streets over from Bourbon Street. The Williams Research Center was no different from the previous research adventures documented earlier in the book. There was a cart set aside with my name on it covered in several of the same boxes I'd seen countless times over the last three years. *Oh, goody!* The materials in the boxes were extensive, and as predicted, most dealt with the Milne Home for Destitute Women. And there were a ton of pictures of women. *Yeah!* But many of them didn't have names or dates. *Booo!* I was able to establish, though, that most of the photos were of young women who lived at the facility. After reading some of the other written materials, I learned that these young women were not orphaned or homeless like many of those at the other private facilities, but they had been placed there for mental capacity reasons. Having worked in public schools for most of my professional teaching career, I knew of countless young adults who—for a variety of reasons—were placed outside of their homes and, by default, outside of the local school system. The Milne Home was much the same. These women had some sort of mental disability, and their home situation was not suitable for adequate care.

There were lots and lots of photos of these women doing various inside and outside chores (cooking, textiles, animal care, etc.), and I can only assume that they served as some sort of promotional component, given that these types of homes survived on private donations only.

Additionally, there were a few photos of much older women who didn't look like clients but rather women who worked there. Could Helen have been in one of these photos? *Definitely.* Did I know for sure? *No.* I found no photo with her name associated with it. *Bummer. Moving on!*

Fortunately, I did find a few hints as to why Helen Seymour only lasted just over a year (1922-23) at this location. Initially, I assumed that she'd simply found a better job. But that probably wasn't the case.

The first clue was a district civil court case summary dated January 1923—meaning the actual case was tried sometime in 1922. I found Helen's name referenced in the summary, so I assume that she testified. It seems that one of the Milne Home's clients went home for a spell, and the parents and extended family wanted to keep her at home rather than have her return to the facility. The home was suing the parents for her return based on a law that was written several years before outlining the treatment of "feeble-minded" people in the state of Louisiana. The judge agreed with the Milne Home, and the woman was, I suppose, returned there. I did learn later that the parents appealed the case to the Louisiana Supreme Court and won.

But what could this court case have done to Helen Seymour's psyche? Could she have testified for the Milne Home though her heart wasn't in it? Perhaps she supported the parents' rights in this case. Ultimately, though, it was one written sentence that perhaps made everything else moot.

Surprisingly, I was not the first person to dig through these files. Very late in the process, I found one sheet of legal paper with a bunch of notes accompanying an old-time ledger book that contained minutes from the Milne Home board of directors' meetings. Unfortunately, this particular book only went up to 1919. I found no others. Thankfully, the person doing research had written a note on the legal paper that read, "Miss Helen Seymour Apr. 15, 1922—Board not satisfied with her." It appears that the researcher was listing all the previous superintendents of the Home with any notes that he or she could find in the minutes. *So many questions.* Where was the ledger that would corroborate this statement? What caused the board to be dissatisfied? Was she fired or did she resign? Was the civil case a part of their dissatisfaction? Not sure. But it does seem to fit with her short stay at the Milne Home.

In about two hours, I had trudged through all of the documents, newspaper clippings, and photos. While I still hadn't found a picture of Helen Seymour, I did know a little bit more about her, and she became even more human to me. It's rare that we don't have a run-in with "The Man" at some point in our professional careers, and in some cases, this can lead to a parting of ways. While I was not sure of the exact nature of Helen's problems with the Milne board, it did ultimately lead to another similar job that lasted far longer. From 1924 to 1928, she was the matron of the Home for Homeless. Perhaps it was a mutual separation for the benefit for all parties.

Dark, Again

After 1928, I found no more references in city directories, and I suppose that she had retired from any official social service. In the 1930 census, she was again living as a boarder with two others and their two hosts on 1440 Camp Street.

In the meantime, Anna kept reaching out. In the next letter in my possession, September 8, 1920, Anna and Frank Crocker were now living at 72 Green Acre Avenue in Longmeadow, Massachusetts, which is just south of their previous house in Springfield. They, according to Anna, had recently moved there, and again I assume that the desk—as well as Helen's other items—was still with them. The next letter, the last Anna Crocker one in my care, was dated October 8, 1922, and it carries the same themes. Helen had gone dark on Anna. Both letters also are quite short compared to the other letters in my possession—only a paragraph long. In the 1920 letter, Anna comments, "I want to write you a letter; but wish to be sure you receive it." Yes, she indeed underlined for emphasis. I am not sure the letter made it to Helen, but the 1922 letter does perhaps answer that.

The 1922 letter is the last in my possession from Anna to Helen, and it's also quick and easy. She comments that "It is a long time since I heard from you." Without any of Helen's letters, I do not have an idea of the time frame Anna is talking about, but I can only surmise it had been years rather than months.

I have no correspondence after this letter, at least from Anna. Unfortunately, Anna Crocker died on June 7, 1928.

I pity Anna's plight as she neared the end. On one hand, she wanted to do right by her relative and dear friend and do with Helen's inheritance as Helen wished. On the other, Anna wanted to make sure all of the family heirlooms got passed down the line appropriately. Helen, based solely on Anna's words, frustrated the heck out of both Crockers. *If you're nodding right now because you also have a similar relative/friend, you're not alone.* Keep in mind that if my math and logical interpretation of the desk's movements are correct, then the Crockers held on to the desk and other possessions for Helen for almost thirty years. *I'd be frustrated, too.*

For Helen, 1928 is significant as well. Based on my research, this was the year she stopped working at the Home for Homeless Young Women and did not return to the field again. While she might have retired from the group home settings, she continued to nurse well into the 1930s. She also moved several more times.

In terms of her relationship with Anna Crocker, it's tough to say what was true or not. I simply do not have letters going the other way to verify anything. But there appear to be huge gaps of time when Helen would not write. Years upon years of silence. I initially attributed her dysfunctional life to my dad's character reference. Being in a situation to write on a timely basis might be asking a lot if she was living on the fringe of society. But that was far from the case. Not by a long shot. She was gainfully employed through much of the time in question, and in many cases, she served in a supervisory position. She had the means and even the motive (it was her furniture, after all) to write Anna and Frank, for that matter. So why didn't she?

Assuming that there weren't horrible issues with mail delivery and she had the correct addresses for the most part, it could be that she was busy as hell. *Yeah. I ain't buying it either.* We've all been in those situations, but for years on end? Reaching, I believe that it was her health keeping her silent, and specifically her mental health. It would explain lots of things. One, her possible addiction to opioids that would have been the prescribed medication for mental health issues. Two, the countless examples of others asking or commenting about her health without any specific mention of a certain ailment. *Ding! Ding! Ding! Major red flag, says the educator of over 40 years.* Three, the simple fact that she didn't write. *Mental health coping strategy 101. Separate oneself from those things that create one's demons.* Again, I'm not buying it totally, but it could explain a lot.

Unfortunately, with Anna now gone and Helen still in New Orleans (I don't think she was swinging by anytime soon to pick up her stuff), it was now Anna's husband, Frank, who had to pick up the ball and try to deal with the Seymour desk.

9

Frankly, My Dear Helen...

Frank Crocker was immediately an intriguing character to me, based only on his and Anna's letters to Helen and any other information I could find about the couple. In my dad's eyes, Frank comes off as a self-serving jerk who's seemingly doing everything in his power to sell the desk for Helen between 1928 and 1930—and perhaps hoping to keep a broker's fee in the process. As mentioned, my dad had written some notes relating to many aspects of the desk on May 8, 2019, a year and a half before his death. One of the notes reads, "There was an increasing mistrust from Helen Seymour to Anna and then Frank Crocker. I get the feeling that Frank may have been an entrepreneur and not above trying to make a buck." After reading the same letters for the first time, I initially came to the same conclusion. But over time and multiple readings later, I softened on that view. I simply couldn't go as far as Dirck goes—implicating the two (Anna and Frank) in some sort of conspiracy. Anna's letters were too personal to make that stretch. While Frank's were definitely more formal and focused mostly on the desk's sale, I couldn't help but feel some sympathy for the plight of the widower.

Part of the deal of any marriage is that you get the other's baggage, which includes their bloodline. The Crockers were no different. Picture this. Frank marries Anna, and at some point, he's given the responsibility of holding on to his wife's relative's inherited possessions—a woman whom he barely knows and who goes dark for years on end. Frank, for quite a long time, watches this charade from the backseat and is probably none too happy to inherit the same charade upon his wife's death. While these situations are part of the deal of marriage, this may be a bit too much. Still, even with the few letters I have, Frank clearly missed Anna deeply and wanted to do the right thing by her. I'm not giving him a total free pass, but he was simply looking to wash his hands of the whole mess. If he could make a buck off the deal, then so be it. I wonder, if I was put in a similar situation, would I act any differently? Probably not.

Unlike Anna's letters, which had some fleeting comments about the desk, Frank's letters focus extensively on it. Thus, summarizing each letter individually seems appropriate. Since the majority of the letters between 1928 and 1930 are from Frank Crocker to Helen Seymour, I'll simply head each passage with a date. With the random other few, I'll give more information as needed.

October 14, 1928

Obviously, the most eye-opening point of the letter is the date—almost six years to the day since the last letter from Anna in 1922. I'm not sure whether there was correspondence between the two parties (the Crockers and Helen) over that time period.

The initial intent of the letter is clear. He's informing Helen of Anna's passing the previous April. Whether Helen knew of Anna's death prior to this letter, I am not sure. He states, "I have been given the above as your address, but before writing <u>fully</u>. I must know if this address is correct & mail would reach you in <u>person</u>." The tone of this letter is very different from Anna's. Was he merely not the touchy-feely person that Anna was? Or was he simply angry at this long-lasting situation? I can only imagine that as a husband for over thirty-five years, he always got an earful of Anna's frustration second-hand but had no real recourse. *Don't try to fix this problem, Frank, and simply listen to me vent. Been there, done that.* He also had a habit of underlining words for emphasis. Today, it would be perceived as a total jerk move, especially among friends, but perhaps in the early 1900s it was quite a normal emphasis.

October 24, 1928

Per Frank's statement in the October 14 letter, this was a far more extensive correspondence—at seven pages in length. His frustration is immediately apparent when he spouts off that he received a letter from Carlotta Smith (Lottie) instead of Helen directly. While Frank was clearly peeved that he was working through an intermediary rather than Helen herself, I was ecstatic. Here was yet another connection to the Smiths and Ellsworths. While I, at that point, totally understood the link between Lottie and Helen (and probably Anna as well), poor Frank had no clue. *Should have stayed off your cell phone, Frank, and paid more attention to your wife. Oh, wait...*

Whatever the case, Frank Crocker was not happy about the third-party interference. Perhaps, while he ostensibly had Helen's best interests in mind, he was covertly scheming to sell off the desk and give the rest of Helen's possessions to his grandkids as his wife had requested. Anna's request was based upon early letters with Helen, but more importantly, Frank probably had to wonder whether Helen was even alive at that point following years of no contact. At least, up until this most recent letter from Helen. *Whaaaat? You're still kicking?*

He states in the first paragraph, "I was thankful to know I could get into communication with you & get a letter from you. I had a letter from your friend, Charlotta (sp) Smith & as it contained <u>no</u> explanation of any kind as to her writing instead of <u>yourself</u>, I thought best to get in direct contact with you personally." Again the underlines irk me, but perhaps it may have been the norm.

He then continues by playing the wonderful husband: "First, I wish to act for my beloved Anna as I know she would wish me to. And second, to assist you all possible would be her wish." I have no doubt of his love for his recently deceased wife—and hers for him as well—but it is very convenient to do as "she wishes" when she's dead. Are his suggestions her wishes or perhaps his alone? He continues, "The arrangement was that you were to compensate Anna by giving her the choice of a chair or lowboy & that if you never sent for the things left with her [Anna] they were to revert automatically to Anna." I can only think of the age-old expression: *Possession is nine tenths the law."* If true, he has a great case. This becomes the gist of all future correspondence.

It is important to mention at this point that the Crockers were not that well off. Frank had moved from job to job over thirty years, and, at the point of his initial letter, was working at a bank. Perhaps the request shifts from doing a relative a favor to finding out how much he could get for some of the more expensive and historically significant items. I honestly don't blame him. Case in point, he states, "After some 10 years or so, Anna decided to accept the lowboy as her own & sold it when we were in circumstances that made it rather necessary." Financially, it made sense, but morally and historically, it must have made Helen squirm. Ironically, I believe that Helen's own financial issues drove the negotiations of the sale of the Seymour desk that was about to come. But matters get more cantankerous when Frank continues,

> This was after we had gone to Longmeadow [western Massachusetts]. As the years came & went, & Anna could get no word from you. Some letters coming back marked 'not found', 'returned to writer' & etc. *None ever answered.* After every effort had been made to get into communication with you, Anna was forced to conclude that you were no longer living. For about five years before Anna went she had naturally concluded & felt that the things had come into her ownership & from that had governed herself accordingly.

There it is in a nutshell, and I don't really criticize Anna or Frank, by default, for their assumptions—they had the returned letters to prove it. It wouldn't be a stretch to assume that Helen had passed, given the general lack of social networks back in the day.

Their belief that Helen had passed should have ended my eventual ownership of the Seymour desk in 1928. According to Frank, Anna, on her proverbial death bed, had willed the desk to her niece. It seems that Anna wanted to keep the desk in the family, and because she hadn't heard from Helen in a long time, passed it on to the next generation. The Crockers had no children, and her niece seemed like a logical option to inherit. In my mind, all of this makes sense and I, like Frank, would have been a little put off by the reappearance of long-lost Helen. *Oh, hey, about the desk? That crazy woman from New Orleans is apparently still alive.*

In finishing this paragraph, Frank states, "I feel I should wait for your answer to this letter before attempting to make any move in the matter." Thankfully, Frank did wait to hear from Helen in terms of Anna's wishes before passing on the Seymour possessions, or I wouldn't be sitting at it right now.

In a concluding paragraph, Frank states,

> *She would wish me to do what was right & I want you to write to me just what you feel I should do under the circumstances in question. I may add, that to myself hearing from you was like a voice from the beyond & I am more troubled over this unhappy condition than I can express. It is beyond my comprehension why you did not answer this letter which you <u>did</u> receive <u>5 years ago</u> when she [Anna] wrote to you of my recovery from a long dangerous illness. <u>Any</u> letter sent to Anna or myself at Springfield or Longmeadow, would have reached her or myself & all this unhappiness would not exist.*

This last paragraph, as well as the rest of the letter, begs the question: What are Frank's motivations here? I am sure that he simply wants all of this to go away. Anna's passing probably allowed for a light at the end of the tunnel. All of the materials, including the Seymour desk, would be doled out to relatives per Anna's wishes. On the other hand, with Helen's reappearance, he also felt obligated to at least follow through with Anna's historical wishes and make sure that Helen was a part of the decision. On that note, he officially ends the letter with an afterthought. He writes, "You speak of wishing to sell the desk. What price do you feel you should wish for same in selling?" Now, the real fun begins.

November 13, 1928

The first thing that immediately comes to mind with this letter is the difference in tone. Frank is writing on Federal Land Bank of Springfield letterhead, where he mentions he is now employed. He is far more contrite and briefer than in the previous letter almost a month earlier. Apparently, Helen had sent him a letter that he received on November 9 and now he was responding in kind with less angst. He states, "Do not in any way distress yourself in answering the long letter I wrote you. My heart aches for you in your sorrows & troubles, & may God help you & give you comfort. I shall wait patiently until such time as you find it entirely easy to write me fully." *Wow!*

A couple things are clear. Helen wrote a real bummer of a letter that he received on November 9 as a response to his scathing letter from October 24. *More of Helen's health issues?* Again, I feel for Frank in his predicament. How much effort does he put into this, given Helen's limited correspondence over the year? But apparently, he was willing to give her the benefit of the doubt, allow her to digest the issue, and then give him some guidance. You would think that from there, the turnaround in terms of correspondence would be relatively quick. *Not!*

November 22, 1929

The first thing that stands out with this letter is the date. It has been more than a year since the last letter in my possession. Was there other correspondence between the two, or was this the only connection in a year? Gone is the accommodating tone of the November 1928 letter, and back is the curt annoyance from the October 1928 letter. Frank jumps right in with "I was pleased to have your letter & regret more than I can express that you do not feel Mrs. Crocker (no longer Anna) made every possible effort to get into communication with you." *Ouch!* But it gets worse as he states that, according to Helen, she never received any letters from Anna or Frank since 1922. *Strange, because I now have a few of these letters and can only assume that they reached their mark.* He continues in the next paragraph, "In 1928, a communication was received by me from a Charlotta Smith, an entire stranger, a person I had never known or heard from, or of, & through her I got into communication with you." *Same old story!* He continues,

> Now my dear lady, I know that Mrs. Crocker repeatedly wrote [to] you, _af-_ _ter_ the letter you _did_ receive. Some were returned by post office dept., others never came back, & at _all_ times, she was much worried & troubled never to be able to hear from you. She at least two (2) years before she went that recovery was impossible & during that time she arranged her affairs with the belief that her connection to you with regards [to] the things turned over to her by you was _a closed chapter._ That you should believe she did not make every possible effort to get into communication with you is most unjust.

Boom! Having been down the ugly road of misinterpreted *text wars*, I feel for him. He probably heard endlessly about Anna's worry for her dear friend Helen and how she feared the worst when they wrote her letters with no response.

He then changes directions by responding to the questions and points from Helen. He mentions the list of the things currently held by the Crockers that Anna created eighteen years prior. Of course, he goes on to mention that a lot of the items have been "disposed of" or distributed to others per Anna's instructions in her will. He states, "I will at once let you know of anything she did not dispose of."

Finally, there is mention of the desk and the chair previously discussed. He writes, "Please advise me plainly if you wish to sell the desk for $250 or less, & also the price of the chair at the least you would wish to accept for that & I will see what can be done about them. Please state [the] history of the desk, to whom it belonged, & used by & its age." Even with the limited letters that I have from this point on, this aspect of the desk (and the chair) bothers me. The Crockers have held on to these items over multiple decades with no clear directive, and now Helen wants Frank to do the legwork to sell them. Keep in mind that $250 would be about $4000 today. They had value. He continues along in this vein,

> I am most unhappy & perplexed over the existing condition. [I know not what condition he's talking about?] If it was possible I would send the value of the desk & chair to you myself but I can not. If you will let me know the least amount you would wish to accept for the desk & chair. I will see what I can do in obtaining the amt you name & send to you if I can so arrange.

He ends the letter with, "I send to you my sympathy for your ill health & your eye troubles. I enclose [a] stamped addressed envelope for reply." Again, it seems that Helen always lets others know of her health issues as if to justify her lack of correspondence, but wisely, Frank was smart enough to include a self-addressed envelope in the mix. Helen couldn't neglect that, no matter her health.

Western Union Telegraph Message from Frank Crocker to Helen Seymour—December 2, 1929

Apparently, Frank got tired of messing around with unanswered and/or undelivered letters and of being accused of not communicating with Helen, so he telegraphed a message dealing with the same chair and desk. It looks roughly as such, minus the official letterhead:

MISS HELEN E SEYMOUR
1612 PRYTANIA ST NEW ORLEANS LA
TELEGRAPH ME COLLECT HERE IF YOU WISH TO SELL
CHAIR FOR ONE HUNDRED DOLLARS THINK I CAN SELL IT
WRITE AT ONCE HISTORY OF DESK AND IF YOU WISH TO
SEE FOR TWO HUNDRED FIFTY DOLLARS AND I WILL SEE
YOU I CAN SELL
CF CROCKER CARE FEDERAL LAND BANK

It reads more like a text message, but that was the point. Quick, easy, and to the point—especially because you were charged by the letter. I applaud Frank for his efforts.

December 3, 1929

The Western Union telegraph was apparently received, because Frank writes, "I had your wire this AM reading sell chair $100 [about $1700 today], will write at once." I assume that he is referring to the person whom he's selling the chair to. He continues, "I will be able to send you [a] check for $100 in about 10 days, for the chair." Then he switches to the desk and says, "It will be most important that you have already written me giving [the] history of [the] desk. To whom it belonged & was used by & that you will sell for $250 & also state as nearly as you can its age." I find his apparent need for information about the desk a bit humorous. Based on previous letters, Anna knew all about the legacy of the desk and probably repeated the same information to Frank over their time together. Of course, he probably only half listened and never retained the full story. I guess the interplay between husband and wife has passed the test of time. *Who's the idiot now, Frank?*

December 6, 1929

This is a quick turnaround from the previous letter, and its contents explain the follow-up. Frank writes, "In my letter of a few days ago I believe I wrote to you I would send money for the chair in about 10 days. I am just in communication from the lady who purchased same, informing it was not convenient to send a check until January 2nd as her funds were low & she did not receive her quarterly income until Jan. 1st." He goes on to mention that he truly trusts this woman, but if Helen had reservations, then he would front the money himself. He again mentions the need for information about the desk and finishes with, "If I sell the desk, it will be a spot cash transaction."

December 14, 1929

This is a quick note, specifically about the desk. Frank writes, "I am writing to hear from the customer on the desk & trust when I do it will be a 'sale'. I expect to hear by Monday next & at once advise you." Apparently, he had made headway with both the chair and the desk.

December 30, 1929

This is a lengthy letter from Frank with a separate page of questions. My initial feelings are that he is pulling out all the stops to find a buyer for the desk but is a little frustrated by Helen's continual lack of communication. Helen is now at 1440 Camp Street as a boarder. I even found census records verifying her location, and she remained there throughout the remainder of this two-way slugfest.

In this letter, Frank states much the same as he does in previous letters. He needs information about the history of the desk, but this time he adds a new element to the issue. There may be two desks out there. He states that he has a potential buyer, but he continues, "My customer has been informed there is a Governor Seymour desk owned in Hartford or East Hartford is a bit afraid. Your desk is not the genuine Governor Seymour desk & unless the Governor had 2 desks, you & I know the desk my customer knows of must be bogus and a humbug." *Been there. Done that.* This is the same conspiracy theory that I mentioned in a previous chapter. *No worries, Frank. You have the Governor Thomas Seymour desk.*

But Frank did not have the same information that I had, and he needed help from Helen. I don't blame him at all for being persistent about the desk's lineage. Much of the rest of the letter describes how Helen should present the information requested by the potential buyer. All answers should be thorough and written on a separate piece of paper rather than on the original questions listed below. They (Frank and the buyer) wanted an official document that basically clarified the authenticity of the desk. While the issue of a second desk was moot (as explained previously), the information requested was perfectly reasonable and valuable to both Frank and the buyer as well as to me. Unfortunately, at least on my end, the information was never recorded officially or was lost over time. Frank must have rolled his eyes when the potential buyer asked for such detailed information. *She can't even answer my own letters. What makes you think she's going to give a detailed response to these questions?*

January 6, 1930

In this letter, Frank immediately declares that he has enclosed a $100 check for the chair. *Good boy, Frank.* He then states, "Please sign & return enclosed invoice." *One piece of furniture sold, and one to go.* He continues, "Your 3rd inst [?] letter received & you have given me just what I need to sell the Gov. Seymour desk, & I will go right at it & trust to sell the same in the near future." *Grrr. My kingdom for that same information.* I can assume that it reaffirmed the existence of one Governor Seymour desk or he would have more questions.

He then wishes Helen well in relation to her health before he gets to the heart of the letter—the question of Anna's integrity over the last twenty-five years. Without Helen's letter, I can only assume that she had issues with Anna's efforts in trying to communicate with her about the Seymour possessions. *Same old, same old!* Again, I'm sympathetic to Frank's dilemma—defending his wife's memory, and justifiably so, while also trying to sell the desk for his wife's friend and relative. Since I've read many of Anna's letters to Helen and know very well that she tried endlessly to communicate with Helen and get instructions about her possessions, I can only imagine the anger that coursed through Frank's veins. He states,

> *You must know she was a pure clean soul, ever with pure thoughts & actions, with the nearest sense of justice of any human person living or dead & I am so unhappy over your feeling you can or wish to criticize her action in any possible way that it has caused me many unhappy hours, over your feeling that she had or did anything in any way that which was not entirely honorable.*

He was not a happy man, and maybe, at this point, he was totally done with this whole deal. He'd sold the chair for her and sent her a check, and now he simply needed to do the same with the desk.

January 6, 1930

This is a very short and poignant note mailed on the same day as the previous letter. It was probably sent in the afternoon and obviously after receiving Helen's wire. It reads,

> *Dear Miss Seymour*
> *I am just in receipt of your wire reading, "Do not sell the desk until you hear from me."*
> *I received the history statement of the desk this am & wrote to you at once (this am). I will wait to hear from you before I do anything further about selling the desk.*
> *Hastily, CF Crocker*

In one short message, I begin to wonder whether this is the first inkling that the desk may be heading in my direction. On the other side, Frank must be totally confused.

January 9, 1930

Frank acknowledges that he received her instructions to hold off on his sale attempts, and he has telegraphed his potential buyer. He then states, "Naturally I am in a very uncomfortable position with the customer I fully believe intended buying the desk, however I do not see how the conditions admit of my doing anything but accepting with the best grace possible your wishes in the matter." *Amen, brother!!!* Basically, he put in enormous effort to sell the desk at the best price possible, but at the eleventh hour, Helen pulled the plug.

Bill of Sale—May 7, 1930

Without any further ado, it reads:

State of Louisiana
Parish of Orleans
City of New Orleans
Before me, the undersigned authority, personally came and appeared, Miss Helena E. Seymour, of age and a resident of the city of New Orleans, deposes and says:
That she is the owner of a certain antique desk, now in the possession of Mr. C. F. Crocker, of Springfield, Massachusetts; that, as owner of the said antique desk, for and in consideration of the price and sum of Five Dollars ($5.00) cash, she has sold the said antique desk to Mr. W. W. Ellsworth, of Esperanza Farm, New Hartford, Connecticut; and that this affidavit will show the ownership of said desk in the said Mr. W. W. Ellsworth and will be his authority to procure the said desk from the said Mr. C. F. Crocker.
Signed—Helena E. Seymour

Sworn to and authorized before me at New Orleans, LA, this 7th of May, 1930
Signed—Anna Naumann—Notary Public
My commission expires at my death.

With this notarized document, my family owned the desk. W. W. Ellsworth (William Webster) was my great-great-grandfather and the great-grandson of Noah Webster and Oliver Ellsworth. The immediate thing that jumps out at me is the price. Five dollars, which would be about $80.00 today. Without any documentation between Helen and the Ellsworths, I tend to feel that this was an attempt to hold the desk for William Ellsworth and that he would pay her the remaining balance later. Ecstatic that I had finally found the specific link that tied the desk from the Seymours to the Ellsworths, I had so many other emotions.

On one hand, after spending a lot of time looking for some sort of official documentation specific to the desk, I finally had it. But on the other hand, nothing else makes sense. Why was there a three-month gap between the January letter and the sale if Helen asked Frank to back off? Why are the Ellsworths involved now rather than much earlier in the process? Was the desk really something my family wanted at this point, or were they simply easing this burden off of Helen, since the Ellsworths, now in Esperanza, were a lot closer to Longmeadow, Massachusetts, than New Orleans? No matter. The official transition would be right around the corner. *Or would it?*

June 6, 1930

This letter came a month after the bill of sale was official, and it is clear that Frank has no idea that Helen has sold the desk, at least on paper, to the Ellsworths. Perhaps she never let Frank know that she had a bill of sale written up and notarized in New Orleans. So he writes to her, stating that he has one more potential client:

As regards sale of the desk I have to advise you that I have a customer who lives in Boston whom I am daily expecting to complete sale of the desk & is coming to Longmeadow. His son has thoroughly inspected the desk. His father is to come & complete the sale during the next week or at longest 10 days. Your letter changing price of $250 to $300, comes just in time to save complications as to price, & I shall expect to send you that figure $300 when the sale is complete.

Whaaaat? Helen has signed off on a notarized affidavit for all intents and purposes, selling under the legs of Frank's work to William Ellsworth, but she still sends a letter to Frank (he mentioned that he received her letter on the second of June) informing him that the asking price is now $300. *What game is she playing here?* Without her letters and the dates to go with them, I don't know whether she was playing both sides or the mail system was just really slow. She could have written a letter prior to the sale of the desk to the Ellsworths, and Frank had only just received it.

June 20, 1930

In this letter, Frank writes, "I was pleased to have your letter on arrival home last evening. I regret to advise my customer who lives in Boston has been unable to come to Longmeadow (outside of Springfield) as yet but I am expecting him daily & just as soon as he has been here. I trust to be able to send you a check for $300, as per my last letter to you & I have agreed to hold the desk for him." Apparently, the ruse continued. Clearly in her recent letter to him, Helen did not dissuade him away from the potential buyer, even though she had sold the desk to the Ellsworths. Perhaps she was playing both fields. Sell the desk to the Ellsworths out of a moral obligation, but if she could get top dollar, well, so be it. Frank ends with "I trust you will be in better health when this reaches you." Without Helen's letters, I am just guessing, but it seems that she continually packs every letter with her mental and physical ailments. Though it has been almost 100 years since this letter was written, people who need to tell everyone about their poor health or recent problems have existed forever.

Letter from Helen Seymour to Mrs. W.W. Ellsworth (Nellie Smith Ellsworth)—August 5, 1930

This is the first letter in my possession from Helen. All my previous thoughts about Helen were based upon others responding to her letters. Speculation at best. She immediately vents on Frank. She begins, "Mr. Crocker has kept me so upset and worried that I did not know what to do. I wrote to him about sending the desk to you and he wrote on the 6th of June that he had arranged to sell it to a gentleman in Boston and would send me a check for $300.00 in a week or ten days. I waited. He wrote again June 20th and said the gentleman had been delayed in coming to Longmeadow but was expecting him everyday." Indeed, she is playing the money game between two parties. She has an agreement with the Ellsworths, but she's still holding out hope to get $300 from the mysterious buyer. Only after she continues do I truly understand her predicament. She is broke, and $300 would solve that problem, at least temporarily. She writes, "Early in June I went to work, nursed a bed patient for six weeks 7:30 to 1:30. Should have stopped at four weeks. Had to stay in bed two days and now go very slow. I only got 5 dollars [about $90 today] a week, was glad to get it—needed many things." As mentioned, while she is no longer working for the Home of Homeless Young Women, she is still nursing to make ends meet. Alas, she was seventy-seven at the time and Social Security would not become law for another five years.

She continues by mentioning that Mr. Crocker indeed knows about Ellsworth's sale, but she seems okay with the prospect of working both sides. She writes, "I have written to Mr. Crocker and told him to let me know at once if he had the money for me. If not, I wanted the desk sent to you as soon as possible. Will send the letters and paper from the notary." This last line did answer a small question for me. How and when did some of these letters to Helen from Frank wind up in the desk after the fact? Helen must have sent them and the notarized bill of sale at a later point.

She shifts gears in the letter and begins to talk about the Smith sisters (Carlotta/Lottie, Nellie, and Fanny) and their connection to Helen as an adopted member of the family. It appears that Lottie has been sending Helen checks monthly. She writes, "Carlotta wrote me such a dear letter. I hope she realized how much I appreciated her kindness—but you know, Nellie, I could not take money from her every month when I owe her so much already." For the first time, it begins to make some sense in terms of Helen's desk dilemma. If the Smith sisters had been supporting Helen over the years, perhaps this was a way to compensate them for past, and likely future, installments.

August 5, 1930

To my knowledge, this is the last letter between Frank and Helen, at least in my possession. Clearly, he's a little miffed at Helen (as written at the end of the letter) and at himself for not tying up his sale of the desk. Then another twist is added to the mix. He writes, "I communicated with the well-known author, lecturer, and collector of fine antiques Wallace Nutting."

When Frank dropped Nutting's name, I was immediately intrigued. This was no slouch trying to buy the desk. Wallace Nutting is a name I know quite well, simply because I own two of his books. *Well, I inherited the books when my dad died.* I had given the books to my dad (a renowned furniture guru in his own right) as Christmas gifts years earlier. The books are basically an encyclopedia of furniture in the 1700s and 1800s, with hundreds of pictures of furniture of all shapes and sizes. A close replica of the Seymour desk is in the book with a listed date of 1790, giving more credence to the age of my desk.

Frank continues, "He [Nutting] informed he had just purchased for himself a fine old tambour desk, but that he had a number of friends whom would quite likely wish to own the one I have." One of those friends was the same person whom Frank mentioned in a previous letter, when he talked about the son viewing the desk but that the father had not had the opportunity to venture from Boston to Springfield. Frank hadn't heard from the person in over three weeks (thus the time lapse in the letters in my possession), and he reached out to Nutting again to hopefully push things along. He continues,

> *After waiting a suitable time, I put the desk in hands of a very able Longmeadow antique seller who has many wealthy principals & he at once had a man & woman (husband & wife) come to Longmeadow & view & examine the desk. They are wealthy & important people, were much taken or pleased with the desk & when they entered their car to go away plainly said I would hear from them shortly.*

Like before, this led to nothing. Frank waited "a few weeks," heard nothing, and was clearly frustrated. He would never make it as a car salesman. He then went on to detail multiple similar examples of potential buyers with similar results. He shifts gears and states, "Now dear lady I understand you are desirous of having the money for the desk & I am no less desirous of disposing of the same, I assure you I am doing all possible to do so & am very confident with patience for a time longer I will." Slowly and delicately, his frustration with her previous letter begins to seep out. I can only assume that her previous letter had touched a nerve. He then moves on to the Ellsworth issue. He writes, "If I do not & you dispose of it to the lady Mrs. Ellsworth, what would be my standing in the sale to her. Before this is done, it would be necessary for me to know how I would be remunerated in such an event." *Remunerated? Remunerated for what?* Why would he be involved if the Ellsworths would pay Helen directly? Unless he anticipated a middle-man fee. He continues trying to salvage a sale from his end. He writes,

I have my vacation shortly & will spend a week with friends in Hartford & shall work to find a buyer & if the desk is not sold, I feel confident I can place it with the right people there. The desk should find its resting place in Hartford. Hartford is the logical place to sell it & I feel I can find the right purchaser there.

Now, he's getting nostalgic?!

He then goes to the dark side by throwing her under the bus. He states,

When I first started to sell the desk if you had not been so far from facts when you wrote to me, the desk was the property & used in his lifetime by Governor Seymour, one time Mayor of Hartford, it would been sold at that time to an important & wealthy Hartford man, but when he found my statement was not true & that Governor Seymour was never Mayor of Hartford.

First off, any English teacher would have a field day with this sentence. *Captain Run-on Sentence.* Secondly, while he may be right about her version of the Seymour legacy, it seems equally likely that she said that *a* Thomas Seymour was the governor and *another* Thomas Seymour was the mayor. Technically, she was right, but as mentioned, Governor Thomas Hart Seymour was the grandson of Mayor Thomas Seymour III.

Frank finishes this paragraph by stating again that he would "surely" sell the desk if given more patience. He finishes this lengthy letter with the crux of his issues with Helen: "I have written at this length that you may know, 'I am not asleep at the switch', & I shall keep you posted when anything comes & finished." Clearly, she had written the "asleep" quote to him in reference to his efforts to sell the desk. His lengthy details of all his efforts to sell the desk over the last several months were ultimately a response to this quote. From my end, he was not asleep at the switch (today we use wheel) and was doing everything possible to sell the desk at a good price. I can only suspect that Helen was so financially strapped at that point that she could not see the forest for the trees.

Letter from Frank Crocker to a Mrs. William Webster Ellsworth (Nellie)—August 8, 1930

Short and sweet ... this letter reads:

Mrs. W.W. Ellsworth
Esperanza Farm
New Hartford, CT

Dr Madam
Please send me advice if the Seymour desk is to be sent to you via freight or express, & if it is to be insured, please inform the amount. Also if you are to pay Miss Seymour for the desk & have the desk sent to you C.O.D crating & transit.

Yours Truly
C.F. Crocker

P.S. Addressed envelope enclosed for your convenience.

Clearly, Helen has thrown in the towel on Frank and told him to contact the Ellsworths about shipping details.

Letter from Helen Seymour to Nellie Smith Ellsworth—August 16, 1930

Helen quickly broight that letter to bear when she wrote again to Nellie. She writes, "This should have been written several days ago but was so upset by the letter from Mr. Crocker which I enclose with this one." *Bingo.* Things began to click. The letter that she's referring to is the same letter ("asleep at the switch") that I just paraphrased above. She continues,

I had written him that if he did not sell the desk to the Boston man he was to send it to you [Nellie]. He seemed so anxious to do the selling and so sure that I thought it best to give him the chance and then I thought it would save you some trouble. I have written again telling him to send the desk to you, the exact address you gave me. His wife always said that she was glad to keep the things until I wanted them.

She continues to play that game with those around her. She keeps mentioning the "trouble" that this affair has caused Nellie and the others in her family while, at the same time, badmouthing Frank for his lack of effort—though she would surely love the money that he might get for the desk. Her rant continues, "Then they or he sold my lowboy which I think would have paid if there was any question of pay. If I had known when they were leaving Washington, I could and would have taken my things then." *Whaaaat?* Was she in any position to be transporting all of these possessions in 1907, the year the Crockers moved back north? She was in New Orleans at the time. Not easy to transfer her possessions between there and Washington, D.C., especially if she was financially strapped. Of course, had she scooped up her inheritance prior to moving back to New Orleans, I probably wouldn't be sitting at the desk now.

Letter from William Webster Ellsworth to Frank Crocker—August 24, 1930

This is a response to Frank's letter dated August 8th. It reads:

My Dear Mr. Crocker,

Miss Seymour is giving Mrs. Ellsworth the desk referred to in your correspondence. May we trouble you to have it crated and sent here by express (NY NH & H R.R.?), insured for $300, prepaying express (I believe one has to if the goods are to be insured). Enclosed is (a) check for $10—we will pay more if necessary, or you can return the amount due us if it runs that way.

We thank you, and regret putting you to any trouble.
Yours,
William Ellsworth

The quote "giving Mrs. Ellsworth the desk," must have been tough for Frank to hear, and then to request that if he didn't use all of the $10 he could please return the rest must have sent him further over the edge.

But with this, the deal was finally done. Ultimately, the desk was sold to the Ellsworths for $500, based on a note by my grandmother, Carlotta. I believe that there was more correspondence between the Ellsworths and Smiths and Helen to hammer out the details of the final sale. I can only surmise that a check was sent to Helen after the fact, though I do not have the correspondence to prove it. While I do not have official confirmation from Frank or one of the Ellsworths (only a notation from my grandmother), the Seymour desk arrived at Esperanza in October 1930. Frank Crocker died in April of 1931, about six months after his last letter to Helen.

Helen Seymour lived for another ten years. After leaving the Home for Homeless Young Women in 1928, she would live in three different boarder situations (and perhaps more) in New Orleans. Her last place of residence was St. Anna's Asylum—Home for Aged Women, based on a 1940 census. The term "asylum" doesn't speak kindly of those who were staying there—perhaps a sign of the times. It probably would be considered a nursing home today. I am not sure when Helen entered there, but she died the same year—April 9, 1940. She was buried at Lafayette Cemetery Number One in New Orleans, leaving behind four nieces and nephews and two grand-nieces and nephews.

Before leaving the Seymour aspect of the desk for good, I was intrigued by the logistics of all of Helen's movements through the last third of her life. She stayed in nine residences total over a thirty-five-year period and each time she had to move her person and stuff. *Ugh. I hate packing and unpacking for vacations.* After living in the same house for over thirty years, I can't imagine doing what she did—especially given the amount of stuff that Cathy and I have accumulated over the years. But times were different back then, and Helen's single lifestyle limited her possessions. Then it dawned on me. Helen Seymour *did* have lots of stuff. It simply resided with Anna and Frank Crocker in Massachusetts.

Testing Jessica in the Garden District

Still not satisfied with my research about Helen's movements in New Orleans after her return even though the Seymour desk was not with her, I figured I'd use my remaining time in New Orleans to re-trace her tracks. Using Google Maps, I locked in her abodes (nine in all) chronologically on my phone. Finished, I was able to see all the saved locations on a map of New Orleans, and all but one (Milne Home) were in and around the Garden District. The Garden District and its immediate surroundings comprise about a half square mile, and it's known for its large Victorian mansions, many of which date back to the late 19th century. This was convenient simply because I was looking at the original buildings that could have housed Helen during the early 1900s.

I spent a good hour or two moving from one saved location to another and many times crossing the same street repeatedly, with Jessica leading the way. We refer to the Google Maps voice as Jessica. *In a quarter of a mile, turn left at the light, and are you lost?* While I was never quite sure that I was at the right place, especially when it came to the personal homes, it was indeed a mental trip back in time. While Jessica was probably a bit frustrated with my indecisiveness, I finally felt at ease with my attempt to try to understand this one mutual owner of the Seymour desk.

The Most Unlikely Sale

Initially, my image of Helena Ellery Seymour's life served as no more than a means to an end. I got a cool desk out of the deal, though through some fairly unorthodox means. But who was this woman who ultimately left me with a historical and cultural heirloom from which I now write? If I believed my dad's notes, she was a drifter druggie who sold the desk to support a habit. But he clearly did not have all the facts, as I do today. She may have had a drug addiction, but it was probably due more to a physical or mental condition and the mere ignorance of the problems of prescribed medication of the time. Because I know so much more about her movements between her two lengthy stints in New Orleans, her addiction is almost an afterthought.

Leaving her addiction question finally behind, I realized that my initial elation and puzzlement over my acquisition of the Seymour desk had evolved into resignation and acknowledgement. While I was happy that the desk wound up in my lap, perhaps for the simple reason I could tell its story, I was equally resigned to that fact as well. Why me? It really should be with one of her relatives.

Additionally, my puzzlement became to acknowledgement simply because a woman I considered a nobody was indeed a somebody. Perhaps it's my life's mission as an educator of young adults that I see beauty in those who spend their lives helping others—like nurses—without the financial and public recognition that should go with it. Helen was a career woman who put aside the pressures of a Victorian society, which may have caused her depression and addiction, to help others. She was somebody, and I proudly own her desk.

While I found solace in the work I did on this project, the desk's sale to my family truly fascinated me. The fact that this desk is sitting in a room at my house is a miracle—I can't reiterate it any more firmly. Not only because the Seymours and the Ellsworths have no blood relationship, but also because of how close the Seymours were to selling it to a third party. Ironically, the lack of frequent communication—both dictated by the times and Helen's own demons—actually helped make it happen. With the desk in Esperanza by the fall of 1930, I could now focus on more familiar ground—the desk's movement through my own family. But I still had one more unanswered question that had been nagging me throughout this process.

Having answered, as best I could, the question of who owned the Seymour desk at various times and in what location, I was continually bugged by what was *in* the desk as well. As elaborated throughout this adventure (*is it an adventure at this point?*), there was a significant amount of stuff, for want of a better term, in the desk itself. One: the notes and assorted papers left to me by my dad. Two: the letters from Anna and Frank Crockers, as well as a few stragglers. I can only assume that Helen Seymour sent them north at some point after the sale of the desk. Three: the letters and a book of calling cards attributed to Mayor Thomas Seymour and his grandson, Thomas Hart Seymour.

Here's where my enigma lies. How the hell did they get there? In theory, they should have been with the same massive group of primary documents that were donated to the Connecticut Museum of Culture and History. My only thought at the time was that the small collection I have was stuffed in the back corner of one of the drawers and overlooked for years. Since neither Anna nor Frank Crocker ever made mention of this paperwork, this was all I had to go on. This remained my standpoint until, yet again, two gifts from heaven fell into my lap that changed everything.

The first nugget materialized when I was perusing my Seymour genealogy book for the umpteenth time and noticed an antique chest that I hadn't really paid much attention to previously. *Old habits die hard.* It turns out that among the other items in the Seymours' inheritance was a huge document chest owned by Mayor Thomas Seymour, which was purchased by a third party part-time antique dealer, either before Mary Seymour died or soon after. The chest supposedly contained a multitude of historical documents dating back to Mayor Thomas Seymour (the late 1700s–early 1800s) all the way to Governor

Seymour, but those documents were no longer in it at the time of transfer. *Holy bat farts!* Could this be the same paperwork that was now in my desk as well as at the Connecticut Museum of Culture and History? It made perfect sense, but it didn't answer how the paperwork got to those locations, until...

The next nugget—more like a boulder—occurred during one of my many visits to the Connecticut Museum of Culture and History. As I was culling through the well-organized folders of letters, I came across a letter from Samuel Morse (the telegraph guy) to Thomas Seymour while Thomas was living in Russia. No surprises. There were several letters from Morse during this time frame. But in this case, there was an index card with the letter. I gave it a quick glance and almost put it aside until I noticed the name on it. It read, "A letter to Thomas H. Seymour at St. Petersburg, dated London, October 13, 1856, from Prof. S. F. B. Morse, from the Atlantic cable. This collection of letters fills fourteen manuscript boxes. Gift of Mrs. George M. Creevey of New Hartford." *Holy double bat farts!* The whole collection was donated by my great-grandmother Lucy Ellsworth Creevey.

On one hand, it absolutely made no sense. But on the other, it fit in very nicely with my attempt to connect these two families and cement my theory that the Seymour inheritance moved from the East Hartford home to Esperanza in 1888.

Before getting too excited about this little development, I needed to verify the premise. I contacted my source at the museum and she did indeed confirm that Lucy Ellsworth Creevey donated the items in 1957. She would have been seventy-eight at the time. She would live for another three years.

Brain churning now, I tried to picture the sequence of all these primary documents. They probably sat in the document chest even while Governor Thomas Seymour was alive. That's what document chests are for. In our house, it's file cabinets and milk crates. *Milk crates? Yeah, they were once used to deliver milk ... never mind.* When the document chest was being sold to the antique dealer, somebody had the smart idea to clear out the chest, and, in theory, the documents moved along the same path as the rest of the inheritance. To Esperanza. The documents never left the estate until they were donated to the museum in 1957. *Very good, Harrison.* But it still didn't answer the question of how a select few documents remained in the desk. *Ugh. And I was doing so well.*

I see three possible options. One, they were purposely set aside and put in the desk when it made its way to my grandmother in Cooperstown, New York, well before 1957. But why? Though obviously these letters were pretty cool to me, they were really no different from a lot of the letters in the donated collection. The second option was that they were discovered at Esperanza after the rest of the collection was donated in 1957 and then sent to my grandmother (or she picked them up during one of her trips to Esperanza). But why not simply add them to the collection at the museum once they were discovered?

The last option was that they were stuck in one of the cubby holes of the desk and thus separate from the bigger collection. This is very plausible since there are plenty of cubby holes and this was a working desk. I love this theory, except, as I stated above, neither Anna nor Frank Crocker ever mentions such documents. Added to this, both Crockers kept asking for proof of provenance, and these letters would have seemingly provided that. *Ugh.* Another big question that will probably remain unsolved. Time to move on to something closer to the present tense.

10

My Man Cave

Once I figured out how the desk got into my family's hands, from there it's a vertical path of ownership between three generations of Harrisons—from my grandparents to my parents to my wife and me. Or better yet from Cooperstown, New York, to two homes in Glens Falls to Northfield, Massachusetts. Easy peasy, lemon squeezy. But if I've learned one thing from all this, it's that nothing is that easy, and it generally isn't what it seems.

If asked, all grandkids will tell you that they're much closer with one set of grandparents than another, and I was no different. In my case—and I'm only speaking for myself—I had a much better relationship with my mom's parents (William and Dorothy Davies) than my dad's.

My mom's parents migrated from England to the United States in the early 1930s with my mom, Joyce, and her twin, Jean. My grandfather Bill (Grandpa to us) served as a chauffeur to the prominent racehorse man Ambrose Clark when he was visiting England. According to my mom, Mr. Clark was so impressed with my grandfather as a driver that he hired Bill permanently and moved the whole family to Long Island where one of his horse farms was located. I also learned that the Clarks owned a horse farm in South Carolina where my grandfather spent much of his time serving the family. According to my sister, Gwyn, my grandmother (Nana to us) was none too happy about raising two twin girls alone in Westbury, New York, while Bill worked in South Carolina. The Clarks spent their summers in Coop-erstown, and by default, the Davies did as well. While my parents did not officially know each other until they both were in their twenties, Cooperstown became the focal point of their initial relationship and eventual marriage.

My closer connection to my mom's parents was due to the simple fact that they visited far more often than my dad's parents did. They would always visit on Thanksgiving cr Christmas, switching off with their other daughter, Jean, who lived with her family in Scituate, Massachusetts. My maternal grandparents were a lovely couple, al-ways doting on each other and showing a general interest in every-thing their grandkids did. Although they claimed to have lost their "Englishness" after decades in the States, they still held on to their ac-cents, had afternoon tea, and Nana made the best shortbread cookies. While they both fell in love with the Mets, Bill's true love was always football (soccer) and the daily scuttlebutt of the English leagues. Thus, both, but especially my grandpa, were curious about our exploits on the athletic fields, and more notably the soccer pitch. I vividly remem-ber how, sometime during my senior year, they came north to watch my brother Matt and I in one of our final soccer games of the year. Before the game, Grandpa gave me a pep talk that ended with some-thing like, "Play a clean game out there, Andy!" Of course, according to many, I really don't know what a clean game is, and I proceeded to *take out* one of my opponents and earn myself a penalty with a yel-low card. *That guy will think twice about moving through my end of the field.* After the game, I apologized to my grandfather about my rough play, to which he responded with a grin and scoff: "That looked per-fectly clean in my book!" *English soccer! You gotta love it.*

Thus, comparing grandparents wasn't a fair fight. In fact, I knew nothing of substance about my dad's parents, Carlotta and Fran Har-rison, other than the basics. We visited Cooperstown once or twice a year—kicking and screaming the whole way—and I don't remember a single time that my grandparents stayed at our house. The plain fact was that Carlotta and Fran were enigmas to me.

Hack It Off!

I knew that Fran and Carlotta had moved to Cooperstown in the late 1920s when Fran, a medical doctor, was hired by the hospital there. He eventually become the chief of medicine and retired at the age of sixty-five. In his retirement, he became a fairly accomplished painter, with many of his works hanging in our house. To me, Fran was simply an aloof and soft-spoken man who rode his big-ass lawn-mower while smoking a pipe. But it was Carlotta who truly baffled me, at least from an adolescent perspective. She sat at her huge dining room table drinking coffee, chain-smoking cigarettes, and working on her huge shell collection; she never seemed to have the time of day for anyone under the age of twenty. Of course, that was the perspective of someone who didn't really have a clue. Having done my homework, I now know better.

My grandfather, Francis French Harrison, was born in 1898 in Montclair, New Jersey, to Benjamin Vincent Harrison and Josephine French Harrison. He graduated from Yale (yup, another one) in 1920 and Columbia University's medical school in 1925. Much like my dad's college experience—and Noah Webster's, for that matter—Fran's Yale years were affected by war. I'm not sure of the details, but I assume he had to forestall his graduation from Yale when he enlisted in the U.S. Army in 1918—about the same time the United States entered the First World War. Fran went on to practice medicine in New York City until he was hired by the Bassett Memorial Hospital in Cooperstown in 1928. Long before specialized medicine was the norm, he was a jack-of-all-trades and practicing general medicine. He would eventually become chief of medicine there, and he served in that capacity until his retirement in 1963. Rumor has it that he also served as the local medical examiner/coroner and performed autopsies for the county. *The forensic science teacher in me grinned when I heard this tidbit.*

When our country entered World War II on December 8, 1941, my grandfather was forty-three and well established at the Bassett Hospital. Still, he felt his patriotic duty call him again, but this time as a medical doctor. He offered his services to the cause and served in three hospitals in North Africa and Italy from 1942 to 1946 as chief of medicine. While it's unique to have a father and son serving during wartime together, and I'm quite honored that both my father and grandfather did so, my grandmother was apparently not too pleased about the situation. By the time I was in the picture and cognizant of things around me, Fran was already retired from the hospital and doing his painting thing. But based on the stories I've heard and my own rare experiences with him, he was quite an interesting man. Two of those stories stayed with me.

First, according to my dad, Fran was not a heavy drinker up until the Prohibition Era (1920-1933). But the fact that the federal government, through a constitutional amendment in 1920, told people that they couldn't make or drink alcohol apparently rubbed Fran the wrong way. His middle finger moment occurred when he built and operated his own still in someone else's garage. Again, according to my dad, that someone else was the local police chief. That simple fact explains one reason why the Prohibition amendment failed miserably and is, to this day, the only amendment that was nullified by a different amendment. The irony doesn't escape me that many from my generation felt the same way about indulging in marijuana. The fact that our toughest drug laws were enacted in the 1970s to '90s gave rise to a new generation of finger raising for the same reason. Of course, as an amateur brewer of beer, I would have loved to talk shop with Fran and perhaps form a connection that I never felt as a young man.

My only personal indelible memory of my grandfather occurred quite out of the blue. As mentioned, Fran ended a successful and fulfilling career as a doctor and, with the same sense of passion, moved on to painting watercolor landscapes. While I may be slightly biased, his works are quite good, and there are many Harrison descendants with rural winter scenes featuring a run-down barn hanging somewhere in their respective houses.

On the rare occasions that we did visit Cooperstown, dinner was always preceded by the cocktail hour. It was quite boring for a ten-year-old. On one such occasion, I looked at Fran, who was holding his drink in his right hand, and noticed that he was missing a finger—his pinkie. I couldn't figure it out. Why was he missing a finger? No one had ever mentioned this to me. I really wanted to break up the festivities with something like *"Hey, Fran. Lose something in the Great War?"* But instead I waited until later to ask my dad. According to legend, Fran had a nasty case of bent finger syndrome (there is a medical term for it) that made holding a paintbrush difficult. So, in the Harrison way, he went into the hospital, used some influence, and persuaded a surgeon to lope it off. *Easy peasy, lemon squeezy.*

Aha Moments

Fran's wife, Carlotta, was born on September 13, 1902, in New York City to Dr. George Mason Creevey and Lucy Ellsworth Creevey. After high school, she attended Smith College in Northampton, Massachusetts, and graduated in 1924. It seemed that all Ellsworth men went to Yale and the women to Smith (a phenomenal school in its own right), but apparently my siblings and I—as well as most of my cousins—never got that memo. Carlotta met Fran while in New York, and they married on August 16, 1924, at, of course, Esperanza in New Hartford. They again moved to Cooperstown in 1928. My Aunt Barbara (1926) and my dad (1927) were born in New York City, but my Aunt Anne (1930) was born in Cooperstown.

While I clearly had some lasting impressions of my grandfather Fran, I was left with little to go on for my grandmother Carlotta—other than the coffee (and something stronger as the day wore on) and cigarettes I mentioned earlier. Prior to digging into my past with this book, I knew relatively nothing else about my grandmother and never bothered to question my dad for more details. *Wash. Rinse. Repeat.*

Thankfully, I found her obituary through Ancestry.com. While there was no need for a career, given her husband's profession and the times she lived in, she was not eating bonbons idly on the couch. In addition to raising three kids, Carlotta became active between 1940 and '60 with the Red Cross—which was in its relative infancy at the time—and served in a variety of administrative roles. During World War II, though not generally happy with her husband's second tour of duty, she was quite active in the war movement at home. Her obituary reads, "She was in charge of the production of dressings and kits to the men in service, from 1942 through 1945. Mrs. Harrison organized the local Red Cross blood program in 1948 and 1949, with the first donations in 1949."

Upon reading that specific quote, I had one of my aha moments (there were many throughout this process). My dad, for as long as I knew him, gave blood on a regular basis. *Like an über donor.* He also served the local chapter of the Red Cross in Glens Falls, New York, as a volunteer. Clearly, he inherited this mission through his mother. I give regularly as well, though I can never match his numbers. My daughter, Sam, has also become a donor. In fact, we'd often plan our donation dates together and have races to see who could fill a pint bag faster. *Something about an apple and a tree.*

Additionally, while my grandfather was out in the woods and farmland of upstate New York sketching and photographing rustic barns so he could put them on canvas, my grandmother was doing her own thing—collecting, organizing, and categorizing the most amazing seashell assemblage. Again, now in hindsight, I realize the enormous effort that she must have put into this endeavor.

She was also an artist in her own right. Rather than paint, she created needlework in the toughest medium possible. Petit point. Having done my own fair share of needlepoint in my earlier days (before kids), the use of petit point is baffling. For novices, it is the use of single threads on a smaller, holed canvas. It was quite popular in the 17th and 18th century in France. The outcome is some of the most intricate pictures possible. Some of Carlotta's landscapes of fine yarn are so detailed that they look like they were painted. Unfortunately, she lost her eyesight as she aged and thus was limited with this hobby, but one has to wonder whether her needlework was somehow a cause. *Amazing woman! And I'm still an idiot.*

A Village of Museums

Cooperstown, known primarily as the birthplace of baseball and now home to the Baseball Hall of Fame, is much more than that. On the Village of Cooperstown website, it reads, "Cooperstown was settled in the late 18th century by William Cooper, father of novelist James Fenimore Cooper, whose novels were set in and around Cooperstown. The aesthetic centerpiece of Cooperstown is beautiful Otsego Lake, which author Cooper nicknamed the Glimmerglass." It is a beautiful place to visit and, not surprisingly, has drawn the wealthy for generations, especially in the summers (take the Clark racing family, for example). The website continues,

> *Today Cooperstown is a village of museums, including the National Baseball Hall of Fame, which opened in 1939 with the induction of Babe Ruth, Cy Young, Ty Cobb, and other baseball legends. The Farmers' Museum, one of the country's oldest outdoor living history museums, showcases rural life in 1845 in its village of historic trade and craft shops. The Fenimore House Museum is home to one of the country's premier folk art collections. Other cultural attractions include the Glimmerglass Opera, New York State Historical Association, National Art Association Show, Gallery 53 Multi-Arts Center, Cooperstown Brush and Palette Club, and several small art galleries.*

Of course, all this didn't matter much in my younger days. Only now do I appreciate the town for all its beauty and what it represents to my heritage. The same can be said for the house and property that my dad was raised in. One Beaver Street, as we referred to it growing up.

Woven into my new revelations about my grandparents is the Seymour desk that sat in 1 Beaver Street, Cooperstown, New York, for about sixty years. Much like the manse of Esperanza, 1 Beaver Street simply refers to a gorgeous home built right next to the Bassett Hospital. According to Aunt Barbara, my grandmother was deeply involved in the design and construction of the house—most likely to the disdain of the workers who had this woman looking over their shoulders. Construction was started in the early 1930s and completed in 1934. An interesting note—which gives the reader some idea of my grandmother's meticulous nature—is that, according to my aunt, Carlotta had shelving purposely built into the walls to accommodate a china set that was originally from the czar of Russia. *Whaaat? China from the czar of Russia? Not another book!*

According to multiple sources, Minister Thomas Seymour became close friends with both Czar Nicholas I and his son, Alexander II, when he served in Russia. So much so that Alexander gave Thomas several impressive gifts—a set of china, a wooden lap desk, and malachite jewelry. These items were never mentioned in the items held by the Crockers, and one can only assume that they remained at Esperanza until they went to my grandmother. But Carlotta went a step further. In a note on one of Julia Smith's letters, she writes, "He [Thomas Seymour] brought back many lovely things amongst which is a very fine porcelain breakfast service for two, Which was presented to him by the Czar and given to me by his niece or grand niece, Helen Seymour many years ago. I also have a bit of his malachite jewelry and his traveling desk, with his calling card." *Wow!* I can only assume that while in New Orleans, Helen Seymour passed word to Carlotta that she could have these items.

Probably no surprise to the reader, I do not remember the items being in the Cooperstown home, but I have seen the china and the malachite jewelry. Aunt Barbara showed me the malachite jewelry and the gold-rimmed china when I visited her home during my research in Cooperstown. The gorgeous wooden lap desk with Thomas Seymour's name on it went to my cousin and one of Barbara's daughters as a wedding gift. *My cousin can write that book!*

Of course, doing special alterations to the new house for the china set begs another question: Was there a location in the house that was designed purposely for the Seymour desk as well? Perhaps, but I simply don't remember seeing it when I visited. According to my Aunt Barbara, she always remembered the desk being in her parents' bedroom at 1 Beaver Street. While I am not totally recusing myself from the idiot label, there weren't many times that I wandered into the primary bedroom of my grandparents' house in Cooperstown.

Following my grandmother's death in 1991, 1 Beaver Street should, in theory, have gone to one of the siblings—and most likely Barbara, since she lived in Cooperstown at that point. But much to my Aunt Barbara's consternation, the house on 1 Beaver Street was donated to the Bassett Memorial Hospital where my grandfather Fran had worked for almost his entire adult life. The house sits right next to the hospital and was turned into prime office space. While the convenience is undeniable and the house from the outside looks much the same, the inside looks like ... well ... offices, especially the first floor. I have never spoken to Barbara about this, nor did I think that our lunch meeting was the best time to pose the question, but it was my understanding that Barbara would have loved to take over the house to pass it on to the next generation. I have visited the manse several times after its transition into the hospital's hands, but the most recent visit was the weekend of my father's interment service in October 2021.

Traveling around Cooperstown with one of my closest college friends, my daughter, and her partner, we decided to visit the house on 1 Beaver Street on the Friday before my father's service. While I was satisfied with simply looking at the place from afar, especially because it was occupied with employees at the time, my friend had other ideas. He quickly strolled up, knocked on the door, and walked in. After a few awkward moments of introductions and an explanation about our connection to the home, we took a tour of the house—though I was ultimately giving the tour while our host followed and asked questions. I didn't mention the ad hoc trip to my aunt.

After talking with my Aunt Barbara, I was pretty comfortable stating that the desk never left 1 Beaver Street until my dad packed it up and moved it to Glens Falls in 1992. But I still wasn't sure of its location before 1 Beaver Street was completed. Where did it sit between 1930—when it was sold to W.W. Ellsworth by Frank Crocker and shipped to Esperanza—and the time when it was moved to Cooperstown? An excellent question with no good answer. There is no record of its movement during that time period. Whether it stayed in New Hartford for a few years or was quickly shipped to Cooperstown prior to the house being built really has no bearing on the story. But it does beg the question: Was the desk purchased just to get Helen Seymour out of her situation with Frank Crocker, or was it specifically purchased with my grandmother in mind? My initial thought was that my grandmother must have seen the desk when it spent some time in Esperanza around 1888, but that wasn't possible since my grandmother was born in 1902, and at that point the desk would have been in the hands of the Crockers.

Then I remembered one of my prized possessions that was included in the desk when I received it—a detailed drawing of the desk created by my great-great-grandfather, William Webster Ellsworth.

The color drawing of the Seymour desk was created on two pieces of paper turned 90 degrees and taped together. The drawing is quite meticulous (I could never hand-draw something like that) with comments and labels identifying the wood used in its various sections.

While I wouldn't give it a second thought under normal circumstances, the fact that it's by my great-great-grandfather of the same desk that I now own makes it special. My question is when it was drawn. I had initially believed that it was drawn in 1930 when the desk changed hands, since William Ellsworth was a big part of that deal. But perhaps it was drawn around 1888 when it sat in Esperanza for the first time. Of course, I don't have any idea. There's no date on it. Maybe my grandmother "fell in love" with the desk based on the drawing, or maybe it spent enough time at Esperanza that my grandmother saw it and requested it sometime between 1930 and 1934. All I know, based on a conversation with Aunt Barbara, is that it was in 1 Beaver Street in 1934. *Good enough.*

But Barbara went further. At least in theory. In one of her many emails to me, she writes,

> *The desk was in my parents' bedroom at One Beaver Street, I would guess from the time that we moved into the house in July, 1934. I might guess that she bought it because she wanted it, put it in storage and then put it in a special place in the house that was many years in the planning, with CCH [my grandmother Carlotta] at the architect's shoulder all along the way. She really cherished that desk: I have never known whether it was the desk itself or its provenance.*

If I was a betting man (which I'm not), I believe that my grandmother probably did have some influence on the eventual sale of the desk to the Ellsworths, which might explain their eleventh-hour involvement. She would have been in her late twenties and newly married with a big house in her future. Additionally, I would also suggest that the desk stayed in Esperanza until the Cooperstown house was completed in 1934. Pure speculation at best, but logically it makes sense.

The 'Rents

My dad, Dirck, was born in 1927 in New York and moved to Cooperstown soon after. He spent most of his childhood at 1 Beaver Street. While he never spoke a lot about his childhood, I never got the impression it was anything but normal, even in the height of the Great Depression. The fact that his father was a successful doctor in a fairly affluent town probably helped. A lot! I do know that while Dirck started his schooling in Cooperstown, he wound up at Berkshire Academy, a private school along the Massachusetts and New York border, from 1938 to 1943. He, as mentioned earlier, moved on to Yale, with a road bump in the middle due to World War II. He finished Yale in 1948, returned home, was eventually hired by Arkell and Smith Paper Bag Company in a town thirty miles from Cooperstown, and fell in love and married my mom, Joyce, in 1953. He was twenty-six, and she was twenty-three.

After my mom, Joyce, moved to the United States in 1933, she spent her school years on Long Island in Westbury, New York, though her family would move with the Clark family to Cooperstown for the summer. Cooperstown was the place to be in the summer, especially for a horse-racing family like the Clarks, given that Saratoga was right down the road. After graduating from Westbury High, my mom and her twin sister, Jean, went to Lasell College in Newton, Massachusetts, and earned two-year degree. Over the course of her life, my mom worked as a medical and legal secretary on top of maintaining a home and raising four very active kids.

Joyce moved to Cooperstown sometime after 1950 to work at the Bassett Hospital. According to my sister, Gwyn, though Dirck knew of the twins since they stayed in Cooperstown for the summer, they didn't officially connect until the fall of 1952. At this point, Dirck was back living in the area after his stint with the U.S. Navy and graduating from Yale in 1948. One of my dad's closest friends lived just down the street from 1 Beaver Street, and he needed a second on a double date. It appears that my dad's close friend had a date with the ever-alluring Joyce Davies (*Can I say that?*), but Joyce had a friend with her at the time. Thus, the need for a second. So, off they went and they wound up listening to the Friday night fights (boxing) on the radio. Again, according to my source, my mom bet on a boxer with the last name Davies, and won. That victory triggered their plans for a second date, but my dad's friend was out of town on that day and my dad agreed to take her out instead. The rest, as they say, is history—though it all sounds a little hinky.

Learning about, or at least paying better attention to, my dad's play on my mom triggered my own recollection of my first date with my future wife, Cathy. Apparently, the adage "like father, like son" is the modus operandi here. Cathy and I both went to Lenoir-Rhyne College, a small school in Hickory, North Carolina. She was two years ahead of me. We initially met in the winter of my freshman year (1980) when I attended a frat party with a close friend who was a member of the fraternity. Cathy was a *little sister* of the same fraternity, partly due to the fact that she was close friends with my same friend and was at the party helping out. Needless to say, I don't remember much about the evening other than that someone kept putting popcorn in the pockets of my hoodie, but I do remember getting a kiss from my future girlfriend and wife. Rumor has it she was also the popcorn dispenser.

A couple weekends later, my buddy had the same dilemma as my dad and his friend in that he had plans to go see a movie with Cathy and he needed a second for her roommate at the time. I agreed, though I decided to make my own Harrison play. When entering the aisle, I discreetly maneuvered myself so I was seated between the two girls with Cathy on my right and my buddy two seats down on the left. I felt like I had pulled a real fast one, though in hindsight there wasn't much argument from anyone. *Hmmmm. Who was playing whom?*

Dirck Dey Harrison (25) and Joyce Davies Harrison (22)-Honeymoon in the
Bahamas (February, 1953).

Whatever the case with my parents, they clearly hit it off in the fall
of 1952 because they married in February 1953. A quick turnaround.
And before you ask the obvious question, their first child—my older
sister, Gwyn—was born in February of 1954, twelve months after
their marriage. The quick turnaround was nothing more than impa-
tience on one or both their parts. When Cathy and I told my parents
that we were engaged in 1983 but we wouldn't get married for another two years, my dad quickly scoffed, "You'll never make it." He
then told me that he and my mom had made a similar proclamation
but clearly didn't reach it. By the way, Cathy and I married on July 13,
1985, two years after the engagement. *Take that, Dirck.*

It seems that my dad's lucky play paid off, but we learned, almost
sixty-five years after their marriage, that there was a bit more to the
story. Following my mom's death in 2017, we had the standard calling
hours and memorial service at a church in Glens Falls. We reserved
the interment service for later that year in Cooperstown. It is only fit-
ting that my mom and dad are buried next to each other in the place
where they first met and each spent a lot of time growing up. Fol-

lowing the interment service, my Aunt Barbara had a lovely lunch in her gorgeous home in the hills looking over Cooperstown. In typical Harrison fashion, stories flowed about Mom. Stories we've told and heard hundreds of times—until Dirck dropped a whopper on us. It seems that in 1952, my mom was already betrothed to another man (Jerry something, according to my sister), but he was off in Korea at the time, fighting for his country. Thus, my dad swooped in while Mr. Jerry was away. Of course, there are countless stories like this of men (and women) serving their country in some faraway place, but it didn't stop us from giving Dirck an earful of grief. We laughed until we cried.

As mentioned, my older sister, Gwyn, was born in February 1954. Unbeknownst to me, there was a miscarriage in the late fall of 1954. My mom was informed by her doctors that another pregnancy in the near future was unlikely, but she fooled the experts and became pregnant with my older brother, Brad, who was born in December of 1955. Defying medical odds became the norm when my mom became pregnant again in the late fall of 1960 with her third child. I was born in July 1961. The five-and-a-half-year gap between Brad and me was not part of the plan. My mom had always wanted four kids, which was quite normal in the baby boom period. But sometime after Brad's birth, Dirck contracted the mumps—which really sucks for any adult to get, but it can be potentially even more devastating for men, as the mumps wreak havoc on the body's glands in general and testicles specifically. *Really, Harrison?* Some men see heavily reduced sperm count levels to the point of sterility, and my dad was one of those unfortunate few. But to my parents' surprise, my dad's plumbing fixed itself several years later and I was born, followed by my brother Matt in December of 1962. My mom had her four kids.

Of course, while there were never any doubts about who the final two belonged to, we couldn't help teasing my parents when Matt and I began to blossom into our adult bodies. While my mom and dad and the first two kids all averaged about 5'9" in height, Matt and I blew the proverbial bell curve out of the water. We are both a tad under 6'5" (*though I'm taller by a quarter inch. Just saying.*). We always commented that it was the mailman, a year and a half apart. It has become the on-going Harrison inside joke. When my dad told us about my mom's first engagement at my aunt's house, I even asked: "How tall was Mr. Jerry?" We laughed again until we cried.

As mentioned, my dad's professional career was all business (pun intended), and while it wasn't the normal track of the Harrison/Ellsworth males, he, by all rights, was successful at what he did. Rumor has it that he indeed was destined to become a medical doctor and follow in both his father's and grandfather's footsteps. He realized soon enough that while he was probably smart enough, he did not have the academic discipline to stay the course. No matter. He found his niche in business.

Dirck took a job in 1950 at Arkell and Smith Company in Cana-joharie, New York, and he and my mom lived there (following their marriage in 1953) until 1955. Then they moved back to Cooperstown, and my dad commuted to work for the next three years—a half hour drive. In 1958, Dirck was transferred—with family in tow—to a branch near Glens Falls, and my parents would never leave the area again. Arkell and Smith Company was eventually bought out by Chase Bag Company in 1968. Dirck was clearly on the fast track, and he eventually became vice president of production. He stayed with the company for the rest of his professional career. In 1989, when he was sixty-two years old, he opted for an early retirement buyout rather than be transferred to *East Something*, Ohio. While financially it wasn't the smartest decision and my parents allegedly had to do some bootstrap-pulling to make things work, they never regretted it.

While my dad lived in an age when men were generally defined by the career they chose, Dirck never fell into that hole. He could com-partmentalize; work was work and everything else was really impor-tant to him. Outside of the daily grind of work, he was a modern-day Renaissance man. While he was never a gifted athlete, he was a fit-ness machine well before it became a thing. We (the four kids) all remember him doing morning calisthenics, including something called "The Birds," where he would lie prone on the ground with his arms out wide and proceed to lift all four limbs simultaneously as far as they would go. Over and over again. *Try this right now. I'll wait.* He would then bag his healthy lunch (in the reject airplane vomit bags from work), ride almost five miles to work on his bike in his business suit, and return later in the afternoon—often just in time to watch his kids' sporting events. He played tennis, ran until his legs gave out, rode his bike until his balance did the same, and swam at the YMCA well into his late eighties.

While growing up, I knew that Dirck was ultimately the second man in charge at Chase Bag and the go-to guy when anything mechanical at the plant malfunctioned. He essentially served as the connection between the blue- and white-collar employees. He, in his own words, was a "get your hands dirty" man who happened to be wearing a coat and tie. Beyond that, I knew relatively nothing about what he did for work for almost forty years of his life. Before you say, "Here's the idiot mantra all over again," I may have had some sort of excuse in this regard. While I might not have been paying much attention, or perhaps I never really cared, Dirck never made it his mission (nor did my mom, for that matter) to share his daily grind with his kids. We never would have thought to call or text him at work (think about that, Gen Z'ers), and I can only remember one time that I visited him there. Coming from two educators like Cathy and I who needed to occasionally vent or share with a full family audience, his stoicism was remarkable. But again, those were different times.

Though my parents never left the Glens Falls area after 1958, they would purchase five different homes during their lifetime. This was initially to accommodate their growing family and then eventually their shrinking family as well. Glens Falls, which sits along the Hudson River, has a history dating back to the middle 1700s, and it eventually became a prominent city with a strong industrial base. As in a lot of mill towns across the northern United States, industry ebbed and was eventually replaced by service industries. Location is everything, and Glens Falls' close neighbor to the north, Queensbury, has become a desirable place to live. With the state capital, Albany, and Saratoga a short distance to the south and the Adirondack Mountains and Lake George an even shorter distance to the north, the Glens Falls area continues to be a popular place to raise a family. For my parents and especially my dad, the Glens Falls area was perfect for their lifestyle even after they retired from their jobs.

I would be totally remiss and probably disowned if I didn't mention my dad's true love—strapping a pair of boards to his feet and careening down a mountain covered in snow. Both Fran and Carlotta were crucial to opening a ski mountain in the Cooperstown area. In 1938-39, they helped open the first ski mountain in the area named Mt. Otsego. They passed their love of the sport on to their three kids, including Dirck, who proudly skied until his eighties. Only when his legs and his stability gave out did he finally hang up the boots and skis. It was a sad moment.

**Dirck Dey Harrison (31) at Mt. Otsego
in Cooperstown, New York (1958).**

When the winter season gave way to the summer, Dirck's thoughts would move from snow to water. Raised on Lake Otsego in Cooperstown and blessed with parents with resources, he learned to sail. His love of competitive sailing was always a close second to his love of skiing, but he continued to do it well into his late adulthood on Lake George, just north of Glens Falls. Unfortunately, he eventually had to forgo this part of his life as well. Lack of stability on choppy lake water was not a good mix, though drowning or perhaps dying on a ski mountain probably would have suited Dirck just fine. He also took up golf when my mom did. A little less conducive to injury. Some of my fondest memories are playing golf together with my dad, my two brothers, and my son, Noah. Dirck wasn't very good, but he was competitive as hell.

Like his mother, he dedicated his life after retirement to volunteer work. In addition to his work with the American Red Cross, he gave his free time to the YMCA, a local art museum, a local tennis and swim club, Hickory Hill Ski Mountain, the ski patrol, and eventually Meals on Wheels. He truly was his mother's son.

Interestingly, none of these hobbies and exploits following retirement could compare to his second career refinishing furniture and caning wooden chairs. Nothing. Beginning sometime around his retirement in 1989, he began to find a niche. What began as a simple hobby to occupy his time quickly became a passion. He, on multiple occasions, mentioned that he liked working with furniture growing up, and he realized later in life that the itch never died. That itch intensified when he and my mom decided to move for the last time. When they moved into a brand-new duplex in an expanding part of Glens Falls, they not only insisted on as little maintenance as possible but on having a home with a full basement. In one of the bigger rooms of the basement, Dirck created his version of a man cave—or a hermit hole, as I referred to it. For him, however, it was a woodworker's paradise.

Dirck became a known entity in the area for his craftsmanship, especially for caning chairs. I have countless items in my house to prove it. He, admittedly and especially after losing the ability to ski and sail, felt that his work with wood and cane gave him a purpose in life.

There's not a sole person in our family or among close friends who doesn't have at least one piece of furniture that Dirck refinished. I probably have two in every room in the house. He branched out into rebuilding broken pieces, caning and rushing chairs, and even building pieces from scratch. The man continued to work until a few months before his death.

Ironically, though, to my knowledge, he never touched the Seymour desk other than his OCD tendencies to keep every piece of his furniture as clean as a whistle. It's embarrassing to look at that same desk while I'm typing this very sentence and see a slight layer of dust. *It's on my to-do list for tomorrow.*

The Better Half

My mom, Joyce, was born three years later than my dad in 1930 but died three years earlier. While she may have died from a heart attack, she, as previously mentioned, was slowly losing herself to the evils of Alzheimer's. Having gone down that road with Cathy's mom years before, I knew that losing my mom suddenly to a heart attack was a blessing in disguise. While my dad was distraught at losing her after almost sixty-five years of marriage, in the end, we knew that caring for her as her mind deteriorated was taking a heavy toll on him.

Following her marriage to Dirck in 1953 and the birth of their four children, Joyce established herself as a medical and legal secretary for all the years I was growing up in Glens Falls. While Dirck was the significant breadwinner in a professional sense and everything fun in a personal one, my mom was the rock in the family—the caregiver, the disciplinarian, the cook, the accountant, and the keeper of the family calendar. If you wanted an answer about how to fix something in the house, you asked my dad. Everything else, you asked my mom, and I pitied the man or woman who trod too heavily on one of her four kids.

Only when we kids were out of the house did she finally begin to let her guard down and find her own niche in life. She was always the better athlete of the two and was quite competent on the golf course and tennis court. She, like her parents, was an ardent sports fan—especially when it came to her beloved Yankees. Things got real when my brother Matt got drafted by the Yankees in the spring of 1984, following his junior year at Le Moyne College. Matt progressed through all levels of the minor leagues as a Yankee but never made it to the Bigs. *Alas.* By the same token, I, ever the rebel, had become an equally ardent Red Sox fan growing up. Mom was not happy. It wouldn't have surprised me if she'd changed the locks on me after I returned home from college. She really loved her Yankees.

Whether due to the necessity of her profession or not, Joyce developed the most gorgeous handwriting, and she eventually taught herself calligraphy. She, until the evils of dementia kicked in, would spend hours doing wedding invitations and such for others, mostly pro bono. Additionally, she began knitting like a demon, created her own trademark called Joyce's Choices, and specialized in hats and sweaters. Much like my grandfather's paintings and my dad's furniture refinishing, there isn't a kid or grandkid in the family who doesn't have one of her sweaters in their closet. Finally and most importantly, the woman who ran a very tight ship—so much so that none of the kids dared to rock the boat—became the most loving and caring grandmother to her six grandchildren. Much like how I felt about her parents, it was always a special time when she and my dad made the trip to Northfield from Glens Falls to watch my two kids compete in sports. We all miss both of them greatly.

A Mentor

While I can't speak for my sister and my two brothers, I was much closer to my dad than my mom, and we tended to view the world through the same poor eyesight. I could go on and on about his influence—and perhaps there's even another book out there. In the simplest terms, he taught me how to be a man in a modern society. How to treat women. How to work hard at everything you do. How to have fun. How to be open minded and firm in your beliefs at the same time. He was a role model when role models are so hard to find these days.

Which brings me back to the beginning. If I could call my dad about anything for advice, especially home projects (he once walked me through replacing a toilet after my toddler daughter decided to flush one of her toy boats and got it stuck halfway down), why didn't I heed his advice about researching the desk while he was alive? I don't really have a good answer other than the excuses I gave earlier. None of which cut it.

Without my dad to fill in the details, I was left to quiz my Aunt Barbara. I initially asked her: when were the One Beaver Street possessions dispersed after Carlotta's death in September 1991? Barbara seemed to think that most of the house's wares were doled out by early 1992, which was consistent with my assumption around the desk's movement. While I do not remember much about my grandmother's memorial service in Cooperstown, I do remember the broader details of my own life at that moment. In the winter of 1992, Cathy was very pregnant with Sam. My son, Noah, our first, was three-and-a-half and rambunctious as hell. We had just moved into our first home, and I was in my first year as a middle school teacher. If the Seymour desk moved to Glens Falls sometime in the winter of 1992, I probably don't remember it. I was definitely in my own time warp.

The Seymour desk sat at my parents' home at the time—20 Linden Avenue—for the next ten years or so until they moved out of that house and into their last home in a different part of town. Not surprisingly, I don't remember where the desk sat at 20 Linden Avenue, though I had a good idea. Thankfully, my brother Matt helped me out. According to him, it sat in the family dining room. My brother purchased that home when my parents moved out in 2003. For the next eighteen years, the desk also sat in the dining room of their final home. Again, I always admired it when we visited but never gave it much thought, even as my parents urged me to do so. If the desk could talk, it would have told me to get my shit together and start the research while my dad was still alive. *Alas.*

My Man Den

Things got real for me in the winter of 2021. With my parents' home now on the market, the desk was packed snug as a bug in a U-Haul along with a bunch of other items. It moved into the basement of our house in Northfield, Massachusetts. Northfield, though settled earlier than both Cooperstown or Glen Falls, never had the same cultural, industrial, or recreational foundation as the other two. It quite simply is a very quaint town along the Connecticut River that abuts both Vermont and New Hampshire. Nevertheless, the town—like my grandparents in Cooperstown and my parents in Glens Falls—served Cathy and me quite well, especially when it came to raising two kids.

So, the Seymour desk sat in our basement for another year with all the other knickknacks that we'd accumulated. Not very nice treatment for a historical desk, I know, but we simply didn't really know what to do with it. As I've said, during this time I was ready to donate it to either the Ellsworth or Webster estates, since I believed it was surely purchased by one of them. But by the fall of 2021, I had changed my tune for several reasons. First and foremost, I knew, at least in theory, that its legacy did not belong with either Oliver Ellsworth or Noah Webster. Not even close. Second, even if I selectively sold it, it would never sell at its real value. At least, not without some accurate provenance to go with it. Finally and most importantly, it had started to grow on me. So much so that I felt like it needed a real place to live in the house. But where?

As houses go, ours is strange. For lack of a better term. Built in the late 1980s, it's quite modern in design, though it sits in the middle of the woods. A bedroom was added before we purchased it in 1992 and that serves as the primary bedroom on the first floor. We added a third bedroom in the late 1990s when our two kids needed their own separate spaces. The new room turned out to be the prize room in the house, as it looks out among the trees. Noah, our firstborn, lived there until he went off to college, and Sam, four years younger, moved in. It would, for all intents and purposes, be considered her room until my desk came along and we needed a place to put it. I needed a man cave, though I never thought that I would say those words.

The whole concept of a man cave baffles me. As I mentioned, I brew my own beer, so I'm not averse to having a beer or three, and my fridge is readily stocked with my own and others' concoctions. But the kitchen fridge is plenty. I do love to watch sports. A lot. And yes, I'm that guy who can sit for hours and watch golf. But usually most of my viewing is in front of my laptop. We do have two TVs—both relatively small by today's standards. I do have "my couch," as Cathy refers to it, and much of my viewing and academic work occurs on it. But the thought of moving my world to another room for the pure sake of getting away from reality seems a little extreme. Additionally, I can only imagine what would have happened if I'd tried to pull that scenario ten years ago when my daughter, Sam, went off to college and was technically out of the house. The conversation might have gone something like this when she returned home for the first time (she was eight hours away, so it wasn't very often):

Sam: Where's Dad? [after dropping her clothes next to the washer]
Cathy: Up in his Man Cave.
Sam: His what?
Cathy: Man Cave. It's the new thing. Husbands need a place to hang out

by themselves after a long day of work.

Sam: I thought that was what the bathroom was for?

Cathy: Yeah, well, he still camps in there with his crossword puzzle.

Sam: Whatever. What happens if you have guests? I mean, now that he's taken over that room with his really important Man Cave [dripping with sarcasm].

Cathy: Oh, that's still there for guests, or in this case, for you.

Sam: Wait? His Man Cave [dripping with sarcasm] is in my room? What about all my stuff?

Cathy: All boxed up and shoved into various closets around the house.

Sam: WTF, Mom! And my bed, dresser, and other furniture?

Cathy: We had to give them to the Salvation Army. We had to make room for his new couch, massage La-Z-Boy, full-size refrigerator, full bar—including five revolving beer taps—and 150-inch plasma TV. Did I mention his new stereo system? Huge speakers!

Sam: Is he up there now?

Cathy: Of course. He only comes down for dinner.

Sam: Whatever. I'm going over to Chelsea's. Oh, one last question.

Cathy: Yes, honey?

Sam: Does Dad's Man Cave [dripping with sarcasm] have locks on the outside of the door?

You get the gist about where my sentiments lie with the whole Man Cave thing. So the thought of redoing a room in the house to create my own has never crossed my mind. Until I inherited the desk.

Rather than even consider a Man Cave in its true ugly sense, I set to work on my Man Den, for lack of a better term. I cleared everything out of the vacant room, and yes, I packed Sam's world into several boxes and put them into closets. *Shame. Shame.* I repainted everything, including the trim and ceiling and the walls, with a color of my choice. A light green. *Okay, maybe I got some input.* Then I set to work refurnishing it.

The Seymour desk sits proudly along the only solid wall without windows or closets. Along with the desk are other pieces of furniture with their own stories to tell, including an equally popular family heirloom—the Harrison sleigh bed. It's a beautiful hardwood piece, probably refinished by my dad at various points, that has passed through at least three generations. According to Cathy—who does listen much better than her spouse—it was purchased by my grandfather Fran in the New York City area at some point. My dad slept in it as a kid, then his kids (including myself) slept in it, and both Noah and Sam slept in it. It's waiting patiently for my grandson, Charlie, and/or my granddaughter, Elise, to take it over.

The walls also tell stories of their own. I had our (kids' and parents') diplomas framed and matted with all the school's colors and displayed prominently on both sides of the Seymour desk. There are framed artifacts from my past and present that are relatively meaningless to the average person. My most prized inherited painting sits over the Seymour desk. It's a painting by W.B. Romeling, who by all accounts was a renowned painter in upstate New York during the second half of the 20th century. More importantly, he mentored my grandfather as a painter. Every wall holds something that I will occasionally look at and reflect back on with fond memories.

Finally, there is the desk itself. As desired, it has become a working desk, and though my grandmother and perhaps my dad would cringe at the stacks of books and general clutter around it, I truly believe that Thomas Henry Seymour is smiling somewhere. It has served as my safe place as I've worked on this project. On it are other pieces of my life—a petit point needlework piece by grandmother Carlotta, a graduation mug from Yale dated 1920 that came from my grandfather Fran, my copy of Webster's dictionary, a few brass figurines from my mom's collection, a gorgeous clock that I received upon my retirement from Monadnock Regional High School, and, of course, two pictures of my dad. One is of my very young daughter, Sam, in the cutest sundress standing on the couch and combing my dad's hair while he's enjoying the whole process. (For the record, my dad had a buzz cut his entire adult life.) The other is a *formal* picture of my son, Noah, and my daughter-in-law, Larissa, on their wedding day—they are laughing hysterically as my dad gives the photographer the bird.

What will become of the desk in the near and far future, I'm still unsure. My daughter, Sam, has already called dibs on it, but who's to know? I'll be dead, and they can deal with it. Or not. I still sometimes think that it should sit somewhere more prominent than it does currently. Perhaps someone down the line who reads this will have a better solution. I'm open to suggestions. In terms of closure for the time being, I feel like holding on to the desk and using it regularly is the only way to finally come to grips with the idiocy I detailed in chapter 1. But I still had one more chapter to write before I put this thing to bed.

11

Epilogue: Dear Dirck

Dear Dirck,

I've always tried to live my life without regrets, and I suppose that I got that mentality from you and Mom. We all make choices in our lifetime and then we live with them. We try not to look back with regret on what's been done but always look forward to make things right. There's a lot less stress that way. But the events around the Seymour desk that I inherited upon your passing are my exception. I regret not sharing my experience with you. I needed to make things right. I needed to finish what you started. I needed to answer the questions you had about the Seymour desk.

For the last three years, I have been immersed in a project to try to understand the legacy of the Seymour desk that I inherited. It has consumed me. While I've grumbled and cursed continually throughout the three-year process (Cathy can attest to that), I have truly enjoyed being consumed by the adventure. Much like one of your furniture endeavors, it may have been a huge effort to see it through to the end, but the effort was worth it. Unfortunately, I truly regret not acting on your urging to look beyond the simple piece of furniture while you were still alive. I now realize that your urging was coming less from a persistent parent and more from an aging man trying to do his own investigative research before he couldn't do it anymore. Your lengthy notes about the contents of the desk and the questions that followed were equally gut-punch worthy. You hoped that I would be bitten by the same curiosity that nagged you and that we could solve the desk's mysteries together. I will always regret that I missed that opportunity while you were alive.

My only consolation is that I probably would not have been able to take on this project while I was working full time at the school. My shift to teaching part-time in the fall of 2021 afforded me the time to do the research needed for this adventure. It is not an excuse, but the simple reality of the enormity of this process. Throughout these past three years, I've traveled extensively throughout New England back to your old stomping grounds, Cooperstown, New York, and even to New Orleans. I spent hours at three different research facilities, and reconnected with your cousin Jamie and your sister, Barbara. All of this is in search of answers. More importantly, I've written, edited, and revised, trying to tell the desk's story as well as answer some of your own questions for days on end—while most of the time sitting at the aforementioned desk. In the end, I believe I was successful.

One result of this opus was that it gave me a front row seat to one side of my family that I'd never had the time nor the desire to research. Thinking that the Seymour desk must have been owned by either Oliver Ellsworth or Noah Webster, I started with them. *I know. I know. If I had just asked you a few questions, I would have known differently years ago.* But there is a silver lining. If I had known that those two gentlemen hadn't owned the desk, nor had their immediate descendants, I would not have delved so deeply into their lives. I'm glad I did. They were truly amazing men.

Of course, once I realized my mistakes with the desk's lineage, it opened a new can of worms: the Seymours. The Seymour desk had nothing to do with our family initially, and it wouldn't for another 140 years after its construction. Everything began with Thomas Seymour III and his gift to his wife, Mary Ledyard Seymour, around 1790. *But you probably already knew that. Ugh.* As you mentioned several times, the letters in the desk relating to his grandson, Thomas Hart Seymour, were not only amazing but perplexing as well. Why and how they were put in the desk is one question that I could never really answer. But I'm glad that they were there. Each, minus a few outliers, opened doors to research that I could never have imagined. While they had nothing to do with the desk's movements other than to prove its provenance, many shed some light on a time period that previously was a blip on my historical inclinations. The process of un-raveling each letter's bigger picture was nerve-racking and exhilarat-ing at the same time. Governor and Minister Thomas Seymour was truly an amazing man—a family man, a career politician, and a war hero. More than anyone who may have worked at the desk (assuming that you did not), the desk's history awed me at times. It may not be the same as sleeping in the Lincoln bedroom, but it is close.

Additionally, it was fascinating to work with your cousin Jamie as my research took me to Esperanza—both literally and figuratively. If my knowledge of Noah Webster and Oliver Ellsworth was limited, my knowledge of their descendants, including your parents, was shame-fully weak. But with Jamie's help, a little yellow book about Esperanza that he gave me, and hundreds of letters between Morris Smith (your great-great-grandfather), his wife, Julie, and their four daughters, I was not only able to get a clearer picture of my past but also to estab-lish a connection between the two families and the eventual move-ment of the desk from one to the other.

Of course, the biggest question mark was the desk's final Seymour owner: Helen Ellery Seymour. Based on your notes and questions, she was a paradox to you and initially to me as well. While I was unable to answer every question about her as a person, I was able to fill in a lot of gaps about the woman's life—though it took a lot of persistence. The simple answer is that she was not the woman you perceived she was through the letters in the desk or through hearsay from your mother, Carlotta. Like most things in life, only through more infor-mation does a clearer picture emerge.

Of course, knowing you as I do, you don't want any more pomp and circumstance but rather the gory details of the desk's travels. Here it is again, in simple terms:

The Seymour desk was built for Thomas Seymour III sometime between 1790 and 1800, perhaps for his wife, Mary. They built a home in downtown Hartford, Connecticut, on Arch Street and remained there until Thomas died in 1829. Mary's death preceded his passing by more than twenty years. At that point, the house and desk were willed to their third son, Henry. He and his wife, Jane, remained in the same house until their deaths—Henry (1846) and Jane (1851). The house and the desk were passed to their oldest son, Thomas Hart Seymour, around that time. Thomas and his sister, Mary, then built their own home across the Connecticut River in East Hartford sometime after Jane's death. A rough estimate would conclude that the Seymour desk lived on Arch Street in Hartford for almost sixty years.

Thomas Hart Seymour, former governor of Connecticut and minister to Russia, died in 1868, and he gave everything, including the desk, to his older sister, Mary Ellery Seymour, who lived with him on Governor Street in East Hartford. Neither of these two ever married nor had children. When Mary died in 1887, she passed everything to her niece, Helen Ellery Seymour. In theory, the desk stayed at the East Hartford address for more than twenty-five years.

Helen Seymour was the daughter of William Ellery Seymour, Thomas Hart and Mary Ellery Seymour's younger brother. She, with the help of your great-grand-aunt, Lottie Smith, moved everything out of the East Hartford home and into the Esperanza estate in New Hartford, Connecticut, in 1888, on a temporary basis. Not long after, Helen took up a nursing position in Washington, D.C., sometime around 1890, and the desk went with her. She remained in Washington for another twelve years or so until she took another nursing position in the northeast, perhaps in Gloucester, Massachusetts. The desk did not make the trip with her but was given to a close family friend, Anna Crocker, and her husband, Frank, for safekeeping. They were also living in Washington, D.C., at the time.

The Seymour desk remained in the Crockers' custody for almost thirty years. They moved from Washington to Lynn, Massachusetts, to Springfield and eventually to Longmeadow, Massschusetts—and the desk went with them the whole time. After a great deal of drama, the desk was eventually sold to your great-grandparents, William and Nellie Ellsworth, in the summer of 1930 and then shipped to the Esperanza estate in New Hartford soon after.

The desk would remain at Esperanza (again) for another couple of years until its move to your house in Cooperstown, New York, was completed in 1934. Your parents, Carlotta and Fran Harrison, would own the desk and keep it there for almost another sixty years. When Carlotta died in 1991 (Fran had died five years earlier), the Seymour desk was willed to you and Mom. The desk would remain in your possession in two different homes in Glens Falls, New York, until 2020.

In the winter of 2021, the Seymour desk was moved from Glens Falls to my home in Northfield, Massachusetts. While unsure what to do with it for a year, we finally decided to refinish one of the bedrooms upstairs and move the desk there. Though the 1790 heirloom seems somewhat out of place given our modern-designed home, it seems to fit right in with the antique sleigh bed you slept in as a kid. If the two pieces of furniture could talk...

Finally, it goes without saying that I (we) miss you and Mom greatly. I know that you were never a deeply religious man and that the thought of an afterlife was poppycock, and, I suppose, I feel the same. But if we're both wrong, please give my love to Mom and tell her that the Yankees kicked some Red Sox ass again this year.

Love, Andy

Works Cited

I'm an Idiot

The Associated Press. (1998, January 19). *Card Table, a $25 Garage Sale Bargain, Is Sold for $541,500.* The New York Times. https://www.nytimes.com/1998/01/19/nyregion/card-table-a-25-garage-sale-bargain-is-sold-for-541500.html

Cobb, C. (2021, March 1). *Seymour Desk* [Email].

Cobb, C. (2021, March 10). *Seymour Desk* [Email]

Harrison, M. (2021, February). *Matthew Harrison conversation* [Phone call].

Hipkiss, E. J. (1930, April). *An American Secretary.* Bulletin of the Museum of Fine Arts, Vol. 28, No. 166. http://www.jstor.org/stable/4170226

Museum of Fine Arts. (2000). *Recent Acquisition—On View in the Federal Corridor. Tambour Desk, About 1796-98, John Seymour & Son.* Museum of Fine Arts. www.mfa.org

PBS Antiques Roadshow. (2012, June 14). *Appraisal of Seymour Card Table, ca. 1794.* PBS Antiques Roadshow. https://www.pbs.org/video/antiques-roadshow-appraisal-seymour-card-table-ca-1794/

Traditional Fine Arts Organization. (2012). *Luxury and innovation: Furniture masterworks by John and Thomas Seymour.* Traditional Fine Arts Organization. https://tfaoi.org/aa/4aa/4aa210.htm

Ships in the Night

Castro, William R. (1997). *Oliver Ellsworth and the Creation of the Federal Republic.* Second Circuit Committee on History and Commemorative Events.

Esolen, A. (2015, June 26). *The Practical Wisdom of Chief Justice Ellsworth: Reconsidering the separation of church and state.* Public Discourse. https://www.thepublicdiscourse.com/2015/06/14490/

The Constitution of the United States with the Declaration of Independence and the Articles of Confederation. (2002). Barnes and Noble.

Kendall, Joshua. (2010). *The Forgotten Founding Father: Noah Webster's Obsession and the Creation of an American Culture.* Berkeley Books.

Landrigan, L. (2017, October 4). Mary Webster, the witch of Hadley, survives a hanging. New England Historical Society. https://newenglandhistoricalsociety.com/mary-webster-witch-hadley-survives-hanging/

Oliver Ellsworth Homestead—Connecticut DAR. https://ellsworthhomestead-dar.org

Noah Webster House and West Hartford Historical Society. https://noahwebster-house.org

Rosen, Jeffrey. (2006). *The Most Democratic Branch: How the Courts Serve America.* Oxford University Press.

Siemiatkoski, Donna H. (1992). *The Ancestors and Descendants of Chief Justice Oliver Ellsworth and His Wife Abigail Wolcott and the Story of Elmwood, their Homestead.* Gateway Press.

Smith, A. (2019, October 15). *The Witch of Hadley: Mary Webster, the weird, and the wired.* Mass Review. https://www.massreview.org/node/7575

Toth, Michael C. (2011). *Founding Federalist: The Life of Oliver Ellsworth.* ISI Books.

Unger, Harlow G. (1998). *Noah Webster: The Life and Times of an American Patriot.* John Wiley and Sons.

Suddenly Seymour

Arch Street Tavern. https://www.archstreettavern.com/about

Connecticut Museum of Culture and History. *Thomas Henry Seymour Papers—A Guide to the Thomas Henry papers at the Connecticut Historical Society.* https://chs.org/finding_aides/finding_aids/seymt1868.html

Dunham-Wilcox-Trott-Kirk—A Catalog of the Names of the First Puritan Settlers in the Colony of Connecticut. http://dunhamwilcox.net/ct/puritan1.htm

Isham, J., Jr. (1787, July 19). *Letter in Andrew Harrison's collection* [Written letter and bill to Major Thomas Seymour].

Joslin, J. (2017, February 22). *Phoenix Iron Works, Geo. S. Lincoln & Co.—History.* Vintagemachinery.org. http://vintagemachinery.org/

Seymour, George D. and Jacobus, Donald L. (1939). *A History of the Seymour Family: Descendants of Richard Seymour of Hartford, Connecticut, for Six Generations.* Literary Licensing.

Seymour, Major Thomas, III. (1824, March 17). *Letter in Andrew Harrison's collection* [Written letter to Mary Eliza Seymour].

When Andy Met Harry

Allen, S.S. (1862, December 10). *Letter in Andrew Harrison's collection.* [Written Letter to Governor Thomas Seymour].

American Journal of Psychiatry. (Volume 12, January 1856). *Journal of Insanity. Trial of Willard Clark.* Pages 212-37.

Bonham, Milledge Luke. (1850, May 30). *Letter in Andrew Harrison's collection.* [Written letter to Governor Thomas Seymour].

Clark, W. (1861, August 4). Connecticut Museum of Culture and History [Written letter to Thomas Seymour].

Connecticut General Assembly. *Thomas Hart Seymour. Governors of Connecticut.* https://www.cga.ct.gov/hco/books/The_Governors_of_Connecticut_1905.pdf

Connecticut Museum of Culture and History. *Thomas Henry Seymour Papers—A Guide to the Thomas Henry Seymour papers at the Connecticut Historical Society.* https://chs.org/finding_aides/finding_aids/seymt1868.html

Connecticut's Old State House. *About Connecticut's Old State House.* https://wp.cga.ct.gov/osh/about/

Economic History Association. *History of the U.S. Telegraph Industry.* https://eh.net/encyclopedia/history-of-the-u-s-telegraph-industry

Elliott, E. B. and H., John., & Hunter, J. (1952, May). *Letter in Andrew Harrison's collection* [Written letter to Count Alexander Bodisco].

Emerging Civil War. Mexican-American War 170th: The Storming of Chapultepec. https://emergingcivilwar.com/

Emily. (1865, Thursday). *Letter in Andrew Harrison's collection.* [Written letter to Governor Thomas Seymour].

Erving, A. (1855, November 22). *Letter in Andrew Harrison's collection.* [Written letter to Governor Thomas Seymour].

Erving, A. (1856, January). Connecticut Museum of Culture and History [Written letter to Thomas Seymour].

History.com. *Franklin Pierce.* https://www.history.com/topics/us-presidents/franklin-pierce

History.com. *Mexican-American War.* https://www.history.com/topics/19th-century/mexican-american-war

Lynskey, Thomas. (2022). Part-Time Explorer. *The Disappearance of the SS Pacific.* https://www.youtube.com/watch?v=ypUSzCuNCa4

Lynskey, T. (2023, February 27). *S.S. Pacific conversation* [Email to Andrew Harrison].

McFarland, H.H. (1855). *Report of the Trial of Willard Clark, Indicted for the Murder of Richard W. Wight, Before the Superior Court of Connecticut, Holden at New Haven, on Monday, September 17, 1855.* Yale Law Library.

National Governors Association. *Governor Thomas H. Seymour.* https://www.nga.org/governor/thomas-h-seymour/

Pierce, F. (1860, March 17). *Letter in Andrew Harrison's collection.* [Written letter to Governor Thomas Seymour].

Russia Beyond. The Complete List of Russian Tsars, Emperors, and Presidents. https://www.rbth.com/history/334065-complete-list-of-russian-tsars-emperors-rulers-presidents

Seymour, George D. and Jacobus, Donald L. (1939). *A History of the Seymour Family: Descendants of Richard Seymour of Hartford, Connecticut, for Six Generations.* Literary Licensing.

Seymour, M.B. (1865, May 26). *Letter in Andrew Harrison's collection.* [Written letter to Governor Thomas Seymour].

Seymour, Thomas H. (1855-1857). Thomas Seymour Personal Diary While in Russia. Accessed from the Connecticut Museum of Culture and History.

Seymour, Thomas H. (1862-67). Calling card book. Accessed from personal collection.

Today in Connecticut History. *October 15: From Connecticut Governor to Russian Ambassador.* https://todayincthistory.com/2019/10/15/october-15-from-connecticut-governor-to-russian-ambassador/

Trinity College. *Watkinson History.* https://www.trincoll.edu/lits/watkinson/about-the-watkinson/about

Tucker, G. (1860, February 18). *Letter in Andrew Harrison's collection.* [Written letter to Governor Thomas Seymour].

United States Census Bureau. (1850). *1850 United States Federal Census. Connecticut/Hartford/East Hartford.* Ancestry.com

United States Census Bureau. (1860). *1860 United States Federal Census. Connecticut/Hartford/Hartford District 3*, Page 116. Ancestry.com

Unknown. (1843-50?, February 13). *Letter in Andrew Harrison's collection.* [Written letter to Governor Thomas Seymour].

Unknown. (1843-50?, February 14). *Letter in Andrew Harrison's collection.* [Written letter to Governor Thomas Seymour].

Unknown. (1850, February 14). *Letter in Andrew Harrison's collection.* [Written letter to Governor Thomas Seymour].

Unknown (1843-50?, February 14). Connecticut Museum of Culture and History [Written letter to Thomas Seymour].

Unknown (1850, February 14). Connecticut Museum of Culture and History [Written letter to Thomas Seymour].

Unknown. (1915?). *Seymour and Chapultepec essay. Letter in Andrew Harrison's collection.*

Watkinson, E.B. (1860, December 5). *Letter in Andrew Harrison's collection.* [Letter from E.B. Watkinson to Thomas Seymour].

Willard, Warden William. (1866, January 22). *Letter in Andrew Harrison's collection.* [Written letter to Governor Thomas Seymour].

The White House. Franklin Pierce: The 14th President of the United States. https://www.whitehouse.gov/about-the-white-house/presidents/franklin-pierce

Whitney, R. (1957, February). *The unlucky Collins line*. American Heritage. https://www.americanheritage.com/unlucky-collins-line

Sweet Home Esperanza

Noyes, A. (1937). *William W. Ellsworth—member directory—Century Archives*. The Century Association Archives Foundation. https://centuryarchives.org/member-directory/

Creevey, Lucy Morris Ellsworth. (1956). *The Story of Our Esperanza*. Harold S. Case.

Steve. (2016, July 6). *Smith-Worthington Saddlery*. Connecticut Museum Quest. https://www.ctmq.org/smith-worthington-saddlery

Hall, Dr. J. (2021, October 9). *Interview* [Personal communication].

Harrison, A. (2022). *Harrison Family Tree*. Ancestry.com

Harrison, C. C. (1984, May). *Introduction to Nelly's Trip Abroad* [Addendum on the Smith Letters].

Hartford Courant. (1994, November 20). In New Hartford, A House with a History. *Hartford Courant*. https://www.courant.com/1994/11/20/in-new-hartford-a-house-with-a-history

Hartford Courant. (2016, August 2). "Saddle up: Smith-Worthington Saddlery dates back to Washington's Day." *Hartford Courant*. https://www.courant.com/2016/08/02/saddle-up-smith-worthington-saddlery-dates-back-to-washingtons-day

Johnson, K. (2022). *Mulhern Family Tree*. Ancestry.com

Louis, J. B. (2021, October 9). *Interview at Ellsworth House* [Personal communication].

Mulhern, B. (2022, August 4). *Email* [Personal conversation].

Siemiatkoski, Donna H. (1992). *The Ancestors and Descendants of Chief Justice Oliver Ellsworth and His Wife Abigail Wolcott and the Story of Elmwood, Their Homestead*. Gateway Press.

The Smith-Worthington Company. *About. The Smith-Worthington Company Is the Oldest Saddlery in the World*. https://www.smithworthington.com/about

Helen Seymour 1.0

Agnew, Jeremy. (2014). *Alcohol and Opium in the Old West—Use, Abuse and Influence.* McFarland and Company.

Bell, A. (2025, February 12). *Email with Annika Bell, New Orleans Pharmacy Museum* [Personal communication].

Ellen Castelow. (2015, January 26). *Opium in Victorian Britain.* Historic UK. https://www.historic-uk.com/HistoryUK/HistoryofBritain/Opium-in-Victorian-Britain

Courtwright, David T. (2001). *Dark Paradise—A History of Opiate Addiction in America.* Harvard University Press.

Emery, D. (2015). *Emery/Likins Family Tree.* Ancestry.com

Hall, Dr. J. (2023, July 5). *Email* [Personal communication].

Harrison, A. (2023). *Seymour Family Tree.* Ancestry.com

Kennedy, G. (2025, February 6). *Tour of the New Orleans Pharmacy Museum* [Personal communication].

New Orleans Pharmacy Museum. (n.d.). *New Orleans Pharmacy Museum.* NOPM Draft. Retrieved March 2, 2025, from https://pharmacymuseum.org

Seymour, H. E. (1859-1868). *Helena Seymour Letters at Connecticut Museum of Culture and History* [Written letters to Thomas Seymour].

Seymour, M. E. (1850-1868). *Mary Seymour Letters at Connecticut Museum of Culture and History* [Written letters to Thomas Seymour].

Seymour, W. E. (1850-1868). *William Seymour Letters at Connecticut Museum of Culture and History* [Written letters to Thomas Seymour].

Smith, C. (1930, October). *Memo of the Seymour Desk's provenance* [Written letter].

The Times-Picayune. (1883, July 29). *Jul 29, 1833, page 2 - Newspapers.com.* https://www.newspapers.com/image/28273957

United States Census Bureau. (1870). *1870 United States Federal Census. Louisiana/Orleans/New Orleans/Ward #2*, page 177. Ancestry.com

United States Census Bureau. (1880). *1880 United States Federal Census. Louisiana/Orleans/New Orleans*, Page 9. Ancestry.com

Wilcox, B. (2010). *Barbara Wilcox Family Tree*. Ancestry.com

Linkage

Creevey, Lucy Morris Ellsworth. (1956). *The Story of Our Esperanza*. Harold S. Case.

Esperanza Visitation Book. (2023, April 29). *Esperanza Visitation Book (1890-1960)* [Personal communication].

The Times-Picayune. (1890, March 26). *Newspapers.com*. https://www.newspapers.com/article/the-times-picayune/118882775

Harrison, A. (2023). *Seymour Family Tree*. Ancestry.com

Hartford Courant. (August 2, 2016). "Saddle Up: Smith-Worthington Saddlery Dates Back to Washington's Day." https://www.courant.com/2016/08/02/saddle-up-smith-worthington-saddlery-dates-back-to-washingtons-day

Hall, A. (2023, April 27). *Email* [Personal communication].

Hall, Dr. J. (2023, April 29). *Email* [Personal communication].

Hall, Dr. J. (2023, July 5). *Email* [Personal communication].

The New Orleans Crescent. (1849, May 10). page 1 - Newspapers.com. https://www.newspapers.com/image/321418442

The New Orleans Crescent. (1850, January 6). page 2 - Newspapers.com. https://www.newspapers.com/image/321565290

Fenimore Art Museum Library Collection. (1852-1890). *Smith Letters*. Fenimore Art Museum Library Collection in Cooperstown, New York.

Smith, J. (1860, January 29). *Smith Letters* [Written letter to Morris Smith].

Smith, J. (1872, Winter). *Smith Letters* [Written letter to Morris Smith].

Smith, J. (1874, March 11). *Smith Letters* [Written letter to Morris Smith].

Smith, J. (1879, January). *Smith Letters* [Written letter to Morris Smith].

Smith, M. (1863, November 13). *Smith Letters* [Written letter to Julie Smith].

Smith, M. (1878, January). *Smith Letters* [Written letter to Julie Smith].

Smith, M. (1888, May). *Smith Letters* [Written letter to Fanny Smith].

The Smith-Worthington Company. *About. The Smith-Worthington Company Is the Oldest Saddlery in the World.* https://www.smithworthington.com/about

Steve. (2016, July 6). *Smith-Worthington Saddlery.* Connecticut Museum Quest. https://www.ctmq.org/smith-worthington-saddlery

The Times-Picayune. (November 4, 1847). "Ccpartnership on E.R. Stevens and WM. E. Seymour." https://www.newspapers.com/image/25594815

The Times-Picayune. (August 7, 1855). Smith and Brother advertisement. https://www.newspapers.com/image/25555417

The Times-Picayune. (November 1, 1870). Stevens and Seymour advertisement. https://www.newspapers.com/image/26668297

United States Census Bureau. (1910). *1910 United States Federal Census. Louisiana/Orleans/New Orleans*, Sheet 7. Ancestry.com

Williams Research Center. (1849). *New Orleans, North Brothers and Company and Smith Saddlery Engraving* .

Helen Seymour 2.0

The Association of American Publishers. (1903). *The Gloucester Directory.* Page 251. Ancestry.com

Boyd, W. H. (1895). *Boyd's Directory of the District of Columbia.* Page 820. Hathitrust. https://babel.hathitrust.org

Boyd, W. H. (1896). *Boyd's Directory of the District of Columbia.* Page 819. Hathitrust. https://babel.hathitrust.org

Boyd, Wm. H. (1900). *Boyd's Directory of the District of Columbia.* Page 885. Ancestry.com

Boyd, Wm. H. (1902). *Boyd's Directory of the District of Columbia.* Page 882. Ancestry.com

Bscudder. *Bruneau/Corby Scudder/Tinker Family Tree. (Henry Wickes Goodrich).* Ancestry.com. https://www.ancestry.com/family-tree/person/tree/70765263/person/192232968237/facts

Crocker, A. (1904, September). *Anna Crocker's Letters* held by Andrew Harrison. [Written letter to Helena Seymour].

Crocker, A. (1911, January 16). *Anna Crocker's Letters* held by Andrew Harrison. [Written letter to Helena Seymour].

Crocker, A. (1911, February). *Anna Crocker's Letters* held by Andrew Harrison. [Written letter to Helena Seymour].

Crocker, A. (1911, May 7). *Anna Crocker's Letters* held by Andrew Harrison. [Written letter to Helena Seymour].

Crocker, A. (1904, September). *Anna Crocker's Letters* held by Andrew Harrison. [Written letter to Helena Seymour].

Crocker, A. (1920, September 8). *Anna Crocker's Letters* held by Andrew Harrison. [Written letter to Helena Seymour].

Crocker, A. (1922, October 8th). *Anna Crocker's Letters* held by Andrew Harrison. [Written letter to Helena Seymour].

Herwick III, E. B. (2014, May 30). "How Lynn became the shoe capital of the world." *WGBH*. https://www.wgbh.org/news/local/2014-05-30/how-lynn-became-the-shoe-capitol-of-the-world

JMatt50. (2010). *Lang Family Tree.* Ancestry.com

Lisle, Janet. (2012). *The History of Little Compton: A Home by the Sea-1820—1950.* Little Compton Historical Society.

Little Compton Historical Society. (2015). *The Stories Houses Tell: A Collection of Little Compton House Histories.* Little Compton Historical Society.

Research Publications. (1892). *U.S. City Directories—1882-1901: Washington, D.C. 1892-1893,* page 884–885. Ancestry.com.

Research Publications. (1894). *U.S. City Directories—1882-1901: Washington, D.C. 1892-1893,* page 880–881. Ancestry.com.

Research Publications. (1894). *U.S. City Directories—1882-1901: Washington, D.C. 1892-1893,* page 880–881. Ancestry.com.

Old New Orleans. (2005). *NO_Orphans.* Old New Orleans http://old-new-orleans.com/NO_Orphans.html

Smith, M. (1902, Spring). *Smith Letters* [Written letters to Lottie and Fanny Smith].

Soards' Directory Company. (1906). *Soards' New Orleans Business Directory*. Page 879. Ancestry.com

Soards' Directory Company. (1908). *Soards' New Orleans Business Directory*. Page 868. Ancestry.com

Soards' Directory Company. (1911). *Soards' New Orleans Business Directory*. Page 1109. Ancestry.com

Soards' Directory Company. (1918). *Soards' New Orleans Business Directory*. Page 1136. Ancestry.com

Soards' Directory Company. (1919). *Soards' New Orleans Business Directory*. Page 1146. Ancestry.com

Soards' Directory Company. (1920). *Soards' New Orleans Business Directory*. Page 1524. Ancestry.com

Soards' Directory Company. (1922). *Soards' New Orleans Business Directory*. Page 1375. Ancestry.com

Soards' Directory Company. (1923). *Soards' New Orleans Business Directory*. Page 1376. Ancestry.com

Soards' Directory Company. (1924). *Soards' New Orleans Business Directory*. Page 1359. Ancestry.com

Soards' Directory Company. (1925). *Soards' New Orleans Business Directory*. Page 1432. Ancestry.com

Soards' Directory Company. (1926). *Soards' New Orleans Business Directory*. Page 1271. Ancestry.com

Soards' Directory Company. (1927). *Soards' New Orleans Business Directory*. Page 1397. Ancestry.com

Society of Architectural Historians. (2019, September 16). *Orphanage apartments and commercial building (Protestant Orphans Home)*. SAH Archipedia. https://sah-archipedia.org/buildings/LA-02-OR151

Strahan, D. (2018, May 24). *Leander H. Day House, Springfield, Mass.* Lost New England. https://lostnewengland.com/2018/05/leander-h-day-house-springfield-mass

United States Census Bureau. (1860). *1860 United States Federal Census. Connecticut/Hartford/East Hartford*, Sheet 44. Ancestry.com

United States Census Bureau. (1870). *1870 United States Federal Census. Connecticut/Hartford/East Hartford*, Sheet 39. Ancestry.com

United States Census Bureau. (1880). *1880 United States Federal Census. Maine/York/Biddeford*, Sheet 18. Ancestry.com

United States Census Bureau. (1900). *1900 United States Federal Census. New Jersey/Essex/Belleville*, Sheet 13. Ancestry.com

United States Census Bureau. (1900). *1900 United States Federal Census. District of Columbia/Washington/Washington/District 44*, Sheet 14. Ancestry.com

United States Census Bureau. (1910). *1910 United States Federal Census. Massachusetts/Hampden/Springfield 7/District 647*, Sheet 5. Ancestry.com

United States Census Bureau. (1920). *1920 United States Federal Census. Massachusetts/Hampden/Longmeadow /District 74*, Sheet 27. Ancestry.com

United States Census Bureau. (1920). *1920 United States Federal Census. Louisiana/Orleans/New Orleans/Ward 8*, Sheet 2. Ancestry.com

United States Census Bureau. (1930). *1930 United States Federal Census. Louisiana/Orleans/New Orleans/District 7*, Sheet 8. Ancestry.com

United States Census Bureau. (1940). *1940 United States Federal Census. Louisiana/Orleans/New Orleans/District 7*, Sheet 69. Ancestry.com

Frankly, My Dear Helen...

Crocker, F. (1928, April 14). *Frank Crocker Letters* held by Andrew Harrison. [Written letter to Helena Seymour].

Crocker, F. (1928, October 24). *Frank Crocker Letters* held by Andrew Harrison. [Written letter to Helena Seymour].

Crocker, F. (1928, November 13). *Frank Crocker Letters* held by Andrew Harrison. [Written letter to Helena Seymour].

Crocker, F. (1929, November 29). *Frank Crocker Letters* held by Andrew Harrison. [Written letter to Helena Seymour].

Crocker, F. (1929, December 2). *Frank Crocker Letters* held by Andrew Harrison. [Written letter to Helena Seymour].

Crocker, F. (1929, December 3). *Frank Crocker Letters* held by Andrew Harrison. [Written letter to Helena Seymour].

Crocker, F. (1926, December 6). *Frank Crocker Letters* held by Andrew Harrison. [Written letter to Helena Seymour].

Crocker, F. (1928, December 14). *Frank Crocker Letters* held by Andrew Harrison. [WrittenlLetter to Helena Seymour].

Crocker, F. (1930, January 6). *Frank Crocker Letters* held by Andrew Harrison. [Written letter to Helena Seymour].

Crocker, F. (1930, January 6). *Frank Crocker Letters* held by Andrew Harrison. [Written letter to Helena Seymour].

Crocker, F. (1930, January 9). *Frank Crocker Letters* held by Andrew Harrison. [Written letter to Helena Seymour].

Crocker, F. (1930, June 6). *Frank Crocker Letters* held by Andrew Harrison. [Written letter to Helena Seymour].

Crocker, F. (1930, June 20). *Frank Crocker Letters* held by Andrew Harrison. [Written letter to Helena Seymour].

Crocker, F. (1930, August 5). *Frank Crocker Letters* held by Andrew Harrison. [Written letter to Helena Seymour].

Crocker, F. (1930, August 8). *Frank Crocker Letters* held by Andrew Harrison. [Written letter to Nellie Smith Ellsworth].

Dixon, S. (2023, September 27). Connecticut Museum of Culture and History [Email to Andrew Harrison].

Ellsworth, W. W. (1930, August 24). *Frank Crocker Letters* [Written letter].

Hall, Dr. J. (2022, January). *Esperanza Tales*.

Morse, S. F. B. (1856, November 19). Connecticut Museum of Culture and History [Written letter to Thomas Seymour including donation card].

Seymour, George D. and Jacobus, Donald L. (1939). *A History of the Seymour Family: Descendants of Richard Seymour of Hartford, Connecticut, for Six Generations.* Literary Licensing.

Seymour, H. (1930, May 7). *Bill of Sale.*

Seymour, H. (1930, August 3). *Frank Crocker Letters* [Written letter to Nellie Smith Ellsworth].

Seymour, H. (1930, August 16). *Frank Crocker Letters* [Written letter to Nellie Smith Ellsworth].

United States Census Bureau. (1930). *1930 United States Federal Census. Louisiana/Orleans/New Orleans/District 7*, Sheet 8. Ancestry.com

United States Census Bureau. (1940). *1940 United States Federal Census. Louisiana/Orleans/New Orleans/District 7*, Sheet 69. Ancestry.com

Williams Research Center. (1988). *Milne Home Materials.* Alexander Milne and Milne's.

My Man Cave

Chappell, G., & Harrison, M. (2020, November 8). Dirck Dey Harrison obituary. *The Post Star.* https://www.legacy.com/us/obituaries/poststar/name/dirck-harrison-obituary?id=12995204

Davis, J. (2023, July). "Resorts then and now: Mt. Otsego." *Skiing History.* https://www.skiinghistory.org/online-magazine/resorts-then-and-now-mt-otsego

GlensFalls.com. (2024). About Glens Falls, NY. A Historic City in Warren County. https://www.glensfalls.com/about/glens-falls

Harrison, C. (1984). *Memo on an envelope written by Carlotta Smith* [Personal communication].

Harrison, M. (2017, May). Joyce Davies Harrison obituary. *The Post Star.*

Harrison, D. (1991, September 19). Carlotta Creevey Harrison obituary. *The Post Star.*

Mulhern, B. (2023, August 18). *Email* [Personal communication].

Mulhern, B. (2023, June 12). *Interview* [Personal communication].

The Village of Cooperstown. (2024). *About*. The Village of Cooperstown. https://www.cooperstownny.org/about-cooperstown

Photo Credits

Page 17: Library of Congress. (1867). Steel Engraving of Noah Webster, 1758-1843. https://www.loc.gov/pictures/item/2002705096/

Page 19: Library of Congress. (1891). *Photograph of Portrait of Oliver Ellsworth*. https://www.loc.gov/pictures/item/2004665056/

Page 56: Aligata, M. (2016). *Photograph of a statue of Noah Webster (1914) sculpted by Willard D. Paddock*. https://commons.wikimedia.org/wiki/File:Noah_Webster_Statue_(Willard_D._Paddock),_Amherst,_MA_-_May_2016.jpg

Page 76: Library of Congress. (n.d.). *Steel Engraving of Thomas Henry Seymour*. https://www.loc.gov/pictures/item/2003663624/

Page 111: Klotz, J. and R. (2016). *Esperanza, New Hartford, Connecticut*. https://commons.wikimedia.org/wiki/File:ESPERANZA,_NEW_HARTFORD,_LITCHFIELD_COUNTY,_CT.jpg

Page 116: Creevey, Lucy Morris Ellsworth. (1956). *The Story of Our Esperanza*. Harold S. Case.

Page 119: Mulhern, B. (1929). *Ellsworth Family Photo at Esperanza*.

Page 231: Harrison, A. (1953). *Dirck and Joyce Harrison Honeymoon Picture*.

Page 235: Mulhern, B. (1958). *Dirck Harrison at Mt. Otsego, Cooperstoen, New York*.

About the Author

Andrew Harrison, a first-time author resides in Northfield, Massachusetts with his wife, Cathy, and very protective dog, Maggie. After retiring from teaching middle and high school students for over forty years, he now spends his time chasing his next book idea as well as his two grandchildren, a small white ball down a fairway, and the perfect recipe for a homebrew beer. He is currently working on his second book, a who-done-it novel involving a high school teacher.

For more information, visit his website: www.grandywrites.com